# MORE TAPESTRY CROCHET

by

Carol Ventura

Cookeville, Tennessee

2002

A tapestry crochet instructional video is available through
Yarn Barn/Victorian Video
930 Massachusetts
PO Box 334
Lawrence, KS 66044
1-800-848-0284
**http://www.victorianvid.com**

ISBN 0-9721253-0-2

Library of Congress Control Number: 2002-092589



Printed in Cookeville, TN

Designed and Published by

CAROL VENTURA
163 Big Spring Circle
Cookeville, Tennessee 38501

web page: **http://www.tapestrcrochet.com**
email: **cventura@tntech.edu**

**This book is dedicated to all of my students;
you have taught me so much!**

# CONTENTS

Detail of the Rectangular Shoulder Bag project.

# ACKNOWLEDGEMENTS

I am grateful to the collaborative spirit that I encountered from the beginning of this project to its fruition. Several generous thread, yarn, bead, and framing companies (listed in the back of this book) supplied the materials for the projects.

The following people helped me with the content of the book: Mary Cahill, Nancy Nehring, and Marian Nelson of California; Elaine Brown of Connecticut; Kate Coburn of Arizona; David Carrell and Corinne Lilie of Georgia; Ann Harding and Les Harding of Indiana; Cathy Stewart of North Carolina; Therese Honey of Texas; Crystal Smith and Roxane Whisnant of Tennessee, Abdou Mfopa of Cameroon, Anne-Marie Moroney of Ireland; and Aviva Peres of Israel.

When I decided to venture into the publishing world, Dean Carothers, Kim Nash, Lauren Neal, Lana Rossi, Elaine Wells, Mike Wheeler, and Chris Wilson of Tennessee, introduced me to the proper hardware and software for laying out the book and provided me with much appreciated technical support. Nancy Spies of Maryland shared invaluable information about the ins and outs of publishing and selling books.

My family was also instrumental in putting this book into your hands. My father, Vincent Woychowski, bought the computer and software I needed. My husband, Andrzej Gutek, helped me with the editing, and my daughter, Ilsy, modeled the shawl and scarf projects.

Without these incredible people, this book would still be just a dream!

Detail of a shoulder bag from Aguacatan, Guatemala.

# A few words before you begin:

This book can be used alone or with my first book, *Tapestry Crochet,* published under my previous name, Carol Norton. *More Tapestry Crochet* includes new graphs, additional project formats, different motifs (including letter forms), and a variety of natural fibers. To keep the price of the book as low as possible, most of the color photographs have been printed in black and white. I know that color is important, though, so I created a web page at **<http://www.tapestrycrochet.com>** that includes color photographs. All of the illustrations, photographs, and crocheted pieces in this book are from my personal collection.

I hope that you will spread the word about tapestry crochet and that each of you will teach at least one friend how to do tapestry crochet. The instructions to each project are wordy, because I have found that many crocheters have a difficult time following abbreviated instructions. Since some people prefer to crochet the motif by following a chart and others prefer to read instructions, I have included both.

Attention teachers! Tapestry crochet is relatively easy and inexpensive; a perfect vehicle for introducing fiber art to your students. It takes more time than money to create beautiful, original pieces. Colorful patterns and intricate or simple motifs can be worked out with the special graphs in this book. Students can then incorporate their own designs into a variety of projects. They will learn about design, color, *and* fiber art!

If you love crochet, and would like to learn more about it or share your enthusiasm, consider becoming a member of the Crochet Guild of America **<http://www.crochet.org/>**. If you do not have access to the web, you can write to: CGOA at P.O. Box 8043, Rolling Meadows, IL 60008-8043. The CGOA annual conferences, crochet library, and web page are outstanding!

I hope that some of you brave and creative crocheters will design and publish your own projects, too. I have taken a very conservative approach to tapestry crochet. If I do a third tapestry crochet book, it will include a variety of crochet stitches and textured yarns. I dare you to beat me to it!

# What is tapestry crochet?

Tapestry crochet is not found everywhere, although it is becoming more widespread as people move around the world. This type of crochet differs from ordinary crochet in its texture, tension, and how colors are manipulated. Two or more yarns are worked at the same time to create intricate or simple motifs. Depending on the tension and number of yarns carried, the finished fabric can be stiff or supple, and may take any flat or three-dimensional form. Tapestry crochet has the flexibility and portability of crochet, but the finished pieces do not look crocheted. In fact, they look so much like tapestry weaving, that most people think that tapestry crocheted pieces are made on a loom!

# THE HISTORY OF TAPESTRY CROCHET 1

## EUROPE and the MIDDLE EAST

A type of tapestry crochet (pictured below) called Bündnerhäkelei or Mosaikhäkelei (Mosaic Crochet) has been done in Switzerland for several hundred years. With Mosaikhäkelei, the crochet hook is inserted into only the back loop of the stitch, leaving a horizontal line on the face of the piece. Mosaikhäkelei is always worked from right to left, and the yarns are cut at the end of each row. Sometimes the other thread is carried, while other times it is left to run along the back of the stitch.

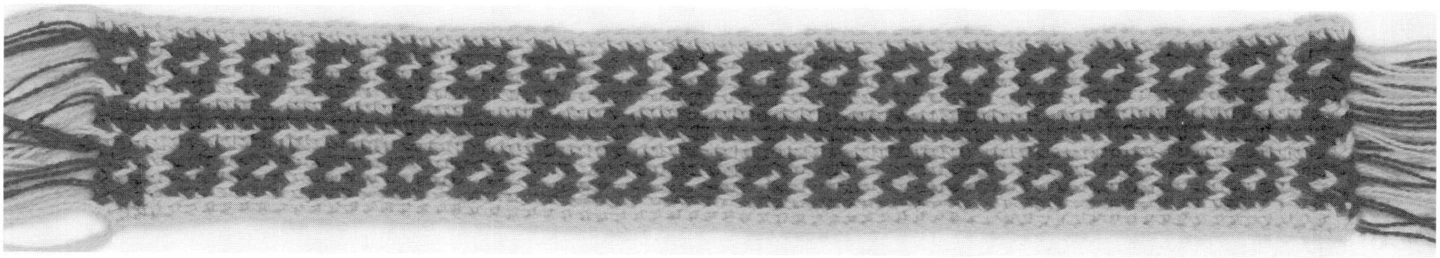

**Anne-Marie Moroney crocheted this 8" x 1" Swiss Bündnerhäkelei with orange and blue cotton thread in 1997. The face is pictured above and the reverse is below. The thread has been carried. The last stitch is worked alternately in one row as a single crochet and in the next row as a slip stitch to keep the crochet work the same height at the beginning and the end of each row. An additional chain stitch is worked in each row so that the last stitch doesn't come out. Both yarns are cut, then the worked yarn is cut and pulled through the chain stitch (Wolf-Bearth, p. 58).**

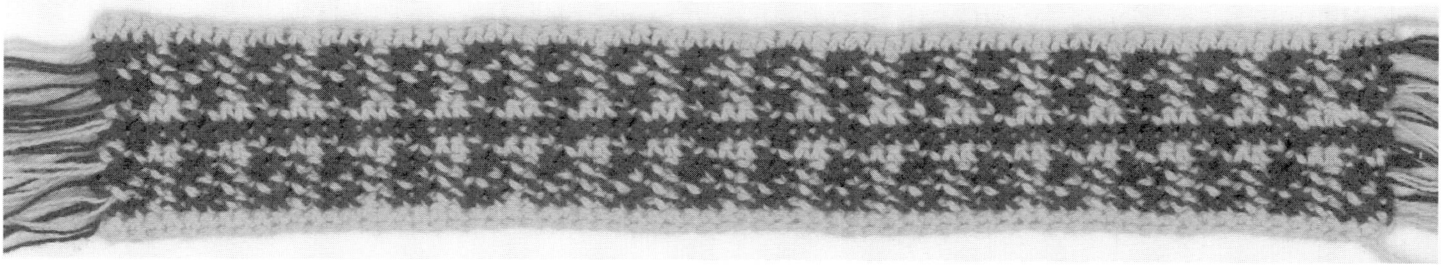

**The 4" diameter Mosaikhäkelei doily on the left is from Graubünden, Switzerland. A crocheted red and white border secures the edges of a piece of white plain-woven cloth. The thread is not carried, but runs along the back of the stitch. It was made by a school girl as a Christmas present around 1950. Anne-Marie Moroney received it from Ms. Regula Hahn of the Rätisches Museum in Chur.**

From the thirteenth to the nineteenth centuries, the Swiss called crochet, "Nun's Work." At that time it was used to border altar cloths and house linens. At the end of the nineteenth and the beginning of the twentieth centuries, Mosaikhäkelei was inset into tablecloths, pillows, and even lingerie. Later, mosaic crochet motifs were used to decorate pillows and the borders of woven cloths (see above). Many of the motifs were copied from cross-stitch and filet crochet pattern books. To create a strong contrast, white and red cotton were often used together. Blue and brown were less common (Wolf-Bearth 1996:55).

Tapestry crocheted *yarmulke* (also called *kippas* and skullcaps) are worn by Jewish men (see below and next page).

**The 6" diameter *yarmulke* on the left is from Israel. It was crocheted with black, white, light blue, dark blue, and brown thread in 1998.**

The 5" diameter *yarmulke* on the left is from Israel. It was crocheted with black, white, and light blue thread in 1998.

The 5" diameter *yarmulke* on the right is from Israel. The dark blue ground is embellished with a rainbow of colors.

The *yarmulke* on the left was bought in a synagogue in Cracow, Poland in 2000. It was crocheted with black and white thread and measures 4 1/4" in diameter.

# AFRICA

Tapestry crocheted hats are popular in Africa. The shape of the hat, the type and color of the thread, and the complexity of the design communicate a number of different messages. Sometimes a crocheted hat denotes a certain social position, other times it marks an ethnic affiliation, and occasionally a hat is simply a fashion statement.

**The hat on the left, called a *kajaya* (pronounced coo faa), is from Marrakech, Morocco. The word, *Allah*, in Arabic script, appears over the animal's back. The hat was crocheted with green, red, white, blue, yellow, and black acrylic yarn. Only two colors are worked on the same row; the yarns are carried. This 6 3/4" diameter hat is unlike the others in this chapter because the entire hat was crocheted with half double crochet stitches. It dates to 1995.**

**The top of the green and white cotton hat on the right does not have a carried thread. The thread is only carried on the side of the hat to work the zig zag motif. A row of green single crochet and a row of white double crochet stitches define the border between the top and side of the 6 1/2" diameter hat. It dates to 1998.**

All three hats on this page were crocheted in Dschang, Western Cameroon, in 2000. The threads were changed after each stitch had been completed (instead of when 2 loops were on the hook).

The 6" diameter hat below was crocheted with red, blue, and white thread.

The 7 1/4" diameter hat above was crocheted with gray and red thread.

The 9" diameter hat below was crocheted (by the man pictured in the lower right) with green, white, blue, and pink acrylic yarn.

The hats and crocheter on this page are from Foumban, West Cameroon, Africa. The yarns are changed after each stitch has been completed (instead of when 2 loops are on the hook). All of the hats on this and the next page date to 2000.

The 7" diameter hat on the left was crocheted with yellow and blue acrylic yarn.

Special clothing is often fabricated to commemorate important events in Cameroon. The 7 3/4" diameter hat below was made in honor of the Foumban Nguon Festival of the year 2000. It was crocheted with white, red, and blue acrylic yarn and a strand of plastic sack fiber (to stiffen the fabric).

Pictured below is a Bamun woman from Foumban tapestry crocheting a hat with cotton and acrylic yarn. In order to make the hat strong, she carries a strand of synthetic fiber from a used sack along with the yarn. A detail of a Bamun hat with two strands of carried sack fiber is pictured in the lower right.

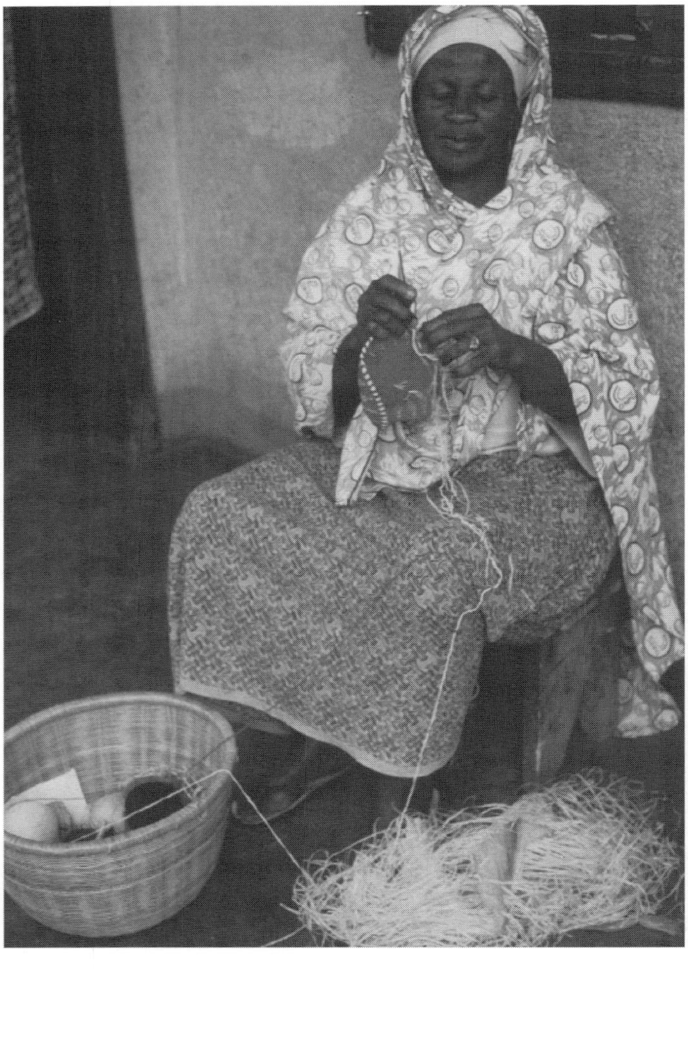

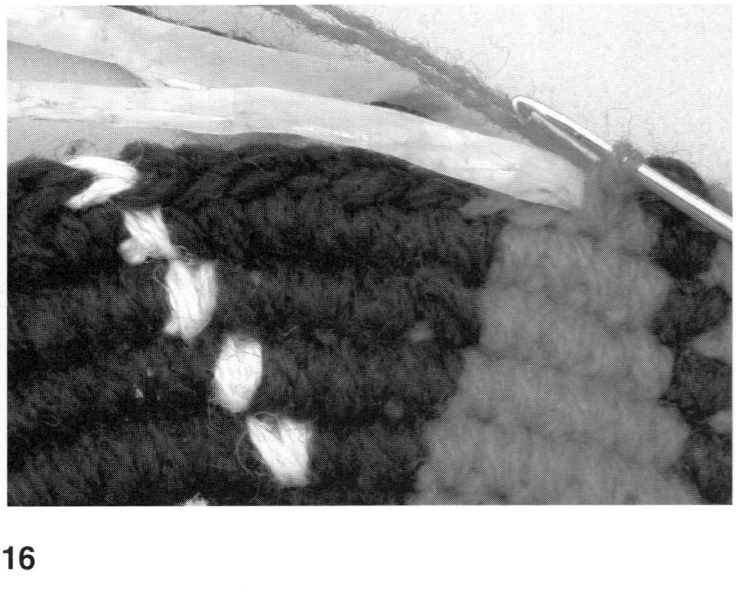

Crocheted hats from Yaounde, Cameroon.

The photograph on the left was taken in Bafut, West Cameroon. The man on the far left wears a crocheted hat; the other wears a looped hat. A variety of hats for sale can be seen hanging on the wall behind the men.

The 5 1/2" diameter black hat (and detail) below was looped from plant fiber in West Cameroon. Looping is one of the oldest fiber techniques in the area, predating crocheting. Looping is a time consuming process because the entire strand needs to be pulled through each loop.

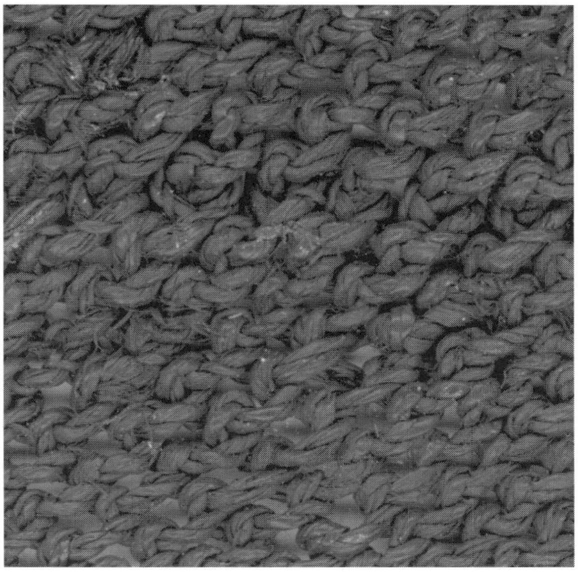

# THE AMERICAS

Crocheting was probably taught to colonial Native Americans by the Spaniards. Although there are very few early examples of tapestry crochet, the Smithsonian Institution has Navajo leggings and a hat from the Southwestern United States that date to 1864 (Taylor 1991:60-61).

While tapestry crocheted hats are popular in the Middle East and Africa, it is the shoulder bag that is tapestry crocheted in Guatemala. In most areas, it was men who traditionally did tapestry crochet, but today, both men and women tapestry crochet.

I have a theory about why tapestry crochet is popular in certain parts of Africa and Guatemala: looping. Looped hats have a long history in Cameroon, while looped shoulder bags share a similar history in Guatemala. Crochet was probably introduced to both Africa and Guatemala during the Colonial Period. I suspect that tapestry crochet really appealed to "loopers" because crochet is more efficient and offers so many more design possibilities. To create a loop, the entire length of thread must be pulled through each loop, whereas with crochet, only a small loop is pulled through to create each stitch. Looping and tapestry crochet are done with different types of fibers and produce very different types of textiles, which is the reason that both techniques are still popular today. Crochet did not replace looping, it was simply added to the technical repertoire, but I believe that it was the loopers who first saw the potential of tapestry crochet in Africa and Guatemala. Both the looped and crocheted shoulder bags are very similar in proportion and appearance and both bags share a similar type of strap, which is attached on one side and tied on the other.

**The 11" wide shoulder bag on the left was crocheted in Todos Santos, Guatemala, with pink, green, purple, and white cotton thread in 1984. The shoulder strap was woven.**

**The 17" wide Guatemalan bag on the left was looped from 2-ply natural, red, blue, brown, and green sisal cord in 1978. A detail of the upper edge can be seen on the right.**

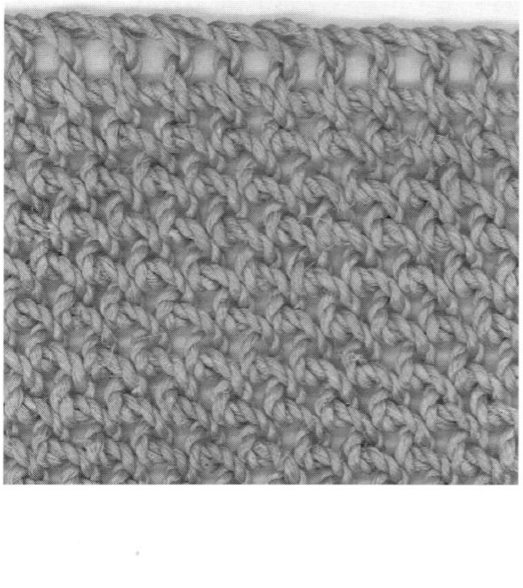

**The Maya man on the right, from Guatemala, tapestry crochets a shoulder bag with four-ply cotton thread. He no longer wears traditional clothes, but has switched to western-style clothing. The photograph was taken in 1984.**

The traditional clothing from each region in Guatemala features distinct color combinations and design motifs. Colonial Spaniards encouraged regional stylistic differences in clothing to help them identify their workers. These differences can be seen in the variety of bags pictured. A tapestry crocheted shoulder bag is an important part of a Guatemalan Mayan Indian man's traditional outfit. Used for carrying seeds in planting season, and for lunch or dinner, these bags are not only beautifully crafted, they are also very functional. Even though most Maya men have switched to more contemporary clothing, they usually still wear a shoulder bag from their town. The shoulder bags are either tapestry crocheted, woven, or knitted. If a man does not crochet his own, he buys one at the local market, since some men produce extra bags to supplement their meager incomes. The shoulder bag is one of the only items of clothing in Guatemala that traditionally is not made by women. The increased demand of the tourist trade, however, has inspired new products and has encouraged Mayan women to tapestry crochet too.

**A traditionally dressed Maya man from San Juan Atitan, Guatemala, crochets a shoulder bag in 1984 with cotton thread as his wife looks on.**

**The 14" wide shoulder bag on the right was crocheted in 1980 in Aguacatan, Guatemala, with purple, white, green, red, and blue cotton thread. The shoulder strap was woven.**

Traditional Guatemalan shoulder bags have distinct regional designs and color schemes. The 15" wide shoulder bag pictured on the right (with a detail on the next page) was crocheted with white, yellow, gold, blue, green, purple, and red cotton threads in Nebaj in 1978. Six threads were carried while another was worked. The shoulder strap was woven.

The Maya woman from Guatemala on the left (with detail below) is tapestry crocheting a change purse with green, yellow, and red acrylic yarn. Her shoulder bag was crocheted with the same vibrant colors in 1984.

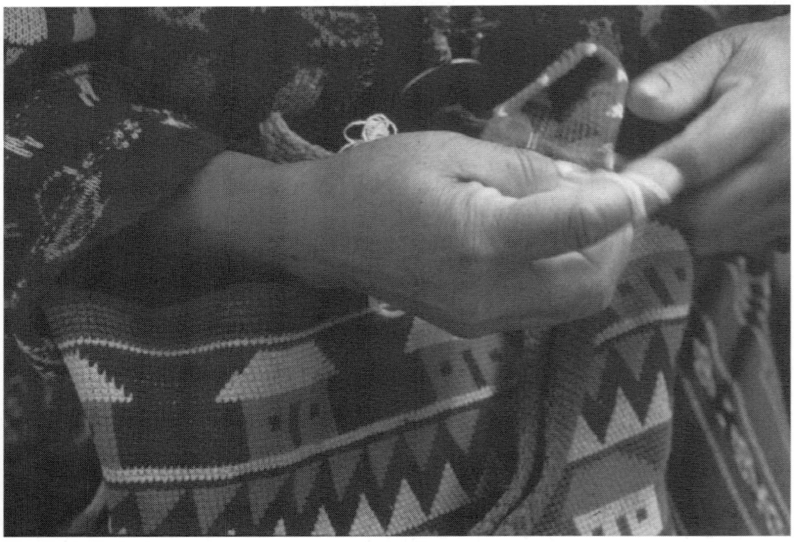

Detail of a shoulder bag from Nebaj, Guatemala.

***The Rules* was crocheted with red, orange, yellow, green, blue, indigo, violet, and white linen in 1998. It measures 15" x 17".**

# MY OWN WORK

I learned about tapestry crochet when I worked with a weaving cooperative from 1976 to 1980 as a Peace Corps volunteer in Guatemala. At the time, I was so interested in backstrap weaving, I ignored tapestry crochet. I already knew how to crochet, so I put my energy into learning the intricacies of backstrap weaving. I bought a number of crocheted shoulder bags, though, and used them when I returned to the States. People that I knew or ran into always asked me about my Guatemalan shoulder bags. They were surprised that the bags were crocheted and not woven. When I realized that tapestry crochet was relatively unknown in the States, I decided to explore its potential.

My first pieces were crocheted in a spiral, like the Guatemalan shoulder bags (and the amulet pouches). Eventually I decided to crochet flat pieces. I had to work out a few kinks first, though. When working in a spiral, the outside of the piece always shows the front of the crochet stitch. I wanted this same look on a flat piece. When a traditionally crocheted flat piece is turned over at the end of each row, the alternate rows show the back of the single crochet stitch. After a lot of experimentation, I realized I could crochet from right to left with my right hand, then from left to right with my left hand, so that the face side of the stitches would always show on the front of the piece.

My first flat piece was designed on square-ruled graph paper, but since the crochet stitch is taller than it is wide, it had an elongated image. I eventually developed the special graphs that are in this book. These graphs take into consideration stitch shape and placement.

Instead of paint, I use thread to reflect my "self". Over the years, my crocheted tapestries have become more intimate; they are more introspective and cathartic. My first pieces, which can be seen in my first *Tapestry Crochet* book, were large and made of heavy wool and cotton. I now prefer to crochet with fine linen.

Like the painter, Monet, I study and restudy a subject, under various emotional states rather than in varying light, though. Color choice is often symbolic, following in the tradition of Paul Gauguin. Like Gauguin's and Frida Kahlo's paintings, words are incorporated into the composition to further clarify the intended message. Like Frida, I do revealing self portraits. These pieces show the various faces I present to the world, which change with each situation.

Some people have mistaken my tapestry crochet portraits for prints. My Master of Fine Arts thesis and exhibition in printmaking featured a series of colorful self-portrait intaglio's, but I never realized the influence until the confusion arose. These crocheted portraits are a logical extension of my prints. I also display them like prints; framed and lined up in a row on the wall. The colors and text vary, but the image is repeated.

When I began teaching color theory in my art appreciation classes, it struck me that the words used to describe color and their relationships to each other can also be used to describe emotions and personality. For instance, we say that someone is green with envy or green can mean that someone is naive. These associations are often culturally bound, however. Although we associate blue with sadness in the Unites States, in Portugal, to be blue is to be happy! *Chameleon Series* includes eighteen pieces that explore the terms used to describe both color theory and personality. The three pieces below were crocheted with black, white, and gray linen in 1993. Each piece measures 5 1/2" x 4 1/8".

*Positive Self*

*Negative Self*

*Neutral Self*

I crocheted *Art Hysterical Triptych* in 1996. Each component measures 9 1/2" x 7 1/2". My frustration about the lack of support for the arts inspired the piece. The cultures we focus on in art history are those that have supported art. What will our legacy be?

*Unenlightened Age* was crocheted with black, white, and gray linen.

*Age of Enlightenment* was crocheted with purple and white linen.

*Priorities and Legacies* was crocheted with yellow and white linen.

# 2 TAPESTRY CROCHET BASICS

## Suitable Yarns and Threads

I have used a variety of threads and yarns for the projects in this book to demonstrate that many types are suitable for tapestry crochet. The important factor is that the stitch be crocheted consistently; either always tight or always loose. Tightness not only hides the carried yarns, but also contributes a stiff quality to the finished piece. Loose stitches allow the carried yarn to show through and produce a more flexible fabric. Experiment to find the degree of tightness that is right for you.

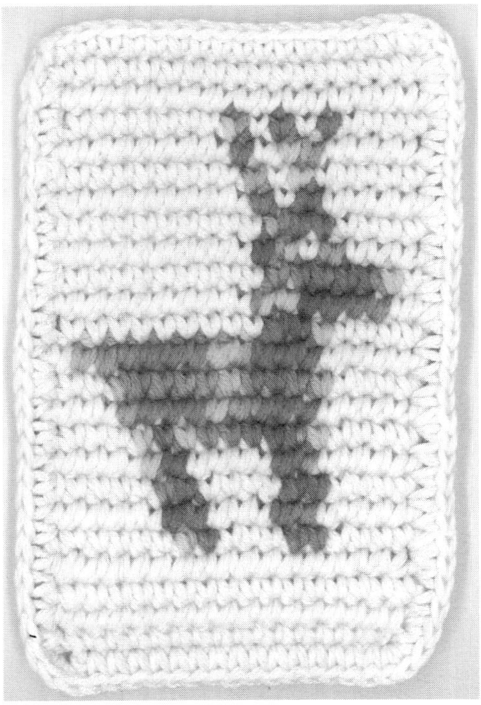

**The sampler above was crocheted tightly with a size "4" steel hook. The fabric is stiff and the carried threads are hidden.**

**The sampler on the right was crocheted loosely with a size "I" hook. The fabric is not as stiff as the first sampler and the carried threads can be seen.**

## *The same thread and graph were used to tapestry crochet the four samplers on these two pages. As you can see, each variation produces a different look.*

**The sampler below was crocheted with a size "4" hook, but the hook was inserted into the back top loop (instead of into both of the top loops). The front loop forms a horizontal line on the top of each row.**

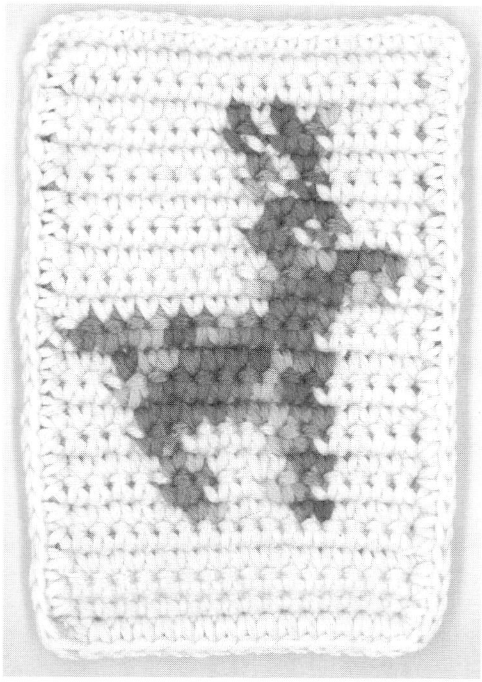

**The sampler on the left was crocheted with a size "4" hook, but it was turned over at the end of each row (instead of being crocheted from right to left and left to right on alternating rows). A ridged texture resulted from alternating rows of the front of the stitch with rows of the back of the stitch.**

Yarns and threads may be substituted for all of the projects in this book. If a thicker one is used, the hook should be proportionately larger; if a finer yarn is selected, a smaller hook should be utilized. Stitches may be increased or decreased at the beginning of each project to accommodate different fibers.

Yarn is commercially dyed in large batches or lots, each with its own "dye lot number." Since dye lots can, and usually do, vary in color from batch to batch, you might want to purchase more than is suggested in the instructions. If you should run out of yarn before finishing a project, you might not be able to rematch the exact color that you need, resulting in a noticeable color variation, or streaking in the piece. When choosing a color, keep in mind that darker colors are harder to work with because they are more difficult to see.

# Crochet Hooks

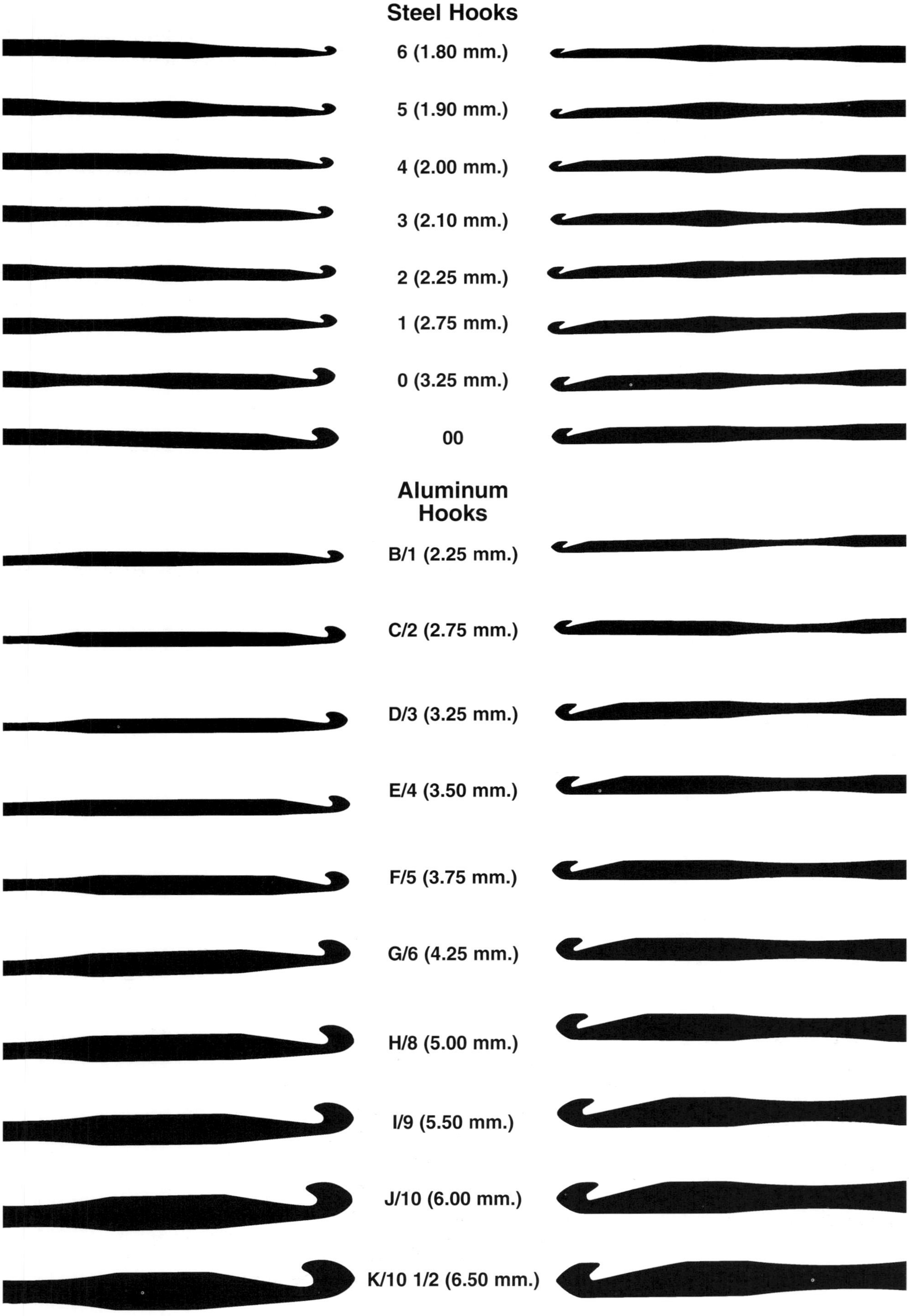

## Crochet Hooks

Two different types of crochet hooks are manufactured. One style is rounder, while the other is more angular. I have found that both styles work well, although each style tends to be slightly different in size. Some crocheters prefer one style over the other, but this is a personal preference.

Steel hooks come in small sizes and are usually used with fine crochet cottons. Aluminum hooks are larger, and usually used with heavier yarns.

A specific hook size is recommended with each project, but you may vary the size of the hook, depending on your needs. If you tend to crochet loosely, increase the tension on the yarn or use a smaller hook to crochet a tighter stitch. Sometimes it is necessary to change both the tension and the size of the crochet hook to achieve the desired result.

Several crochet hook manufacturers produce hooks with large, easy to hold handles. I highly recommend these hooks. You can also buy a soft handle that slips over your hook. The large handles are much easier to grip, especially when crocheting tightly.

Do not be upset if occasionally a crochet hook breaks. I never thought it possible, but I have broken a number of hooks. Sometimes the hooked end will fall off, other times the handle will snap in two.

# Crochet Basics

If you are new to crochet, or wish to brush up on your skills, then practice the following basics before going onto a project. Use a light color yarn (it's easier on the eyes) and a size D crochet hook.

## The Slip Knot

The first step is to make a *slip knot*.

**Begin by making a loop, then . . .**

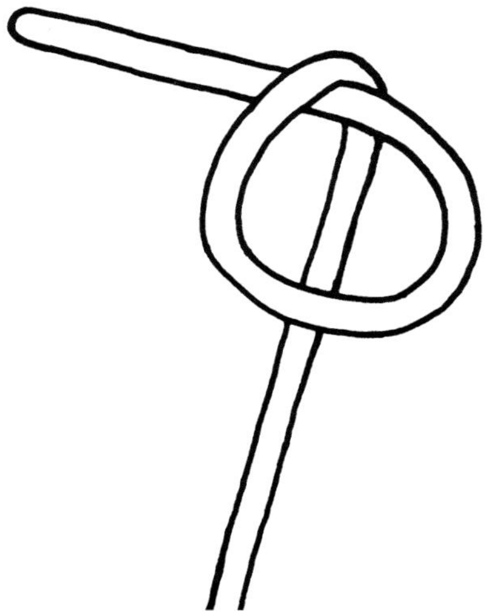

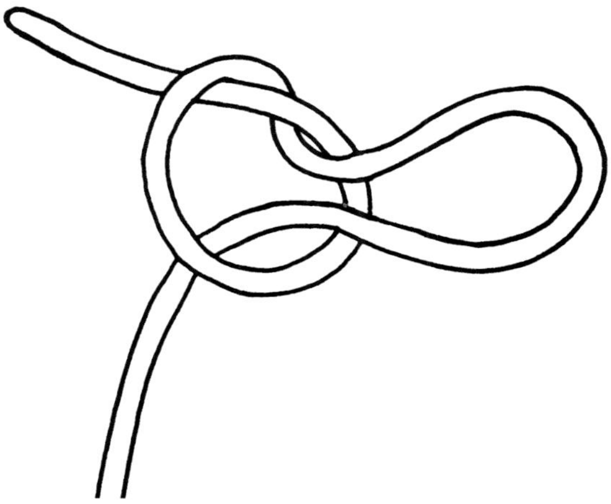

**Pull the yarn from behind the loop through the opening to form another loop. Tighten the *slip knot* by holding the loop to the right while pulling both ends of yarn.**

*Instructions for <u>left-handed crocheters</u> are on pages 34-39.*

# Right-Handed Crochet

## Tensioning

The technique illustrated will allow you to work with consistent tension. To begin:

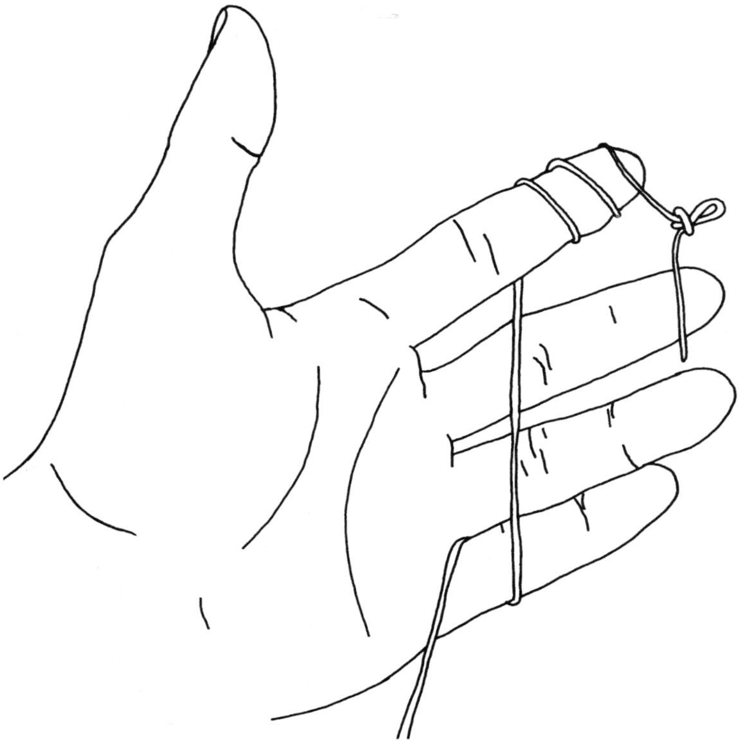

**Loop the yarn around the little finger of your left hand, and then in front of the little, ring, and middle fingers, and then around your index finger a couple of times.**

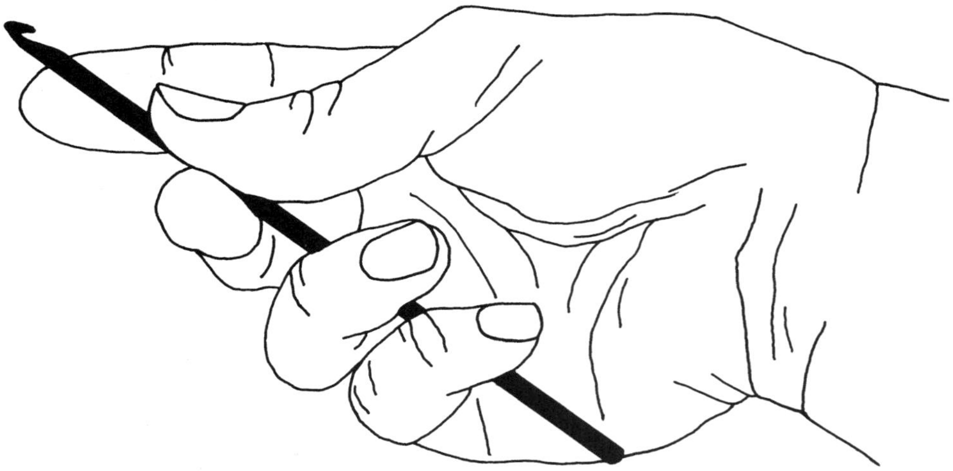

**Grasp the crochet hook with your right hand, resting your thumb and middle fingers on the flat part of the crochet hook. If you are used to holding your hook in a different way, it would be better to change your grip since it is much more difficult to crochet tightly in any other manner.**

# Right-Handed Chain Stitch

To make a *chain stitch:*

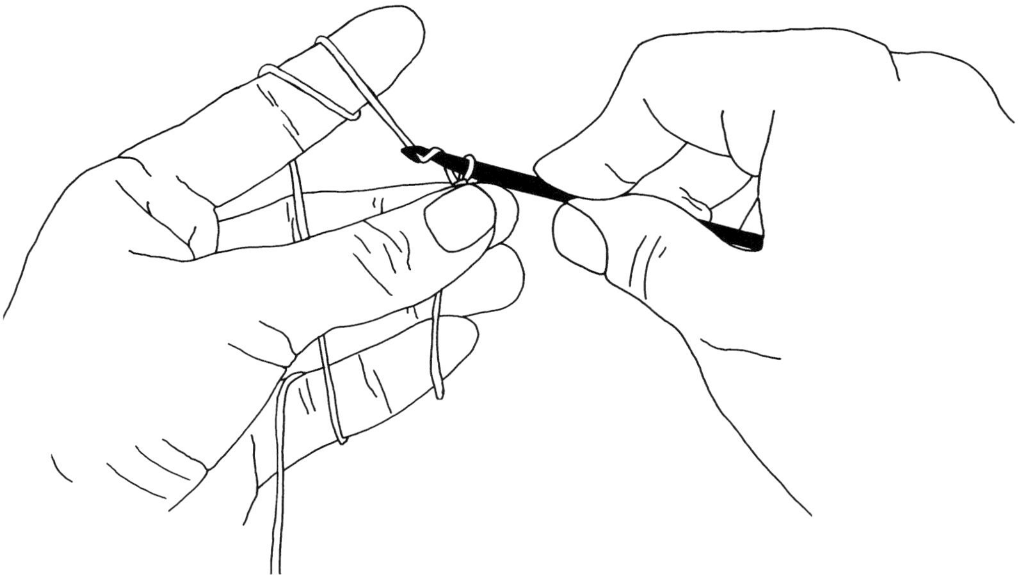

**Hold the slip knot between your thumb and middle fingers. Insert the hook into the loop of the slip knot.**

**Tighten the slip knot around the hook (but not too tight!). Flip the yarn over the hook from right to left and then catch it with the crochet hook. This is called *yarning over.***

**Rotating the hook downward, pull the yarn through the loop of the slip knot. Tighten the new loop on the hook slightly. This makes one *chain stitch.* Yarn over again, and then pull it through the loop on the hook.**

As you use up the yarn, pull up two more inches of yarn and wrap it around your index finger. You can also unloop the yarn around your index finger as you need it.

To continue the chain:

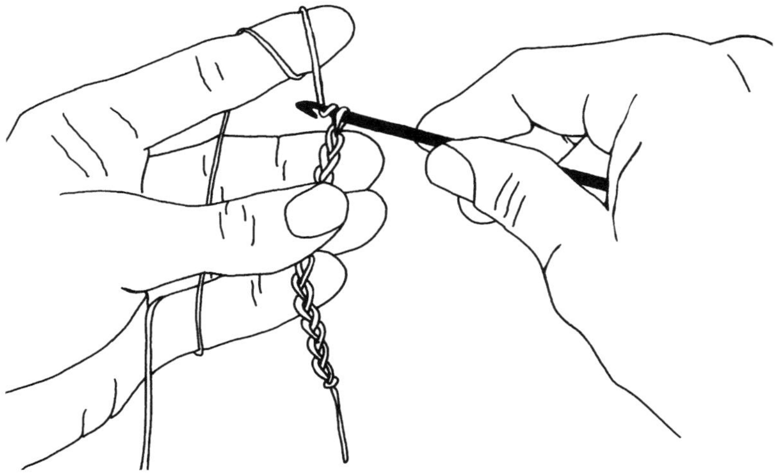

**Hold the chain between the thumb and middle fingers of your left hand.**

**As the chain becomes longer, move it down creating a slight tension between the chain, hook, and index finger. Insert the hook into the remaining loop, being careful not to split the yarn, and then continue to crochet.**

If you should make a mistake, it is easy to *rip out* the crochet stitches. To *rip out* the chain, or any other crochet stitch, remove the hook from the loop and then pull on the yarn. After ripping out, the hook can be reinserted into the remaining loop to keep crocheting.

# Right-Handed Single Crochet in Rounds

The Amulet Pouches, Eyeglass Case, Change Purse, Pillow, Rectangular Shoulder Bag, Shawl, Scarf, and Oval Purse projects are all worked in *rounds.* To practice single crocheting in *rounds*, make a slip knot, then chain 12 stitches.

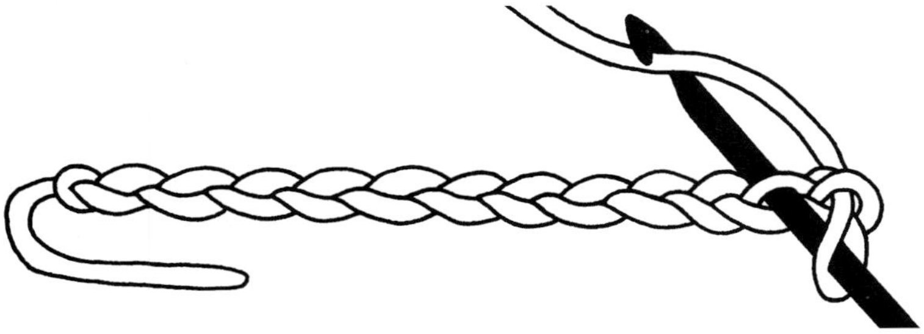

**To start the *round*, insert the hook from front to back through the bottom loop of the second chain to the left of the hook. Yarn over and then pull it through the chain.**

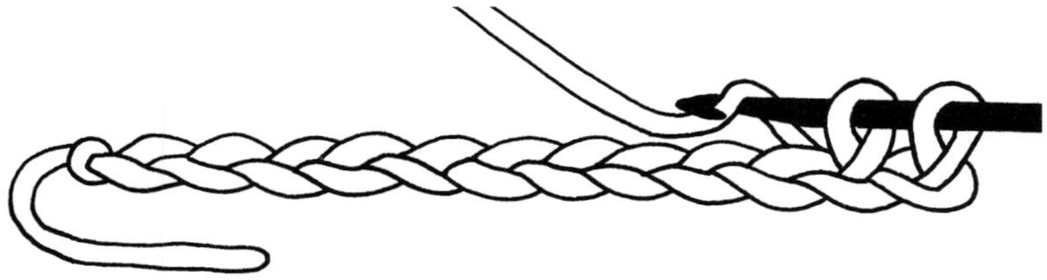

**You now have 2 loops on your hook. Yarn over, and then pull it through the 2 loops on the hook. You have just crocheted a *right-handed single crochet stitch.***

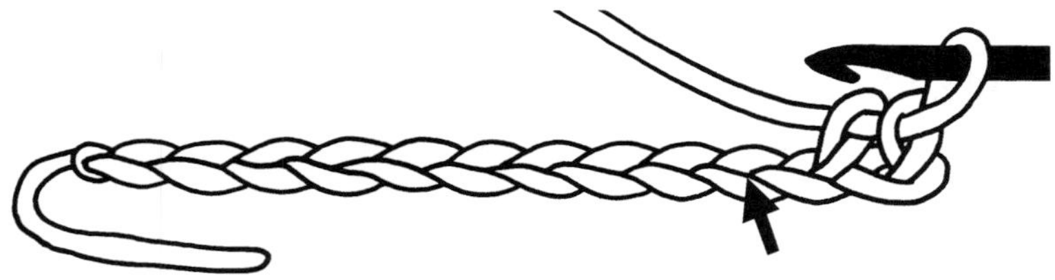

**Single crochet another stitch by inserting the hook at the arrow, again through the bottom loop.**

**Continue to single crochet across the row, working from right to left.**

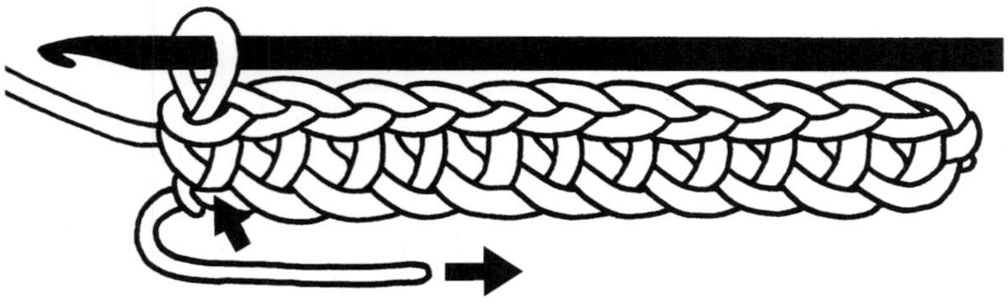

**Work 3 stitches into the last chain stitch in the space indicated by the arrow, then pull the short tail of yarn.**

Turn the piece around so that what was on the top is now on the bottom. Single crochet on the new top through the chain where the arrow indicates. This is a real deviation from traditional crochet.

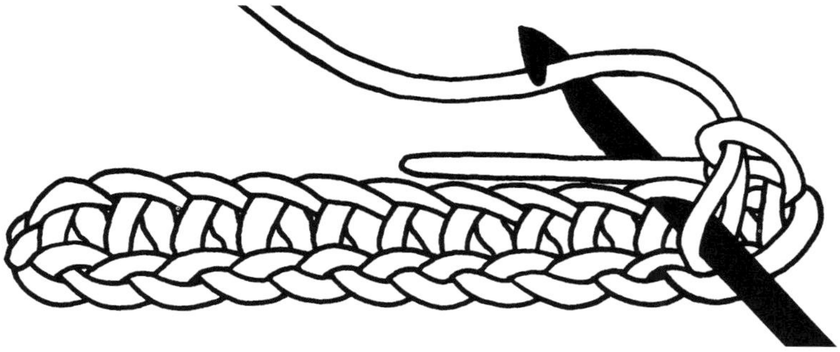

Insert the hook through the new top of the chain and under the end piece of yarn. Continue to single crochet as before, crocheting around the end piece as you go along.

This completes the first *round* of single crochet. Insert the hook where the arrow indicates to start the second *round.*

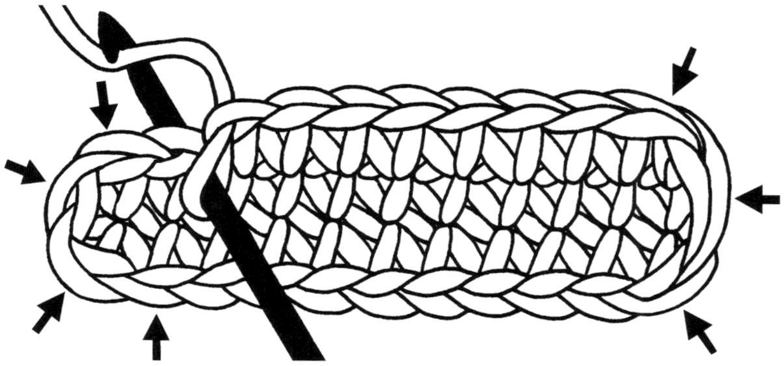

Continue to single crochet around, inserting the hook now under the two top loops of each stitch of the previous row. Care must be taken to crochet *only one stitch into each end stitch* as indicated by the arrows, to create a vertical tube.

*Crochet at least 5 rounds before going on to the tapestry crochet stitch.*

## Right-Handed Tapestry Crochet

The tapestry crochet technique will enable you to crochet a multicolored motif with relative ease. While one yarn is being worked, another yarn is carried. At any point the yarns can be switched. The carried yarn is then crocheted while the previously worked yarn is carried. A graph paper design can be used to indicate the color change sequence, stitch by stitch.

One important consideration is that *all of the yarns being worked should be of the same weight* to avoid a warped appearance. If a thin yarn is used with a thicker yarn, the thick yarn will occupy more space when worked, warping the space.

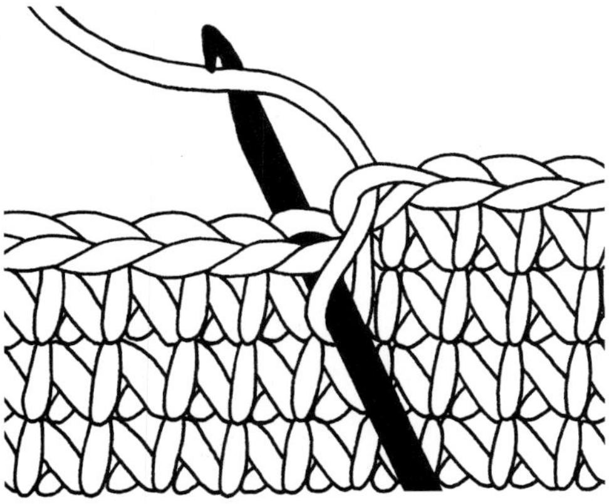

### Inserting the Hook

In tapestry crochet, after the first row or round has been crocheted, the hook is usually inserted from *front to back,* under the 2 top loops of the stitch being crocheted into. If the hook is inserted into only one of the top loops, there will be a horizontal line of yarn over each crochet stitch (see page 25). The *front* of the work will almost always be facing you. The only time it is not facing you is with reverse single crochet stitch.

**Inserting the hook from *front to back,* under 2 top loops.**

## Carrying Yarns

Being able to carry yarns is essential for tapestry crochet, allowing a two - or more - color design to be worked without floats on the back. The concealed yarns make the finished piece more durable. The carrying technique enables knots and loose ends to be eliminated as well.

**To *carry a yarn*, first, lay the additional yarn over the top two loops of the stitches being crocheted into, leaving a one-inch tail sticking out of the back. The carried yarn can be kept in place with the thumb of the left hand.**

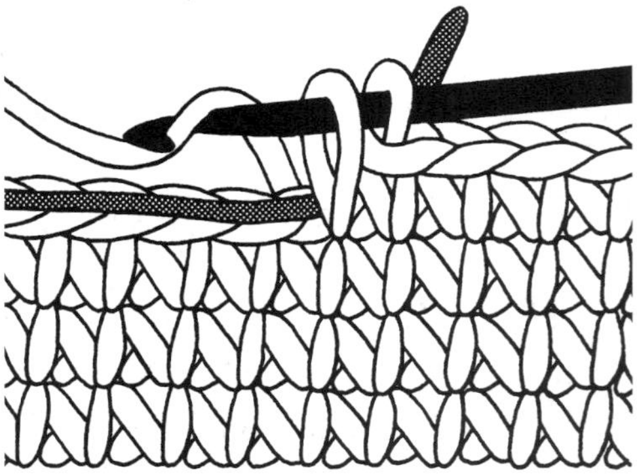

**Single crochet across the row as usual, keeping the carried yarn on top of the loops, crocheting around it. If done correctly, the carried yarn will not be visible from either the front or the back of the work.**

After the row has been completed, the one inch end (that you left sticking out of the back of the piece) can be snipped off.

More than one color yarn can be carried at the same time for a multicolored tapestry crochet motif. Try to limit the carried yarns to two or three to avoid a tangled mess. Each yarn carried will slightly increase the height of the crochet stitch. Page 21 shows a detail of a purse that has 6 carried yarns, making the stitches tall and narrow. For a consistent appearance, start to carry the yarn at the beginning of a project, even if there will not be any color changes for a few rows.

# Joining in New Yarns

If you should run out of the yarn that you are crocheting with, start to carry the new yarn five or more stitches before it is needed, instead of tying on a new piece. Switch to the new yarn, and then carry the tail of the old yarn five or more stitches to secure it before snipping it off.

The carried yarn should be pulled occasionally to assure that it does not stick out of the piece where it becomes slack.

## Right-Handed Tapestry Crochet Stitch

The *tapestry crochet stitch* is similar to the single crochet stitch. One or more yarns are carried while a yarn is being crocheted.

**You have to plan ahead with the tapestry crochet stitch, because the yarn switch occurs while two loops of an incomplete crochet stitch are still on the hook.**

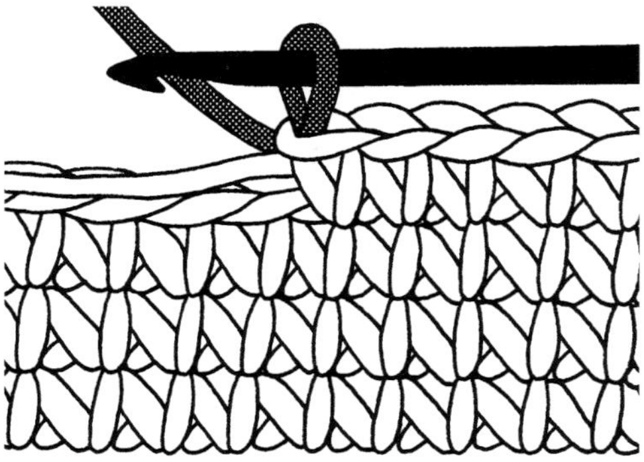

**Make the final *yarn over* and loop with a *carried* yarn.**

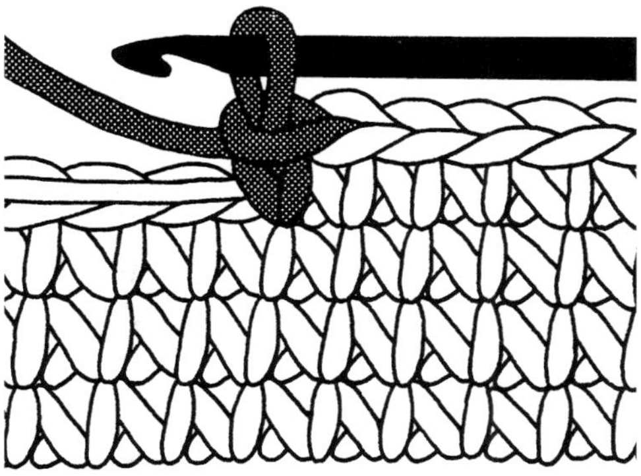

**Continue to crochet across the row while carrying the previously crocheted yarn, until another yarn change is desired.**

After a few yarn switches have been made, the yarns may begin to tangle. Stop and untangle them before it becomes a problem. If you are crocheting with only two yarns, you can untwist them by holding the piece up in the air with one of the yarns while you pull on the other yarn. Let the piece spin around in the air so that the yarns untangle. This is also a good time to check for mistakes.

The various yarns will not tangle together if you separate them while you are crocheting. One way to separate them is to place one yarn to your right and the other to your left. As you change colors, you will see a twist in the yarns where they cross over one another next to the previous stitch. The twist will not show in the finished piece.

*Instructions for right-handed crocheters are on pages 28-33.*

# Left-Handed Crochet

## Tensioning

The technique illustrated will allow you to work with consistent tension. To begin:

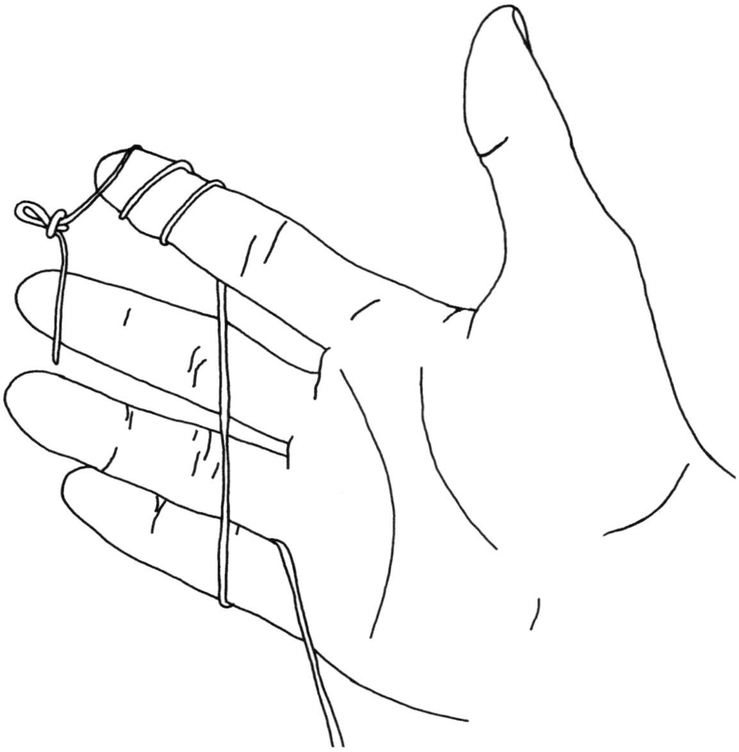

**Loop the yarn around the little finger of your right hand, then in front of the little, ring, and middle fingers, and then around your index finger a couple of times.**

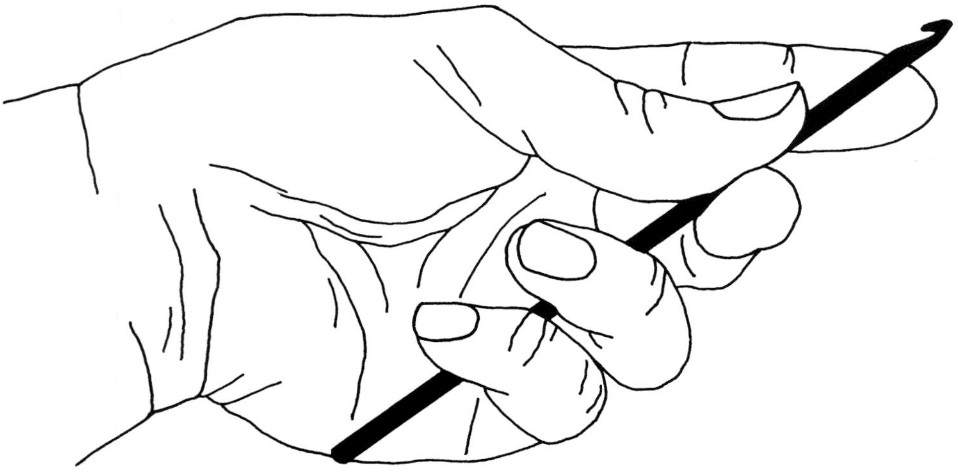

**Grasp the crochet hook with your left hand, resting your thumb and middle fingers on the flat part of the crochet hook. If you are used to holding your hook a different way, it would be better to change your grip since it is much more difficult to crochet tightly in any other manner.**

# Left-Handed Chain Stitch

To make a *chain stitch*:

**Hold the slip knot between your thumb and middle fingers. Insert the hook into the loop of the slip knot.**

**Tighten the slip knot around the hook (but not too tight!). Flip the yarn over the hook from left to right and then catch it with the crochet hook. This is called *yarning over*.**

**Rotating the hook downward, pull the yarn through the loop of the slip knot. Tighten the new loop on the hook slightly. This makes one *chain stitch.* Yarn over again, and then pull it through the loop on the hook.**

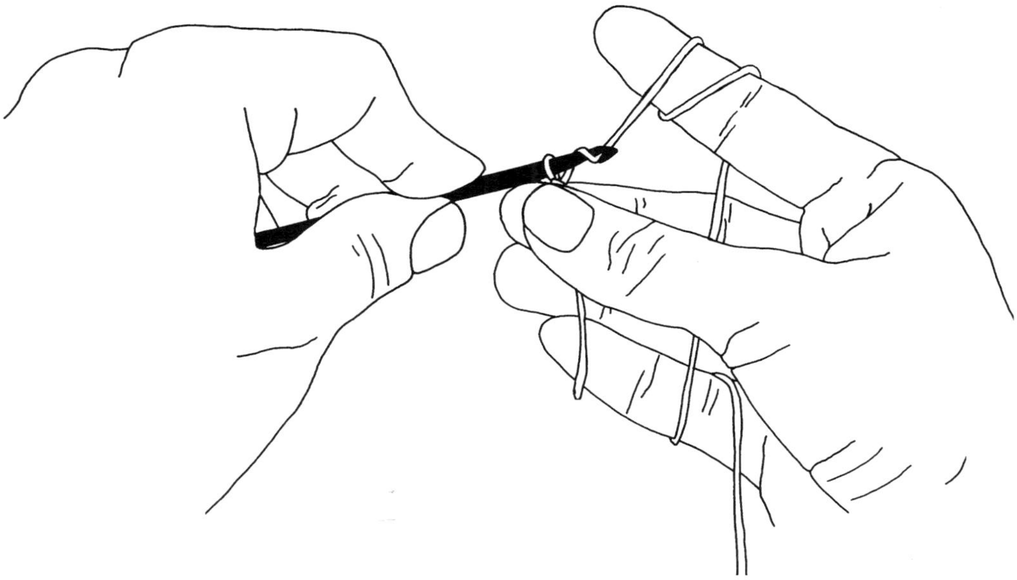

As you use up the yarn, pull up two more inches of yarn and wrap it around your index finger. You can also unloop the yarn around your index finger as you need it.

To continue the chain:

**Hold the chain between the thumb and middle fingers of your right hand.**

**As the chain becomes longer, move it down creating a slight tension between the chain, hook, and index finger. Insert the hook into the remaining loop, being careful not to split the yarn, and then continue to crochet.**

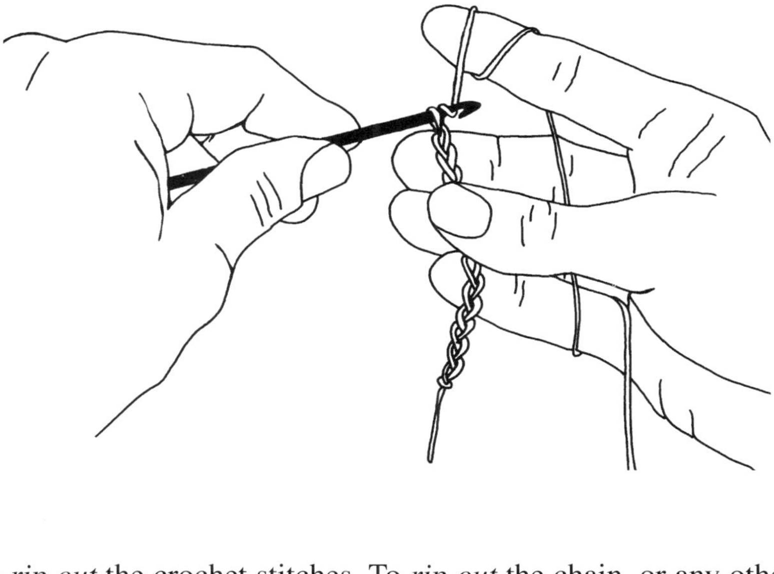

If you should make a mistake, it is easy to *rip out* the crochet stitches. To *rip out* the chain, or any other crochet stitch, remove the hook from the loop and then pull on the yarn. It is then very easy to reinsert the hook and continue to crochet.

# Left-Handed Single Crochet in Rounds

The Amulet Pouches, Eyeglass Case, Change Purse, Pillow, Rectangular Shoulder Bag, Shawl, Scarf, and Oval Purse projects are all worked *in rounds.* To practice single crocheting in *rounds*, make a slip knot, then chain 12 stitches.

**To start the *round,* insert the hook from front to back through the bottom loop of the second chain to the right of the hook. Yarn over and then pull it through the chain.**

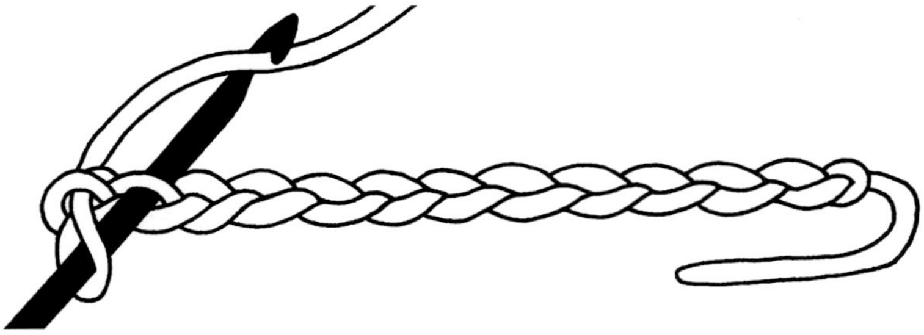

**You now have 2 loops on your hook. Yarn over, and then pull it through the 2 loops on the hook. You have just crocheted a *left-handed single crochet stitch.***

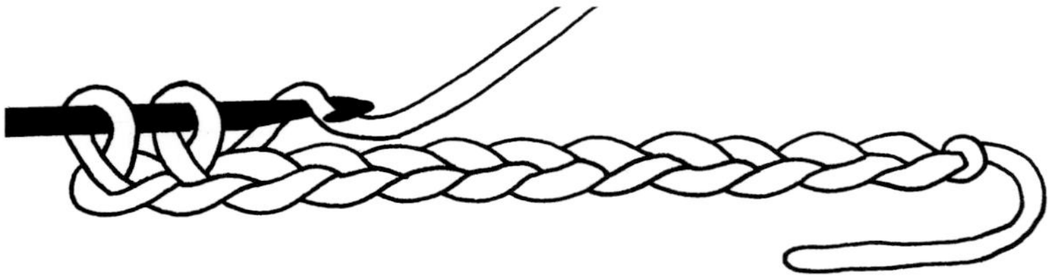

**Single crochet another stitch by inserting the hook at the arrow, again through the bottom loop.**

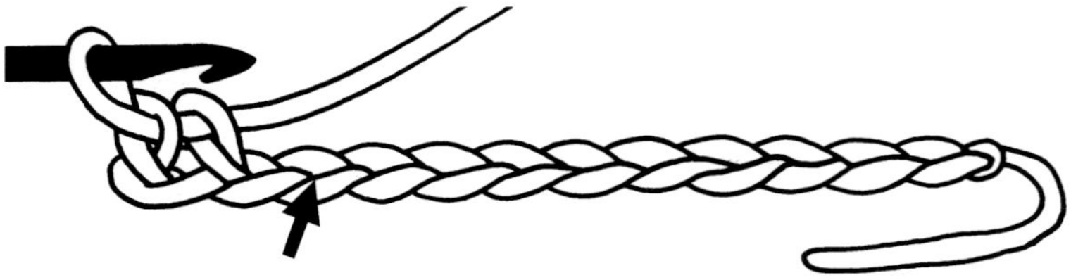

**Continue to single crochet across the row, working from left to right.**

**Work 3 stitches into the last chain stitch in the space indicated by the arrow, then pull the short tail of yarn.**

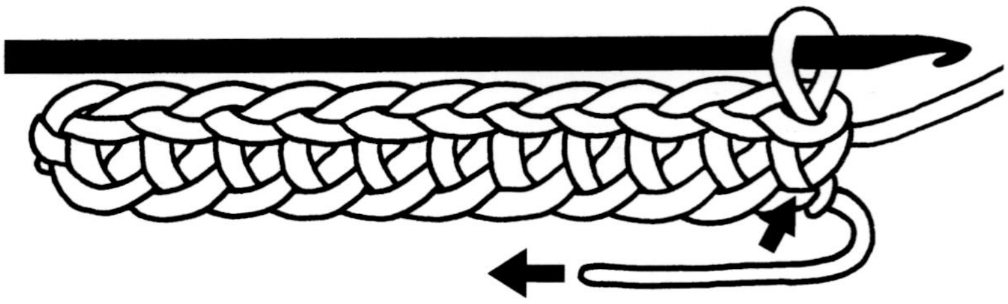

Turn the piece around so that what was on the top is now on the bottom. Single crochet on the new top through the chain where the arrow indicates. This is a real deviation from traditional crochet.

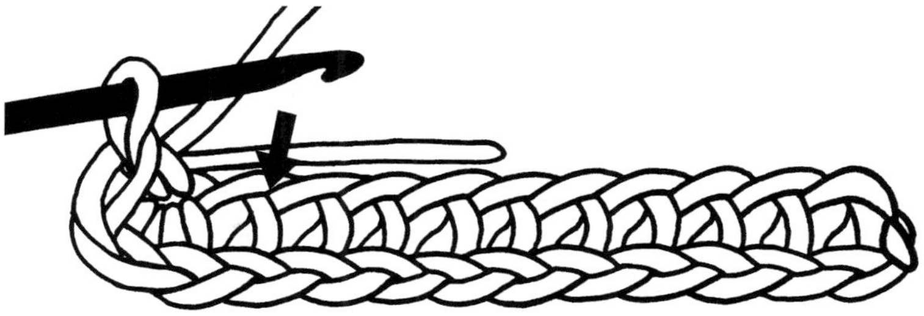

Insert the hook through the new top of the chain and under the end piece of yarn. Continue to single crochet as before, crocheting around the end piece as you go along.

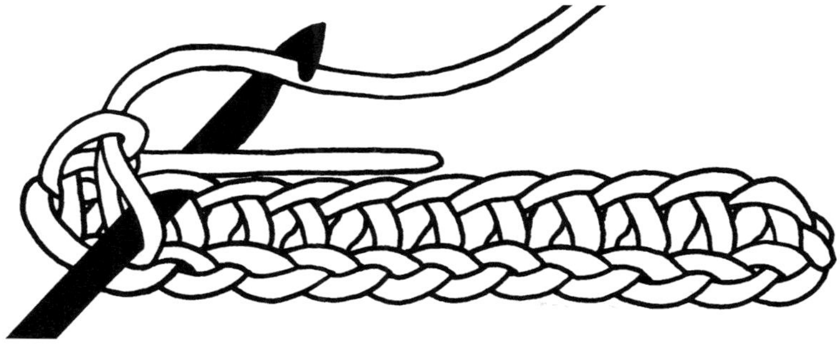

This completes the first round of single crochet. Insert the hook where the arrow indicates to start the second *round.*

Continue to single crochet around, inserting the hook now under the two top loops of each stitch of the previous row. Care must be taken to crochet *only one stitch into each end stitch* as indicated by the arrows, to create a vertical tube.

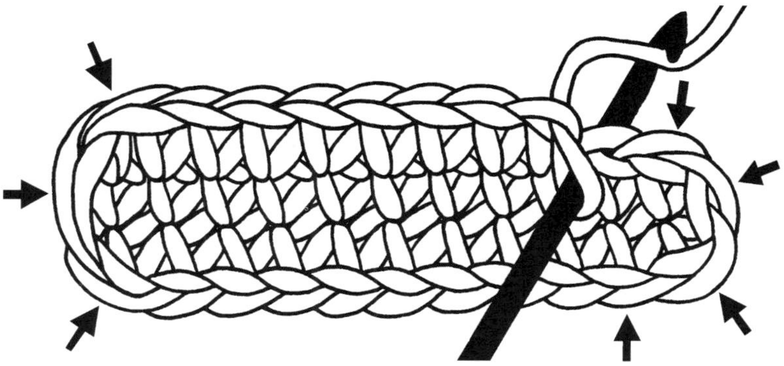

*Crochet at least 5 rounds before going on to the tapestry crochet stitch.*

## Left-Handed Tapestry Crochet

The tapestry crochet technique will enable you to crochet a multicolored motif with relative ease. While one yarn is being worked, another yarn is carried. At any point the yarns can be switched. The carried yarn is then crocheted while the previously worked yarn is carried. A graph paper design can be used to indicate the color change sequence, stitch by stitch.

One important consideration is that *all of the yarns being worked should be of the same weight* to avoid a warped appearance. If a thin yarn is used with a thicker yarn, the thick yarn will occupy more space when worked, warping the space.

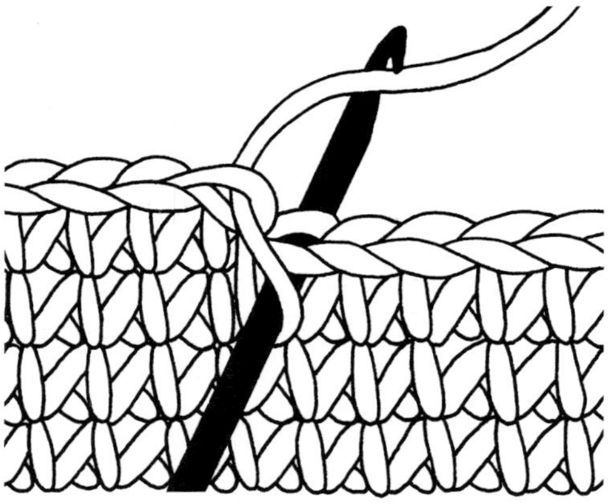

## Inserting The Hook

In tapestry crochet, after the first row or round has been crocheted, the hook is usually inserted from *front to back,* under the 2 top loops of the stitch being crocheted into. If the hook is inserted into only one of the top loops, there will be a horizontal line of yarn over each crochet stitch (see page 25). The *front* of the work will almost always be facing you. The only time it is not facing you is with the reverse single crochet stitch.

## Carrying Yarns

Being able to carry yarns is essential for tapestry crochet, allowing a two - or more - color design to be worked without floats on the back. The concealed colors make the finished piece more durable. The carrying technique enables knots and loose ends to be eliminated as well.

**To *carry a yarn*, first, lay the additional yarn over the top two loops of the stitches being crocheted into, leaving a one-inch tail sticking out of the back. The carried yarn can be kept in place with the thumb of the right hand.**

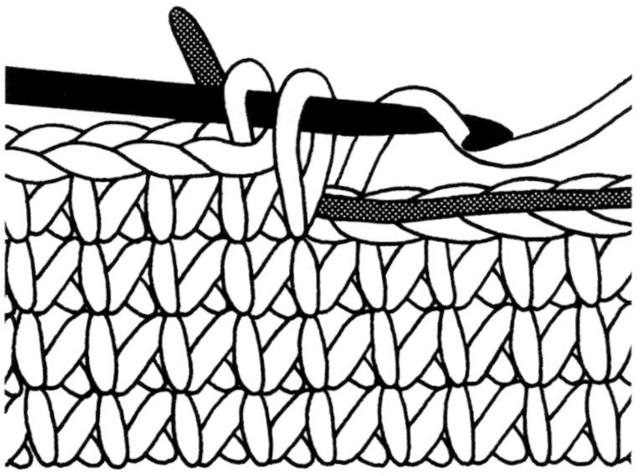

**Single crochet across the row as usual, keeping the carried yarn on top of the loops, crocheting around it. If done correctly, the carried yarn will not be visible from either the front or the back of the work.**

After the row has been completed, the one inch end (that you left sticking out of the back of the piece) can be snipped off.

More than one color yarn can be carried at the same time for a multicolored tapestry crochet motif. Try to limit the carried yarns to two or three to avoid a tangled mess. Each yarn carried will slightly increase the height of the crochet stitch. Page 21 shows a detail of a purse that has 6 carried yarns, making the stitches tall and narrow. For a consistent appearance, start to carry the yarn at the beginning of a project, even if there will not be any color changes for a few rows.

## Joining in New Yarns

If you should run out of the yarn that you are crocheting with, start to carry the new yarn five or more stitches before it is needed, instead of tying on a new piece. Switch to the new yarn, then carry the tail of the old yarn five or more stitches to secure it before snipping it off.

The carried yarn should be pulled occasionally to assure that it does not stick out of the piece where it becomes slack.

## Left-Handed Tapestry Crochet Stitch

The *tapestry crochet stitch* is similar to the single crochet stitch. One or more yarns are carried while a yarn is being crocheted.

**You have to plan ahead with the tapestry crochet stitch, because the yarn switch occurs while two loops of an incomplete crochet stitch are still on the hook.**

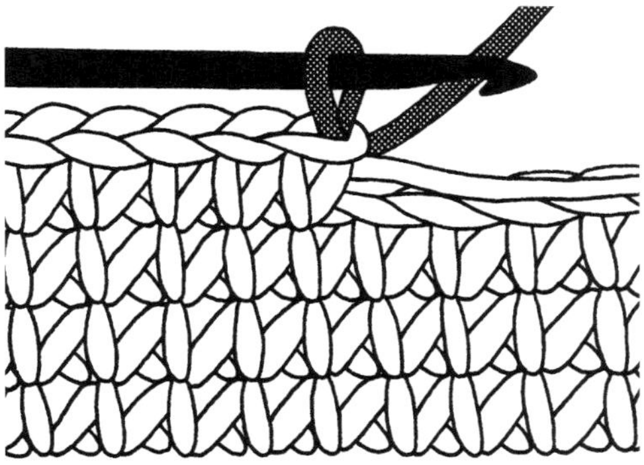

**Make the final *yarn over* and loop with a *carried* yarn.**

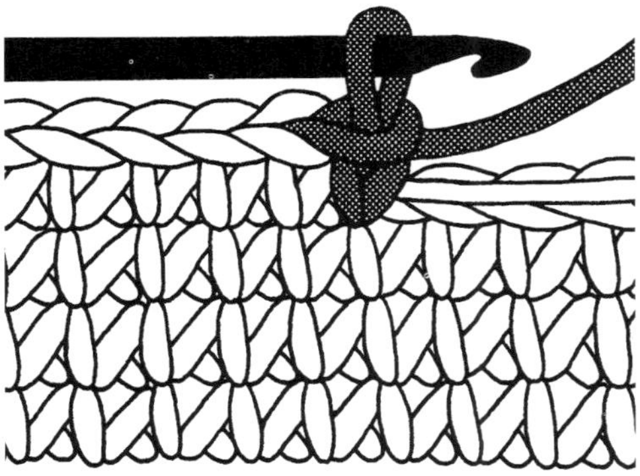

**Continue to crochet across the row while carrying the previously crocheted yarn, until another yarn change is desired.**

After a few yarn switches have been made, the yarns may begin to tangle. Stop and untangle them before it becomes a problem. If you are crocheting with only two yarns, you can untwist them by holding the piece up in the air with one of the yarns while you pull on the other yarn. Let the piece spin around in the air so that the yarns untangle. This is also a good time to check for mistakes.

The various yarns will not tangle together if you separate them while you are crocheting. One way to separate them is to place one yarn to your right and the other to your left. As you change colors, you will see a twist in the yarns where they cross over one another next to the previous stitch. The twist will not show in the finished piece.

# TECHNIQUES FOR ALL CROCHETERS

*The following illustrations are for right-handed crocheters. Left-handed crocheters should place a mirror to the side of each illustration to reverse the image.*

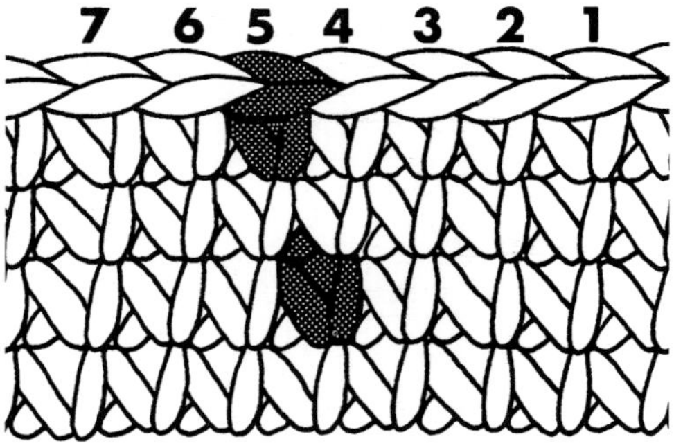


## Counting Tapestry Crochet Stitches

The Tapestry Crochet stitch is a *V*-shaped stitch, topped by two loops which also form a *V.* To count the stitches, either count the *V*s in the body of the piece, or count the *V* loops on top. In the illustration on the left there are seven complete stitches across the top, and four rows.

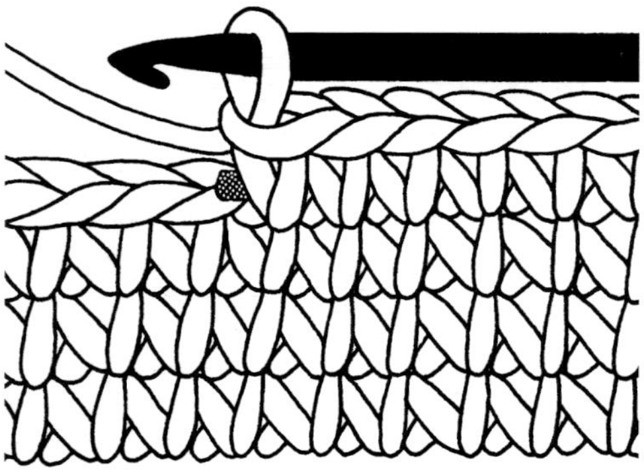

## Cutting a Yarn Flush

Cut the desired yarn as close as possible to the finished piece. Cut only those yarns that have been carried for at least five stitches to assure that they are well-anchored.

## Checking the Gauge

To check the *stitch gauge,* lay a ruler on top of the project that you are working on. Place the ruler parallel to the rows and line up one of the inch markers between any two stitches. Count the number of stitches between the lined up marker and the next inch marker. This will give you the *stitches per inch* measurement.

To check the *row gauge,* lay a ruler on the piece perpendicular to the rows. Line one of the inch markers up between 2 rows. Count the number of rows between the lined-up marker and the next inch marker. This will give you the *rows per inch* measurement.

**On the left, the 10-inch marker is lined up correctly. The *stitch gauge* measurement is 9 stitches per inch since there are 9 stitches between the 10 and 11-inch markers.**

**On the right, the 7-inch marker is lined up correctly. The *row gauge* measurement is 8 rows per inch since there are 8 rows between the 7 and 8 inch markers.**

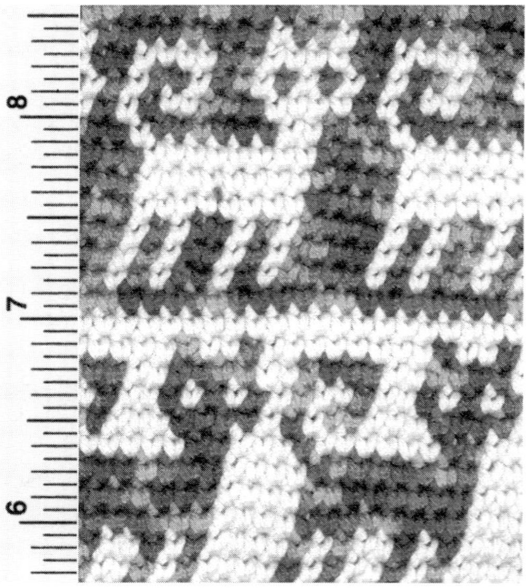

# Increasing Stitches

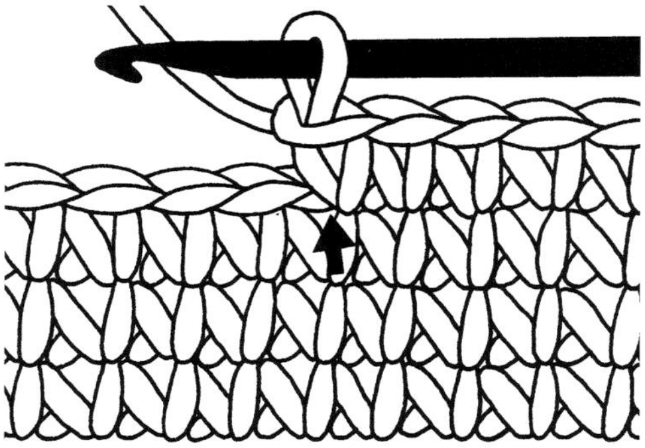

To *increase* the number of stitches in a row or round, crochet two stitches in a spot ordinarily reserved for one stitch. Insert the hook back into the same stitch as indicated by the arrow on the left.

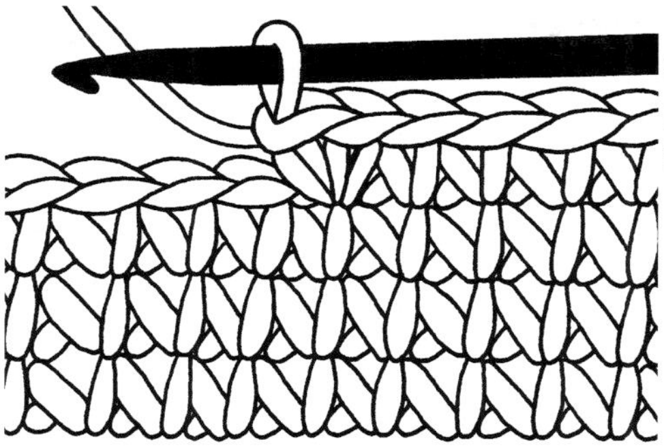

Crochet the second stitch right next to the previous stitch as illustrated on the left.

# Decreasing Stitches:

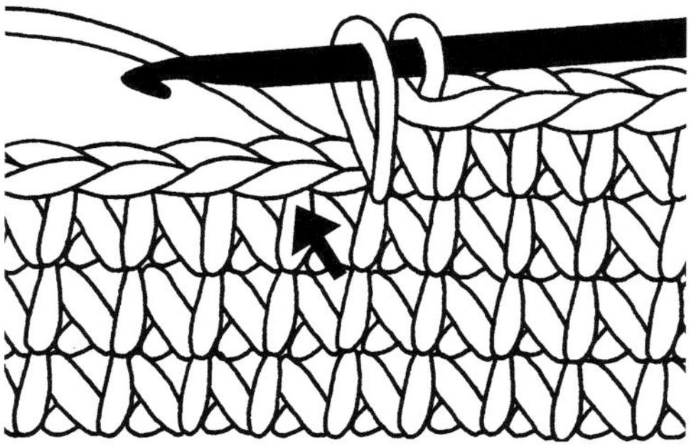

To *decrease* the number of stitches in a row or round, start a normal crochet stitch by inserting the hook under the two loops of the stitch that you are crocheting into. Yarn over and then pull through a loop. Now instead of completing the crochet stitch, insert the hook into the next stitch where the arrow indicates on the left.

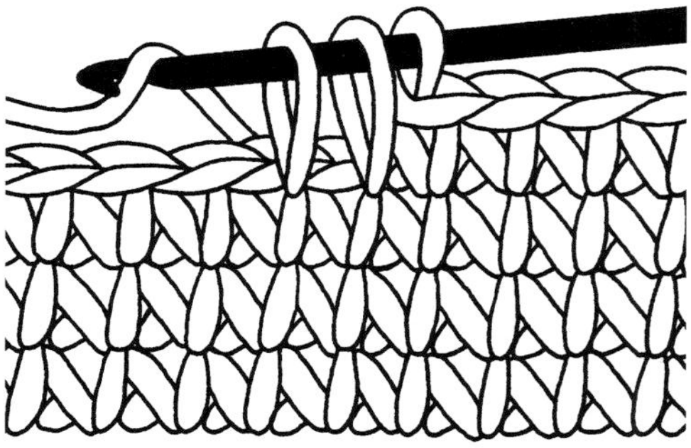

Yarn over and then pull through a loop. You now have three loops on your hook.

Yarn over and then pull it through all three loops.

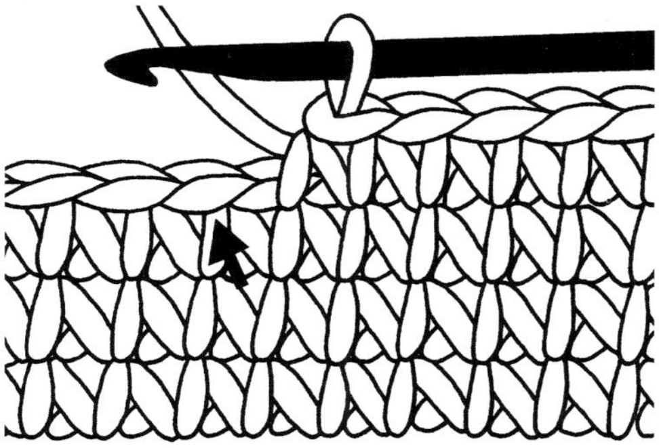

You have now *decreased* one stitch.

Insert the hook into the next stitch as indicated by the arrow to continue crocheting across the row.

# Adjusting the Tension

If you find that you crochet too loose, use a smaller hook, or crochet with more tension. Conversely, if you crochet too tight, use a larger hook or crochet with less tension. The yarn wrapped around your index finger controls the tension. Pull the yarn with this finger after each stitch to increase the tension, or let it slacken to decrease the tension.

# Creating Shapes

Creative use of increasing and/or decreasing was used to make the variety of projects in this book. If a piece is crocheted without any increases or decreases, it will maintain a constant width or diameter. By increasing or decreasing the stitches on a round or row, the width or diameter can be changed.

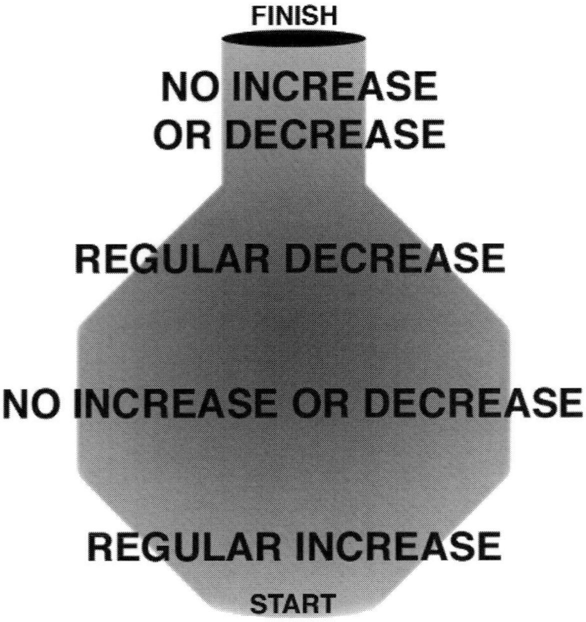


**To crochet a flat, round disk, increases are necessary to increase the diameter. For a proportioned and even look, space the increases and decreases evenly. For instance, if 12 increases are desired in a round of 36 stitches, a stitch should be increased every third stitch.**

**When the increasing is stopped, the rounds will maintain a constant number of stitches and vertical walls will emerge around the flat disk, creating a basket shape. If the number of stitches is again increased or decreased, an interesting shape can be achieved. For sculptural or organic-looking pieces, the increases or decreases can be placed wherever they are needed.**

**On a flat piece, stitches can be increased or decreased at the beginning or end of a row, or evenly or randomly spaced through a row. Each method will create a different look.**

**Frequently the piece will appear warped or lumpy. These minor flaws are easily removed during blocking. A major warp or lump however is usually only slightly lessened through blocking.**

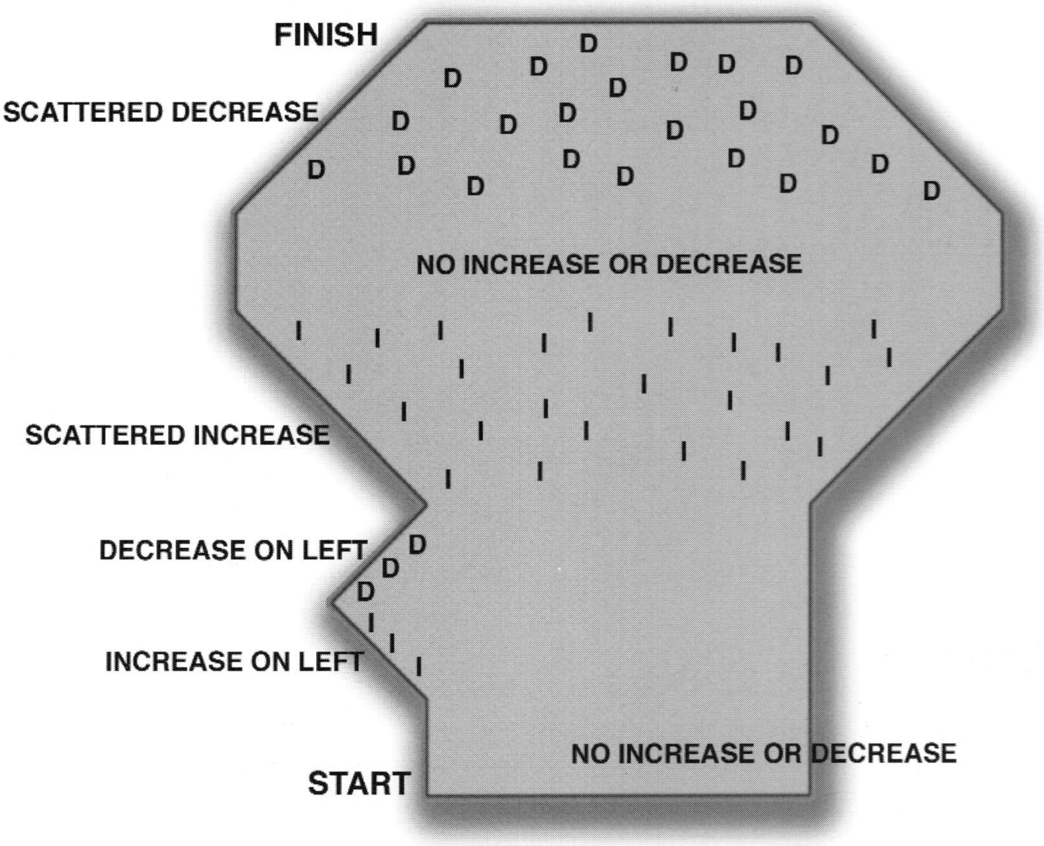

# Crocheting in a Spiral

The Baby Blanket/Throw, Hats/Baskets, Cat's Meow Purses, Beaded Flaring Basket, Beaded Basket, Jewelry Basket, Yarmulke, Hackey Sack/Ball, Scrunchies, and Beaded Bracelet/Necklace projects are all crocheted in a circular spiral.

**To practice crocheting in a spiral, make a slip knot, then chain 8 stitches. Form a circle by inserting the hook into the first chain stitch.**

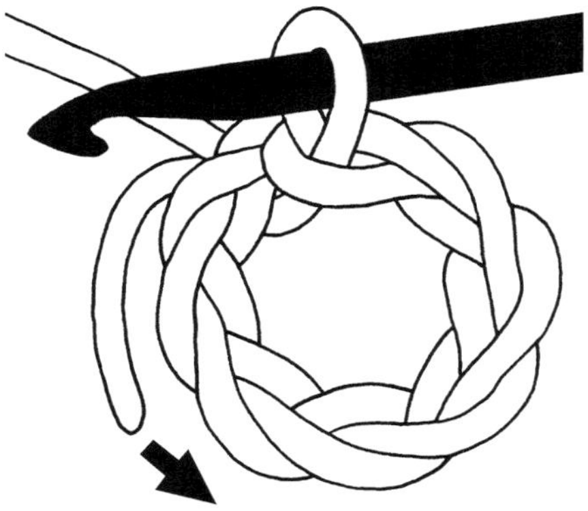

**Yarn over, pull through a loop of yarn, and then continue to pull it right through the loop on the hook. This is a *slip stitch.* Pull the short tail of yarn as illustrated by the arrow.**

**Single crochet 12 stitches onto the circle. Crochet over and under the short tail as you crochet around.**

**Work the next round by inserting the hook under the top two loops of the stitch being crocheted into, as indicated by the arrow.**

**Many increases are required if a flat spiral is desired. A tube can be created by crocheting around without any increases.**

# Crocheting Flat

The Flat Heart and Framed Wall Hanging projects are crocheted flat. Both *reverse crochet* and *alternate-row-switch-hands crochet* produce single-faced, flat pieces with the "knot" side of the stitch on the back of the fabric, for a smoother face. Try both methods and use the technique you find most comfortable.

# Reverse Crochet

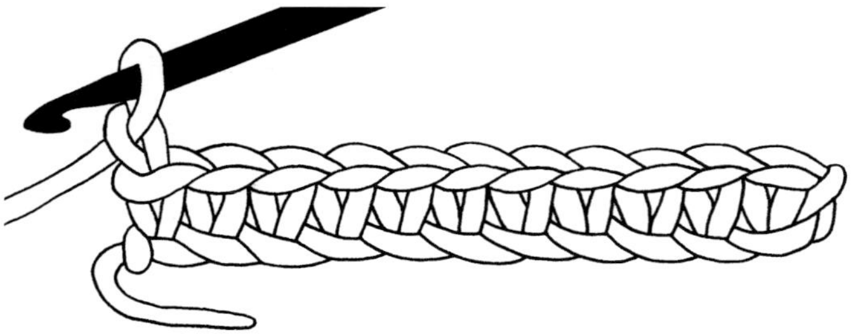

**To practice *reverse crochet*, make a slip knot, then chain twelve stitches.**

**Single crochet eleven stitches onto the chain as you did when crocheting in rounds. Chain one stitch at the end of the row.**

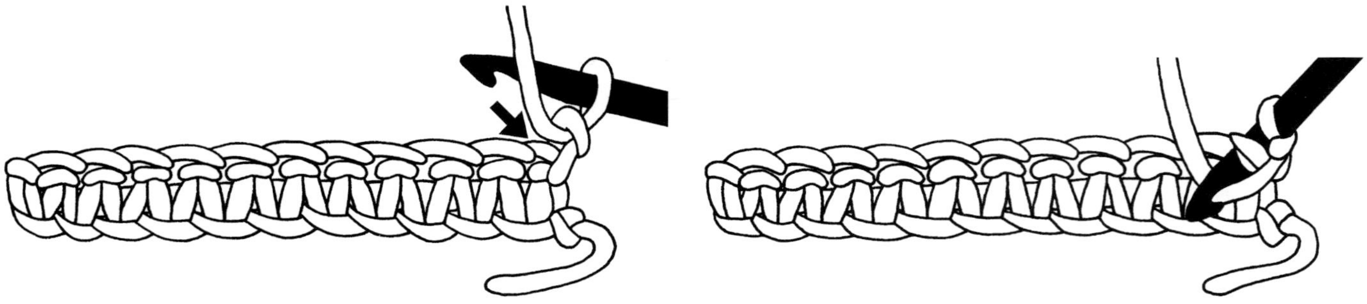

**Turn the piece over. Insert the hook where the arrow indicates from *back to front* and pull through a loop.**

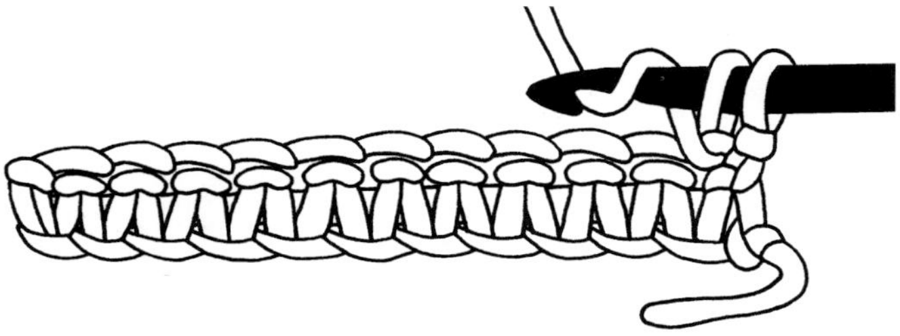

**The hook now has two loops on it. Yarn over, then pull it through the two loops on the hook. This completes one *reverse crochet* stitch.**

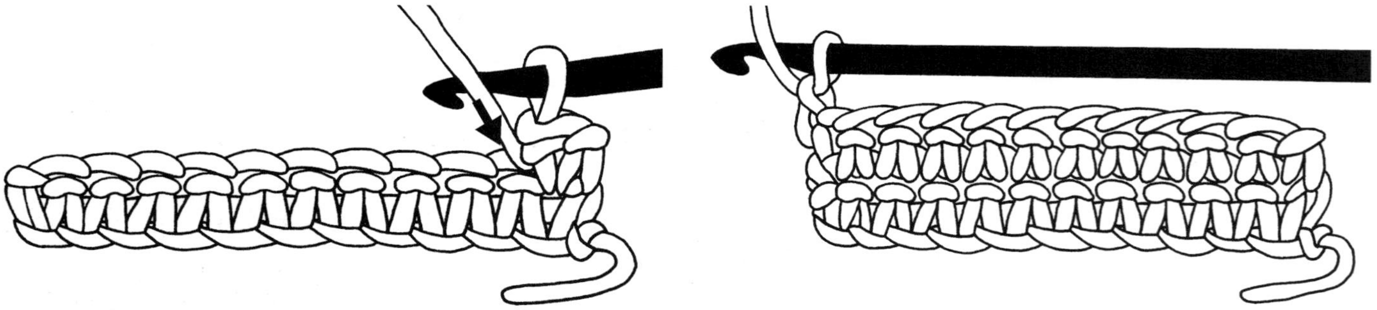

**Insert the hook into the next stitch where the arrow indicates (see above left), again from *back to front. Reverse crochet* across the row. Chain one stitch at the end of the row. Turn the piece over and then crochet normally across the next row.**

# Alternate-Row-Switch-Hands Crochet

You know, it would be great if you had a cooperative friend that crocheted with the opposite hand. That way, you could work together on the same piece and one of you could work across with the right hand, and the other could work across with the left hand. I still find it awkward to crochet back with my other hand, but I have not been able to find my own crochet partner, so until then . . .

**To practice *alternate-row-switch-hands crochet,* make a slip knot, then chain twelve stitches.**

**Single crochet eleven stitches onto the chain as you did when crocheting in rounds. Chain one stitch at the end of the row. Now, *switch hands.* This means that if you are using your right hand to hold the hook, you will now use your left hand. If you are holding the yarn with your left hand, you will now hold it with your right hand.**

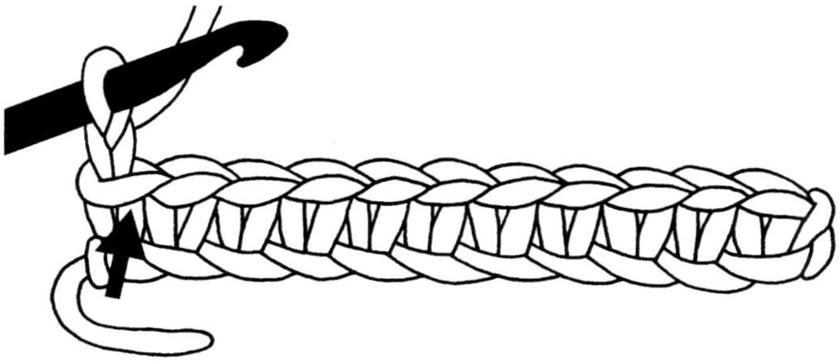

**Turn back to the right- or left-handed crochet instructions to visualize the correct technique. If you are right-handed, you will look at the left-handed instructions on page 34. If you are left-handed, you will look at the right-handed instructions on page 28. At first this technique is very awkward, but with practice you will get used to it.**

**Insert the hook into the stitch indicated by the arrow on the left.**

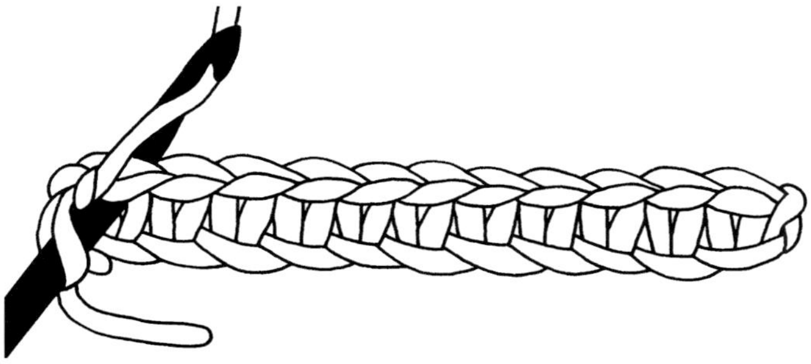

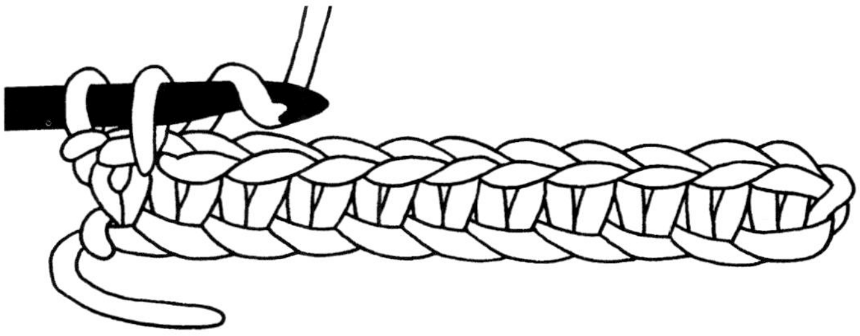

**Insert the hook and pull through a loop. The hook now has two loops on it. Yarn over, and then pull it through the two loops on the hook.**

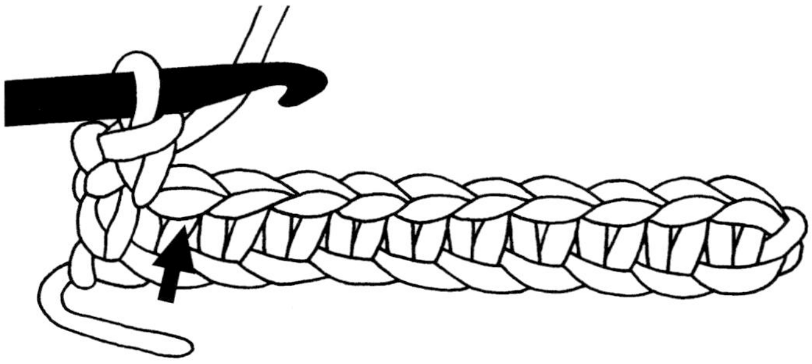

**You have just completed an *alternate-row-switch-hands* crochet stitch.**

**Insert the hook into the next stitch where the arrow indicates on the left. *Alternate-row switch-hands crochet* across the row.**

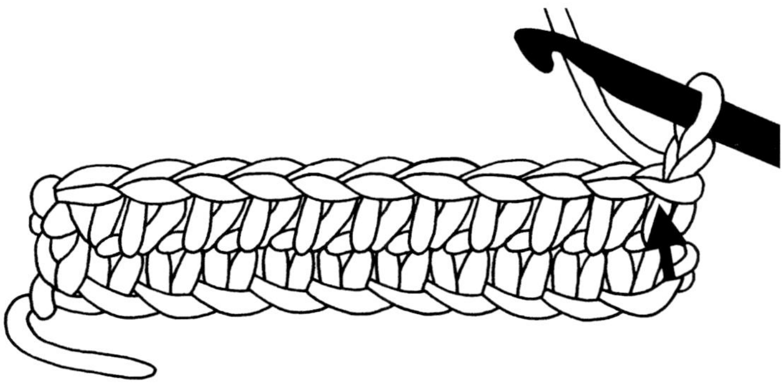

**Chain one stitch at the end of the row. Again, switch hands. Insert the hook where the arrow indicates and crochet normally across the row.**

# Crocheting a Border

The flat pieces in this book have a simple crocheted border to give them a more finished look. Practice crocheting a border around one of your flat sample pieces.

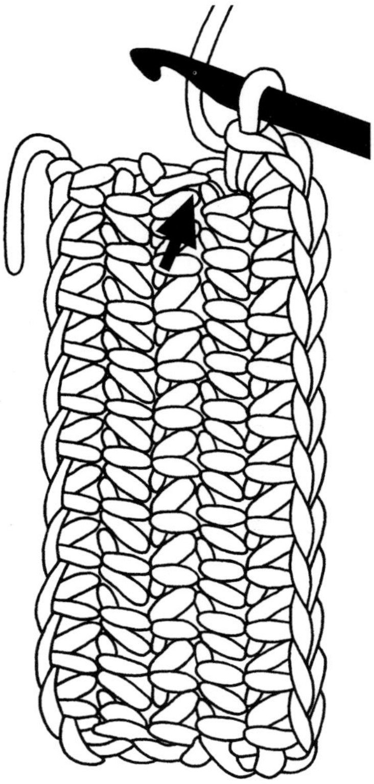

**To begin the border, crochet across the top of the piece.**

**Crochet three stitches into the "corner" stitch.**

**Turn the piece around a quarter of the way (90°) until the left side is on the top. Insert the hook into the space at the end of the row where the arrow indicates for the next stitch.**

**Continue to crochet across the side of the piece, inserting the hook into the spaces at the end of each row.**

**Depending upon your tension, usually one crochet stitch per row is about right. If the piece starts to pucker, increase a stitch or two along the border. If the piece starts to look wavy, decrease a stitch or two along the side border.**

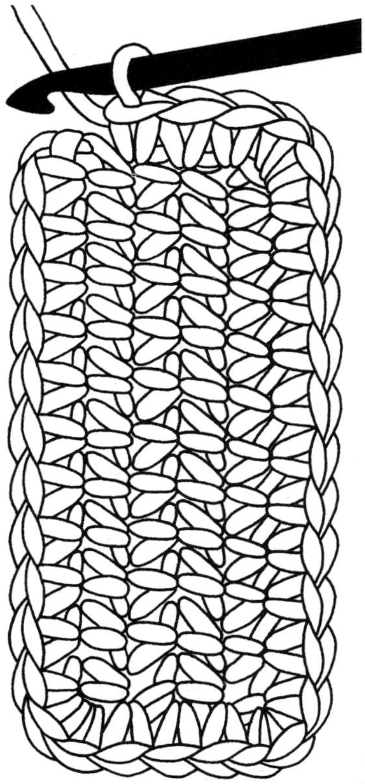

**Crochet three stitches into the next corner stitch.**

**Turn the piece 90° again so that the bottom of the piece is now on the top. Continue to crochet across, inserting the hook into the bottom loop of the original foundation chain. Carry the tail piece along as you crochet to hide and secure it. Again, crochet three stitches into the corner stitch. Turn the piece 90°, then continue to crochet across the side of the piece as you did for the previous side. Crochet three stitches into the corner stitch. The border can be stopped here with a slip stitch or continued indefinitely by crocheting one stitch into every crochet stitch, and three crochet stitches into each corner stitch.**

For a wide frame, crochet a number of border rows. A raised frame will result if only one stitch is worked into each corner stitch. A wavy border will result if the stitches are increased along the sides and on the corners.

# Finishing Off with a Slip Stitch

Tapestry crochet can be finished off very neatly, and the yarn end can be worked into the fabric. To finish off:

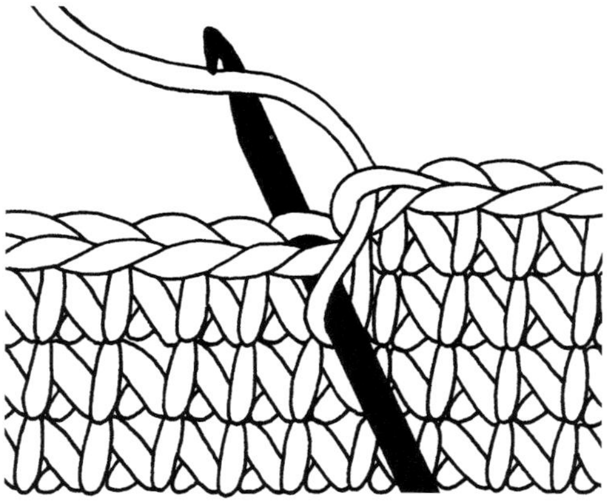

**Insert the hook under the two loops of the stitch being crocheted into as usual. Yarn over, pull through a loop of yarn. Continue to pull the loop right through the loop on the hook. This is a s*lip stitch*.**

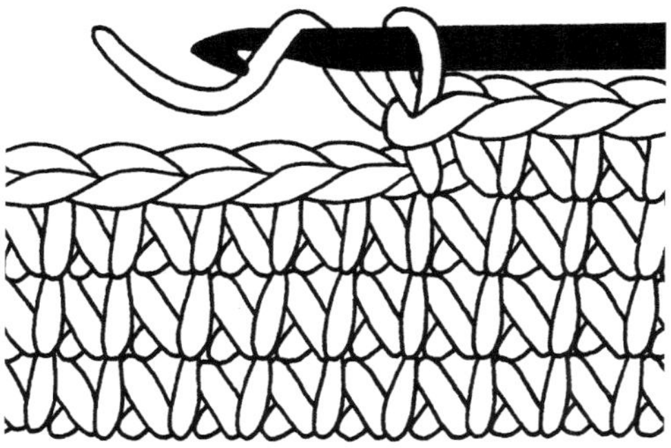

**Cut the yarn, leaving a 6-inch end.**

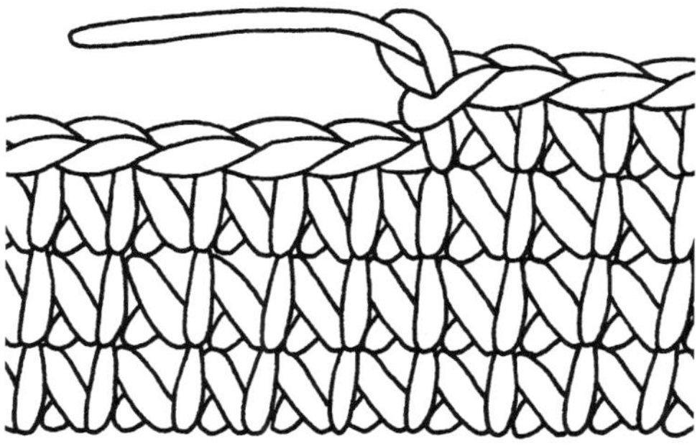

**Yarn over and then pull the 6-inch end completely through the loop on the hook, thereby locking the stitches to prevent any unraveling. The 6-inch end can then be worked into the piece to secure it.**

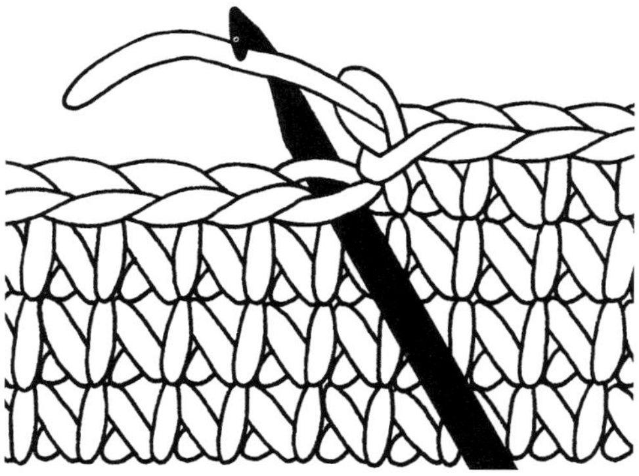

# Working In The Final End

**To work in the end piece, insert the hook under the two loops of the next stitch from front to back, grab the end piece and then pull it all the way through.**

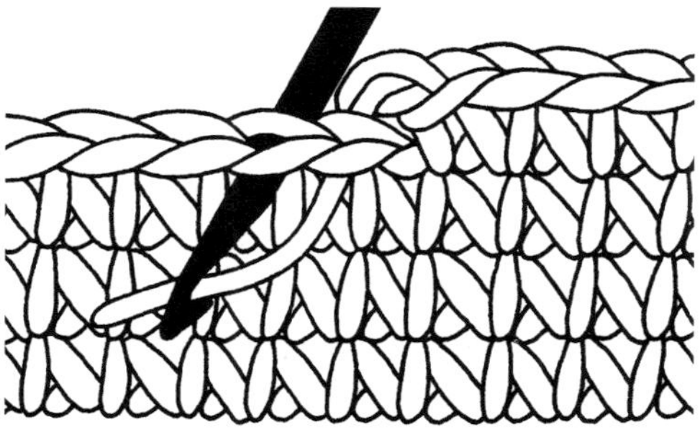

**Now from back to front, insert the hook under the two loops of the next stitch, grab the end piece and then pull it completely through. Repeat these two steps five more times, then cut the end piece flush.**

# Interpreting the Graphs

Two graphs are provided for each project; one actual stitch placement on a tapestry crochet graph and the design transferred to a square-ruled graph. Although the tapestry crochet graph gives a more realistic image of the finished motif, I find it easier to crochet following the square-ruled graph.

The motif graphs included for each project are for right-handed crocheters. Photos are of right-handed work. Left-handed crocheters should place a mirror to the side of the graphs and photographs and then read the mirror images.

Each shell-shape or square on the graphs represents a single tapestry crochet stitch. The dark shells or squares represent dark-colored stitches and the white shells or squares represent light-colored stitches. All of the graphs are read from the bottom up.

# Graphs for Rounds

Right-handed crocheters should read the graphs for rounds from right to left, and left-handed crocheters should read the mirror image from left to right.

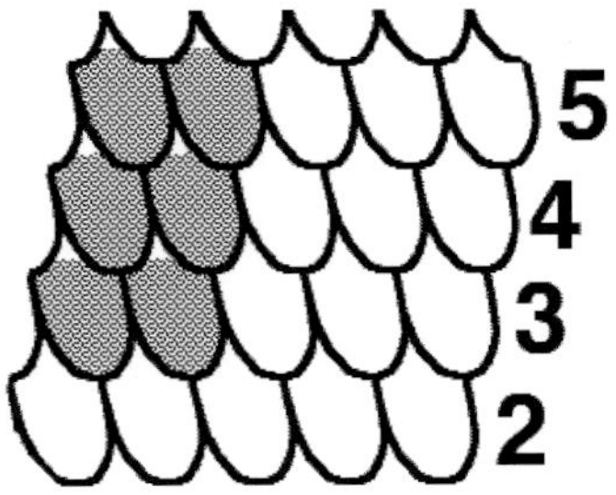


**The bottom row of shells and squares correspond to Round 2 of the Amulet Pouch project, which has no yarn changes.**

**Row 3 corresponds to Round 3 of the written instructions which reads: ". . . Start the stripe pattern as follows: tapestry crochet 3 stitches with the silk thread, then 2 stitches with the metallic thread.. . ."**

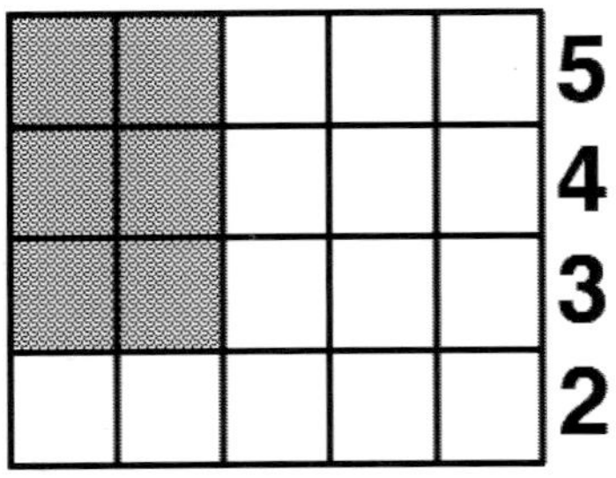


# Graphs for Flat Tapestry Crochet

Flat tapestry crochet graphs are read alternately from right to left and then from left to right, which corresponds to the crocheting technique. Left-handed crocheters should read the mirror image of the graphs to match the rows with the written project instructions.

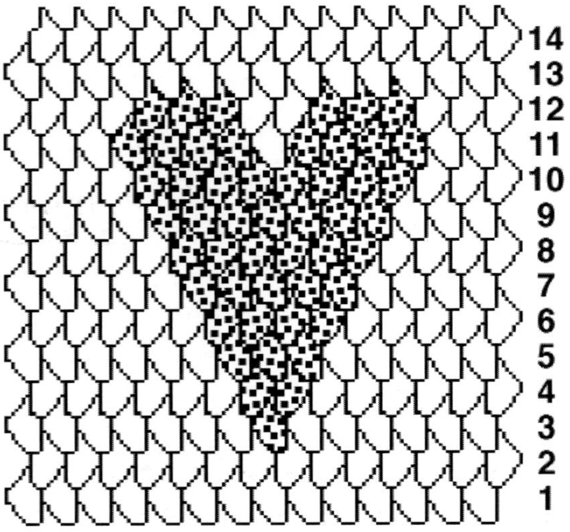


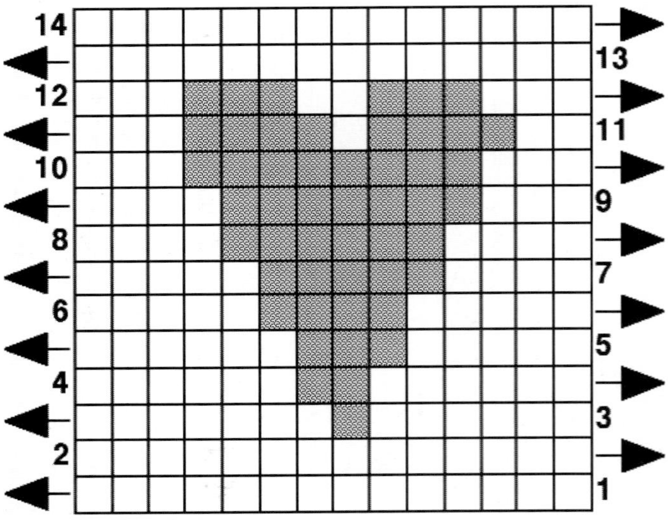


# Keeping in Step with Instructions or Graph Paper

A metal support with a magnetic ruler is very helpful to keep your place with instructions or graph paper. The instructions are sandwiched between the support and the magnetic ruler; the support is placed behind the page and the magnetic ruler is placed on top of the page. The ruler can be easily moved as the work progresses. These helpful tools may be purchased where needleworking supplies are sold.

# Blocking

Most of the projects in this book will require some *blocking*, either to flatten out the piece or to re-shape it. Blocking methods vary, depending on the dimensions of the piece.

If you are using a steam iron, fill it with water and set the iron to *steam*. If you do not have a steam iron, generously spray the towel on top of your piece with water. If you are blocking wool, set the iron on *wool;* if you are blocking cotton, set the iron on *cotton.* If you are blocking synthetic yarn be sure to set the iron on *synthetic* because synthetics will melt at high temperatures. DO NOT STEAM BLOCK a piece made with *metallic* or *silk* thread because these fibers do not like steam and intense heat. For *metallic* or *silk* thread, set the iron on *silk,* cover the piece with a towel, then iron it with dry heat.

Iron back and forth with a steady, downward pressure. When the piece is flat, remove the towel on top and let the piece cool off. Some pieces will require a second or third blocking. Remember, the iron is hot! Don't burn yourself!

Extra large flat pieces are very difficult to block with an ordinary household iron. Some dry cleaners will block the piece for you.

For an irregular shape, such as the shaped basket, use a towel folded a couple of times supported by your hand on the inside of the piece. Steam the piece as usual, rotating it until it is completely blocked. Some pieces will require a second and third blocking. Remember, the iron is hot! Don't burn yourself!

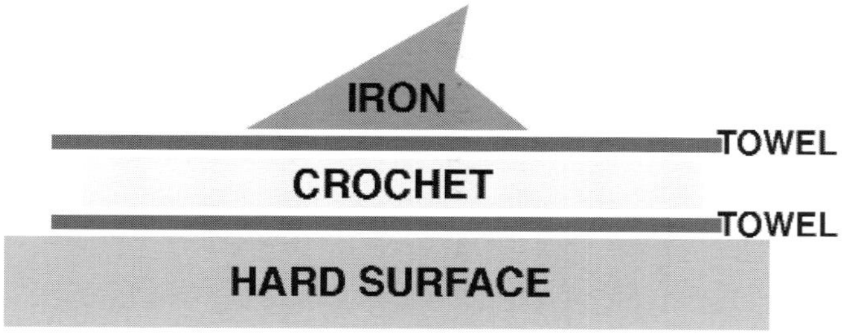


***To block a flat piece,* first you must find a hard, flat surface; I use the floor for large pieces and an ironing board for small pieces. If you decide to use the floor, lay down a towel first, then place your piece face down. Cover the piece with a thin cotton towel.**

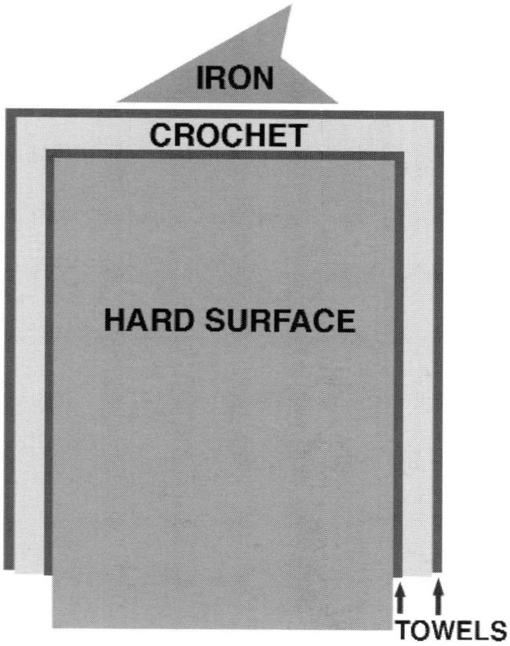


***To block a three-dimensional shape,* such as a basket or shoulder bag, cover a metal can or a block of wood a bit smaller than the interior of the finished project with a towel and insert it inside the piece. Cover the crocheted piece with a thin cotton towel. Steam the piece as previously described for flat pieces, moving the can and towel when needed.**

# Cleaning

Depending on the fiber, tapestry crochet can be either washed or dry cleaned. Very large pieces that are too difficult to handle should be dry cleaned; small pieces can be hand washed.

Keep a record of the type of yarn used for each project so that you can tell the dry cleaner what type of material he or she is dealing with. Some fibers melt at high temperatures, so this is very important.

If you decide to hand-wash the piece, handle it as you would a sweater. Wash it in cold or lukewarm water with a mild soap. Never leave it soaking for a long time or it might shrink. Rinse it well, making sure that all of the soap has been removed. Roll it up in a dry bath towel and then gently squeeze it to remove excess moisture. Lay the piece out on a level surface to dry and reshape if necessary. Never hang the piece up to dry, as this would stretch it out of shape. It is sometimes necessary to reblock a piece once it has dried.

# 3 DESIGN

The pieces in this book are crocheted in a variety of formats with a of number motifs. As you can see from the projects and my own work, my approach is very conservative. One of the fantastic advantages of crochet, though, is that any shape can be executed; flat or three-dimensional. A number of other crochet stitches and fiber techniques can be incorporated with the single crochet and tapestry crochet stitches. It all depends upon the look that you want and your creativity. I encourage you free spirits out there to break the rules I have given you! I hope you will vary your stitch tension, combine tapestry crochet with other stitches, and use yarns of different weights and textures in a single piece!

## Design Sources

Many existing crafts, such as needlepoint, knitting, and embroidery, use motifs that can be transferred to tapestry crochet graphs. Many cultures use design motifs that can be translated into tapestry crochet graphs. A trip to a museum of folk art or natural history will provide many design ideas.

## Designing a Motif on Tapestry Crochet Graph Paper

For working in rounds, photocopy Graph Papers *1R* (page 56) and *2R* (page 57) if you are right-handed, or *1L* (page 58) and *2L* (page 59) if you are left-handed.

To design a motif for a flat piece, photocopy Graph Papers *10 stitches = 7 rows* (page 60), *10 stitches = 8 rows* (page 61), *10 stitches = 9 rows* (page 62), and *10 stitches = 10 rows* (page 63).

If the image that you are designing is larger than one sheet of tapestry crochet graph paper, then join several sheets of paper together. To join the papers, cut off one of the side edges of one of the graph papers, place the two papers side by side, face down on a light table or against a window, line up the pattern (with the cut edge overlapping a half inch on top of the grid pattern of the other paper), then tape them together. Tapestry crochet graph paper can also be enlarged or reduced on a photocopy machine to meet your needs.

I have used five different methods to design motifs. The first method involves doodling (see next page). The motif is drawn onto a photocopy of the appropriate tapestry crochet paper in a free-hand style with a pencil (which allows for experimentation).

The second method involves tracing. Tapestry crochet paper is placed over an image on a light table or against a window and traced with colored pencils.

The third method involves tracing an object onto the tapestry crochet paper. For the *Framed Wall Hanging* project, I placed my husband's left hand on tapestry crochet paper, matching up the edges of his fingers with the edges of the stitches wherever possible, then I traced his hand onto the paper. Next, I traced my right hand onto the paper.

The fourth method also involves tracing. An image is projected onto tapestry crochet paper with either a slide projector or an opaque projector, then the appropriate areas are traced and colored. The design is then visually transferred from the tapestry crochet graph paper onto square-ruled graph paper. Several graph papers may be taped together to form a large sheet. The height of the stitch can distort the image, so a sample piece should be crocheted to determine the correct graph paper needed to reproduce an exact image.

The fifth method involves a computer (see pages 54-55). With a computer and graphics software, images are digitized and then traced or layered onto digital graph paper. The computer can also be programmed with tapestry crochet graph paper that can be stretched or shrunk to match stitch gauges that are not in this book.

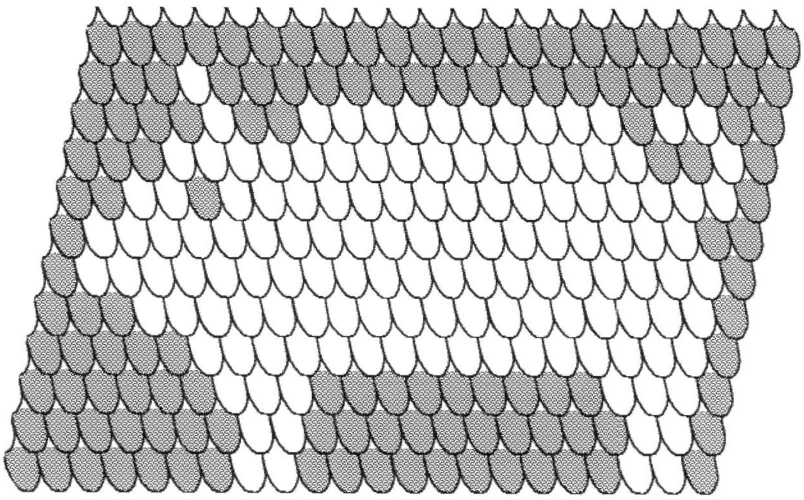

**This pig was designed on a tapestry crochet graph for rounds. Using a pencil, I doodled several different versions, then this one was selected by popular demand (I usually ask for several opinions).**

# Tapestry Crochet Graph Papers

Take a close look at the stitch placement on the tapestry crochet motifs. Notice that each stitch falls slightly to one side of the stitch in the previous row; stitches do not align directly over one another. This is a very important consideration when designing a motif. The stitch configuration is different for a piece worked in the round than for a flat piece. For pieces worked in rounds, the stitches stack up diagonally. On flat pieces, all of the stitches slant to the right on one row, then on the next row they all slant to the left. Graph Papers *1R, 2R, 1L,* and *2L* (designed for tapestry crochet in rounds) are different from the other four graph papers (designed for flat tapestry crochet work) for that reason.

The tapestry crochet graph papers in this book also take into consideration stitch height. The actual stitch height, or rows per inch measurement, will depend on the yarn, tension, and the number of carried yarns. The stitch height can significantly affect the proportion of the finished motif. The stitches will become taller with each additional yarn that is carried. That is the difference between Graph Papers *1R* and *2R, 1L* and *2L,* and *10 stitches = 7 rows, 10 stitches = 8 rows, 10 stitches = 9 rows, and 10 stitches = 10 rows.* The stitches are taller in Graph Papers *1R* and *1L* than in Graph Papers *2R* and *2L.* The stitches are also taller in Graph Paper *10 stitches = 7 rows,* than in Graph Paper *10 stitches = 10 rows.* To determine which graph paper to use for your project, tapestry crochet a two by two inch sample (while carrying the yarns). Measure ten stitches across the row, then use that measurement to see how many rows it equals.

## Charting the Design

After the motif has been worked out on tapestry crochet graph paper, it should be transferred to square-ruled graph paper because it is much easier to follow the pattern on the square-ruled paper. The eye perceives stitch placement much more clearly on square-ruled graph paper, making it easier to count stitches and determine color changes.

Be especially careful when transferring a motif from the tapestry crochet graph papers**.** It is crucial to understand the vertical stitch placement. Look at the edges of the graph papers to see the stitch placement. The stitches along the edge of the graph papers are on top of one another.

The last step is to count the number of horizontal stitches in the motif. The base of the piece should be a multiple of the horizontal measurement if you want the motifs to butt together.

The charted alphabets will allow you to personalize your pieces with your own words. Be sure to choose the correct alphabet; one is for rounds and the other is for flat pieces.

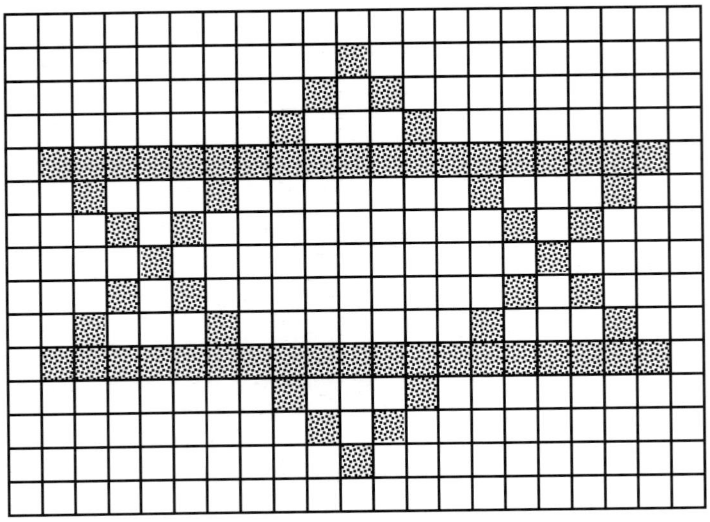

The Star of David motif, with its diagonal and horizontal lines, illustrates some basic tapestry crochet design considerations. The motif on the left was copied from a printed square-ruled graph. The motifs on the next page were designed on tapestry crochet graph papers. As you can see, the motifs are quite different on this and the next page since tapestry crochet stitches are not square and do not fall directly over one another. Horizontal lines look the same, but diagonal lines turn out quite different from what you would expect. So, copy designs from other sources onto tapestry crochet paper, then transfer them to square-ruled paper!

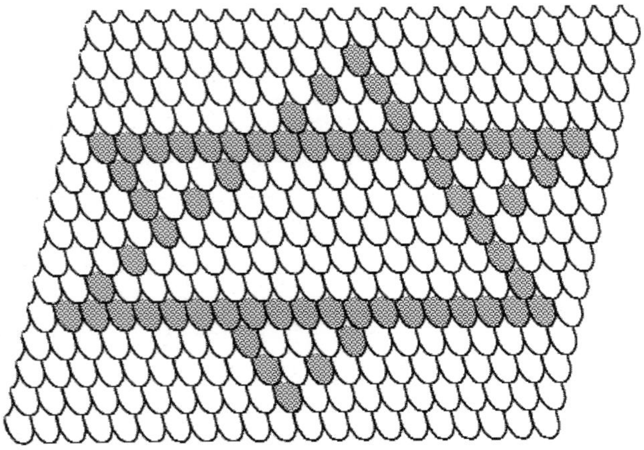

Star of David motif transferred from a square-ruled graph to a tapestry crochet rounds graph (on the left) and a tapestry crochet flat graph (on the right).

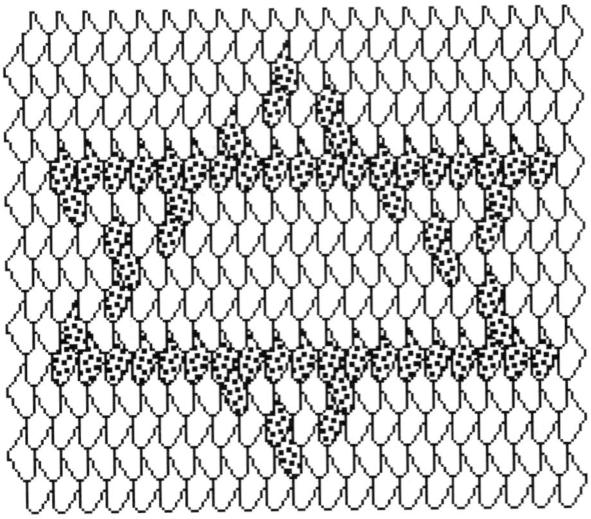

Star of David crocheted in rounds (on the left) and flat (on the right) from the above motif designed on square-ruled graph paper.

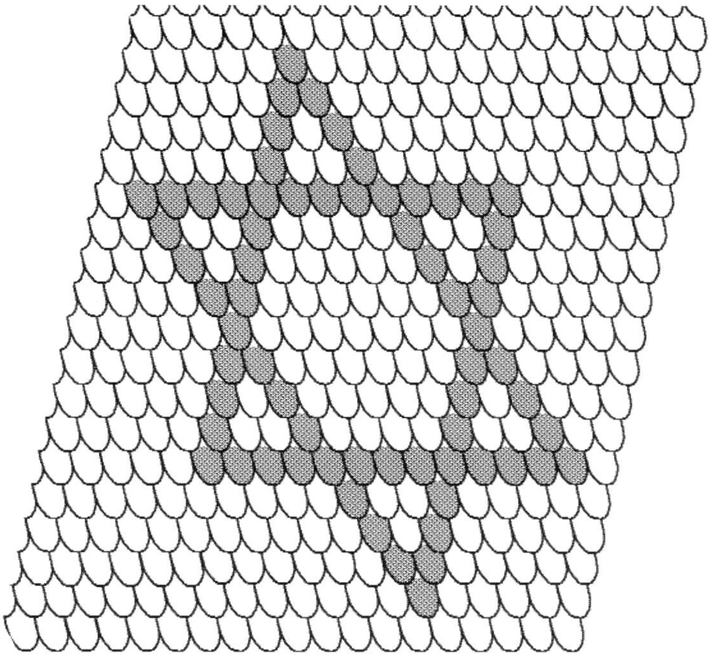

Star of David motif designed on a tapestry crochet graph for rounds (on the left) and a tapestry crochet graph for flat pieces (on the right).

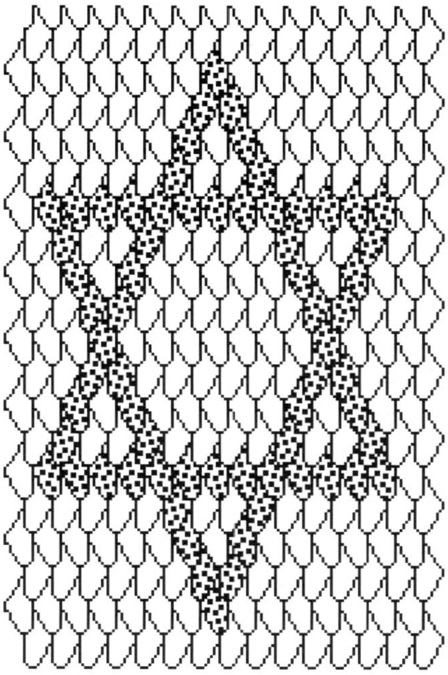

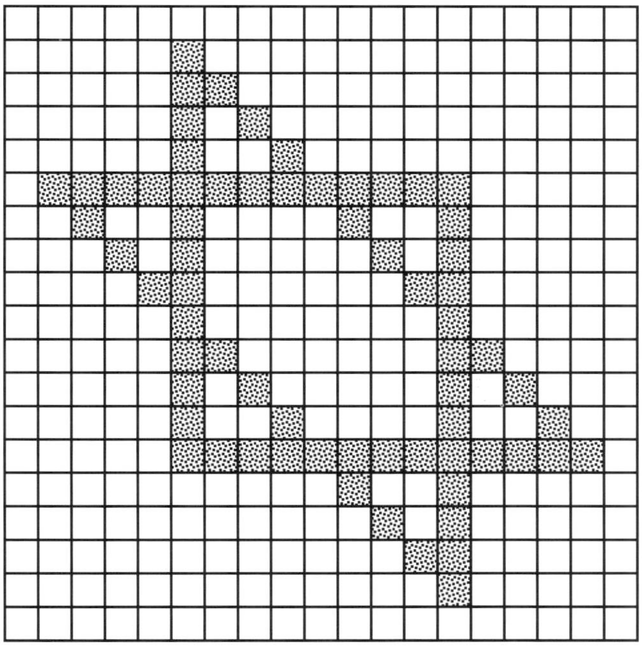

Star of David motif transferred from tapestry crochet graph for rounds (on the left) and for flat (on the right) to square-ruled graph paper.

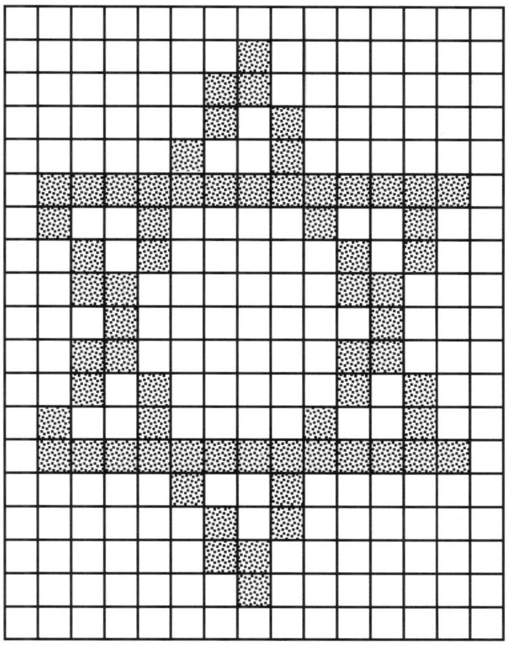

Star of David crocheted in rounds (on the left) and flat (on the right) from motifs designed on tapestry crochet graphs. Notice the smoothness of the diagonal lines.

The image (above left) for *Self Portrait* (right) was captured with a video camera that was hooked up to a Macintosh computer. The image was printed, placed under tapestry crochet graph paper on a light table, traced, visually transferred with a graphics program sititch by stitch, (above right), transferred to square-ruled graph paper (left) then crocheted. Although *Self Portrait* was originally intended to be a necklace, its size made it look more like a bib, so I twisted the straps, mounted, and framed it.

The same graph was used for my next piece, *Cameleon Series* (see page 23).

Self Portrait, 8 1/2" x 7", cotton and metallic thread, 1987.

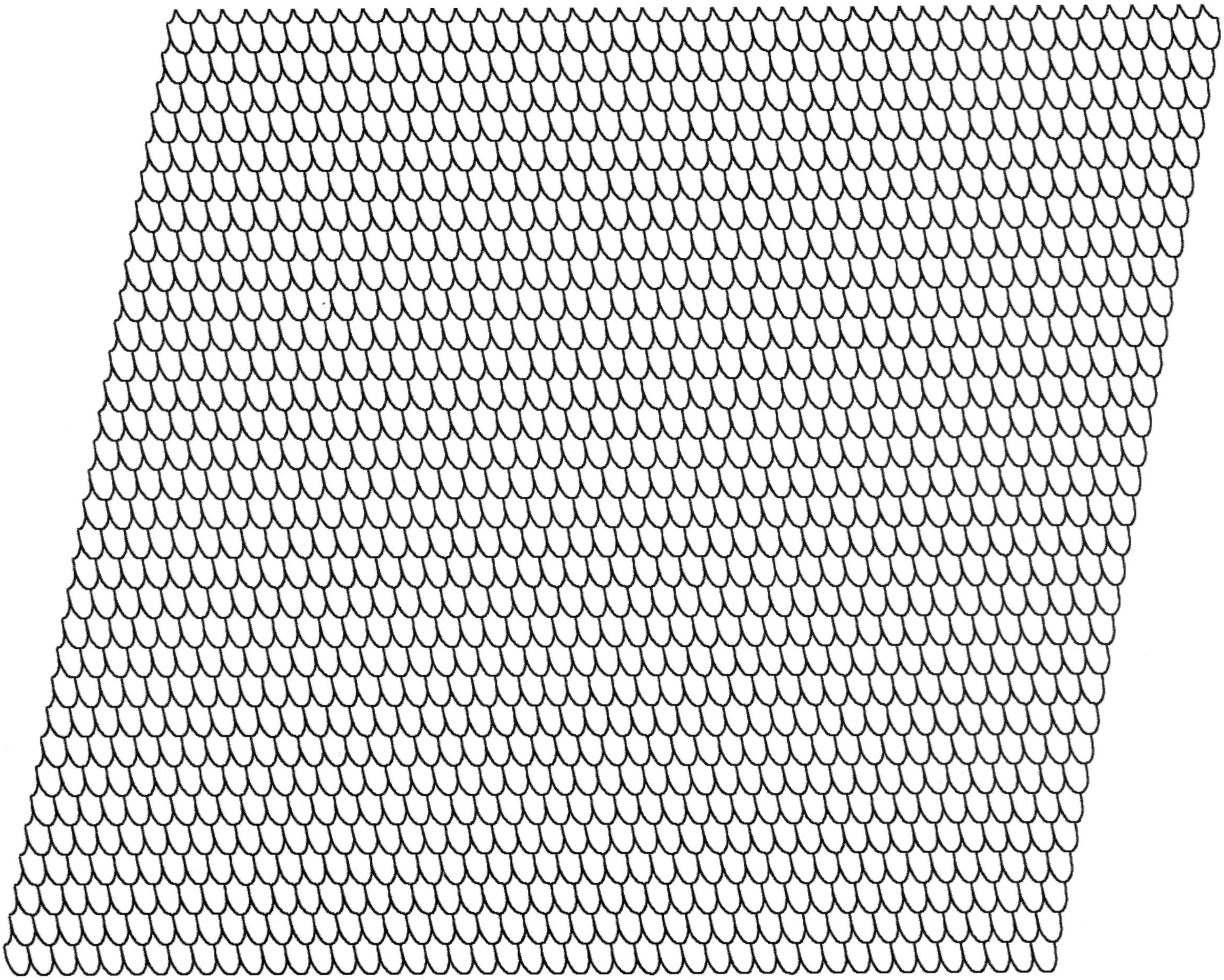

**Graph paper #1R (for right-handed tapestry crochet worked in rounds) 10 stitches = 8 rounds.**
**Feel free to photocopy this paper and use it to design your own motifs.**

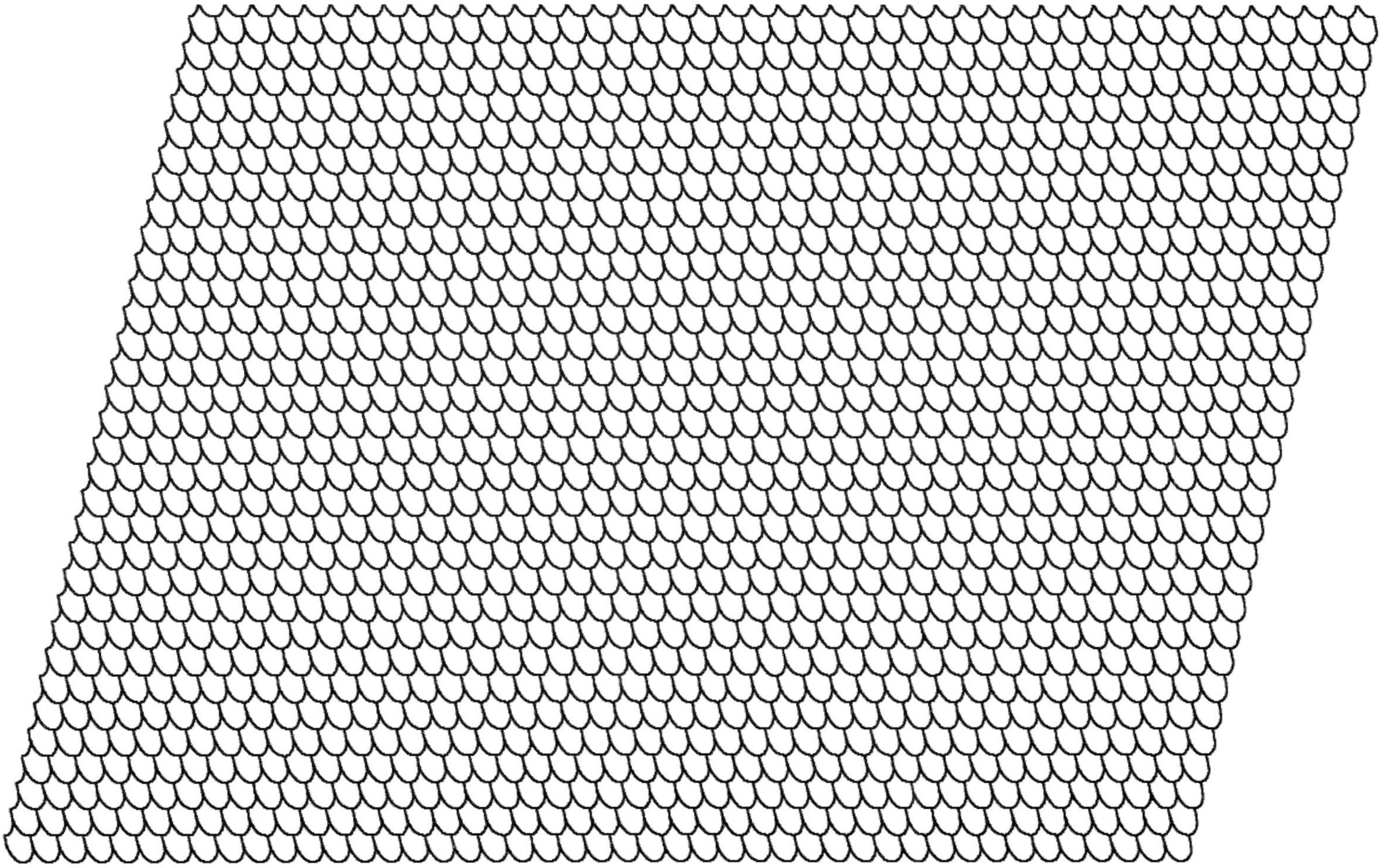

**Graph paper #2R (for right-handed tapestry crochet worked in rounds) 10 stitches = 10 rounds. Feel free to photocopy this paper and use it to design your own motifs.**

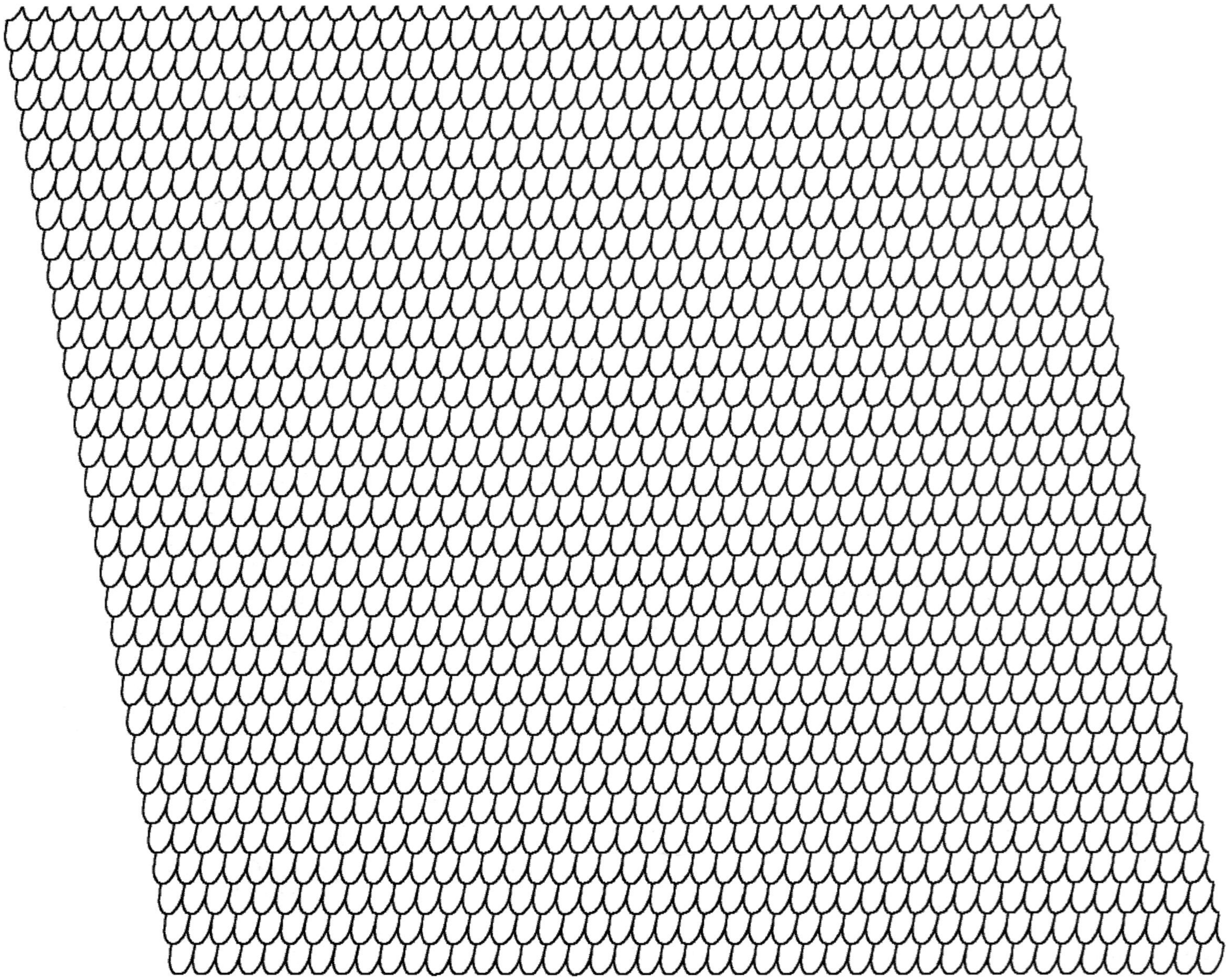

**Graph paper 1L for left-handed tapestry crochet worked in rounds (10 stitches = 8 rounds). Please photocopy this paper and use it to design your own motifs**

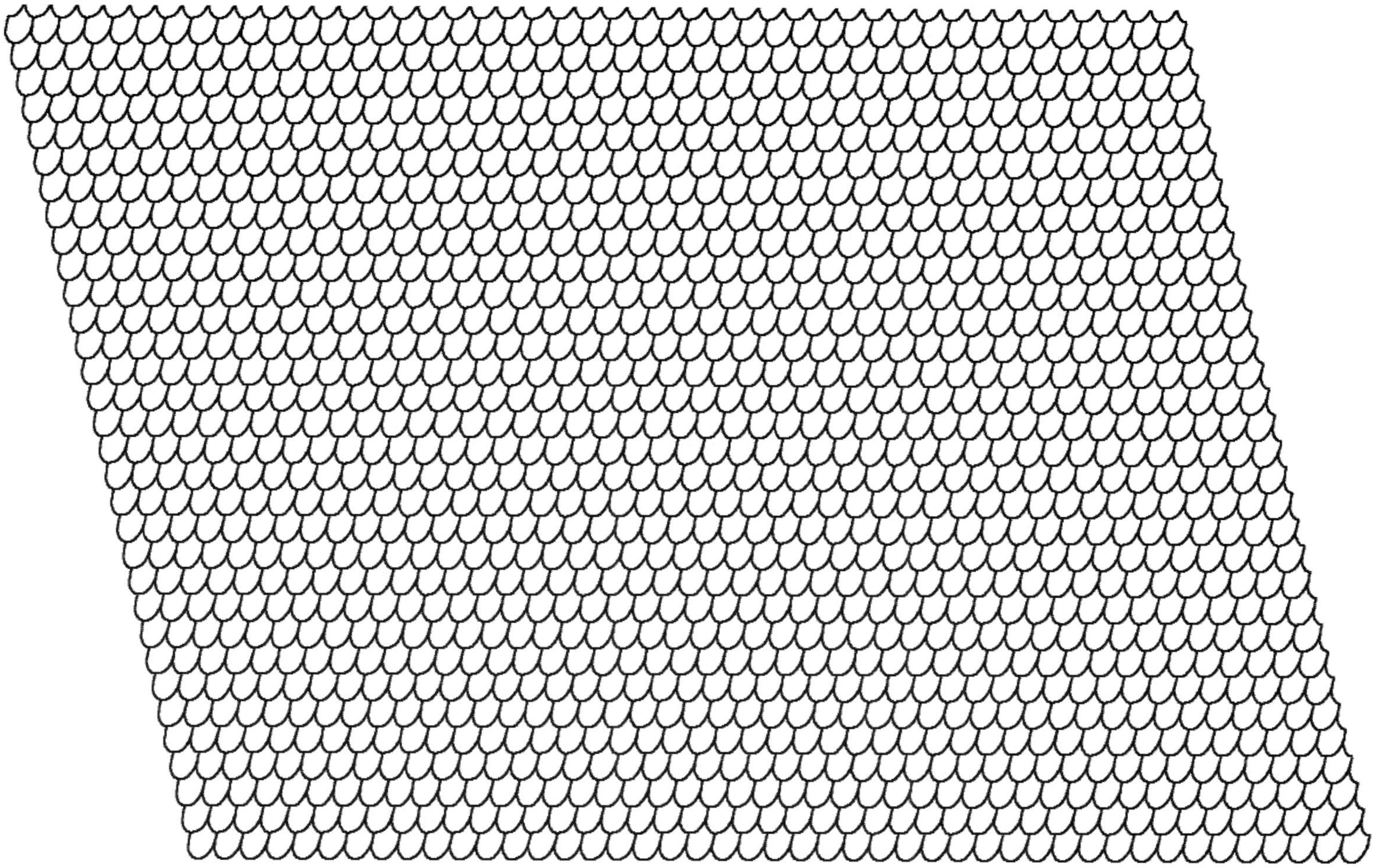

**Graph paper 2L for left-handed tapestry crochet worked in rounds (10 stitches = 10 rounds).
Please photocopy this paper and use it to design your own motifs.**

**Graph paper for flat tapestry crochet (10 stitches=7 rows).**
**Please photocopy this paper and use it to design your own motifs!**

Graph paper for flat tapestry crochet (10 stitches = 8 rows).
Feel free to photocopy this paper and use it to design your own motifs.

**Graph paper for flat tapestry crochet (10 stitches = 9 rows).**
**Please photocopy this paper and use it to design your own motifs.**

**Graph paper for flat tapestry crochet (10 stitches = 10 rows).**
**Please photocopy this paper and use it to design your own motifs.**

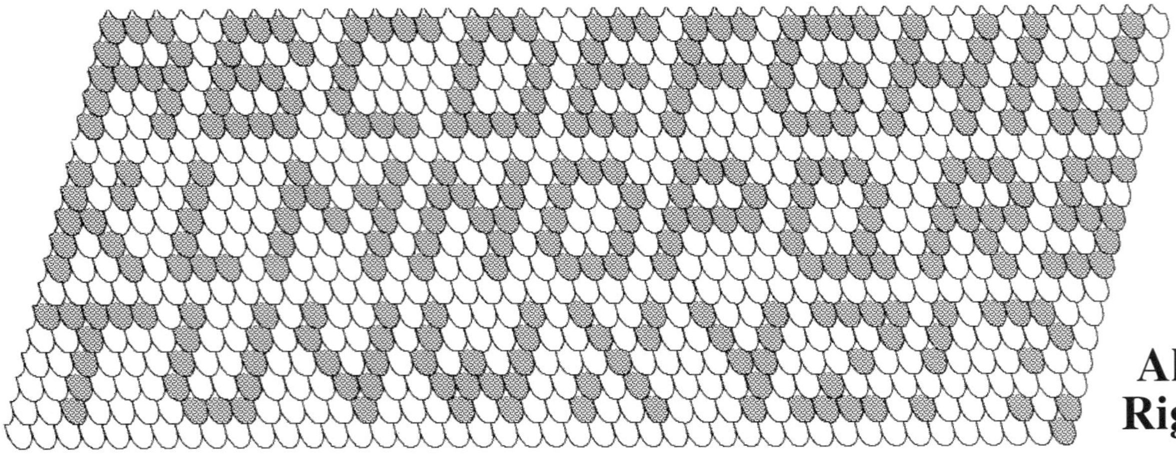

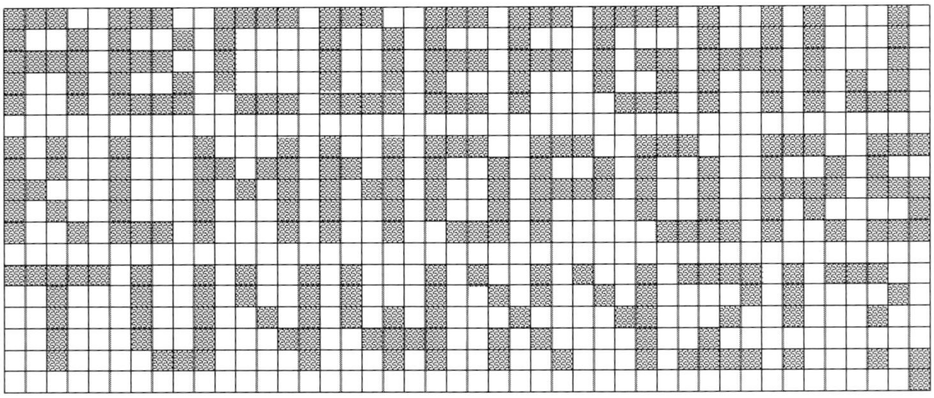

## Alphabet for Right-Handed Rounds

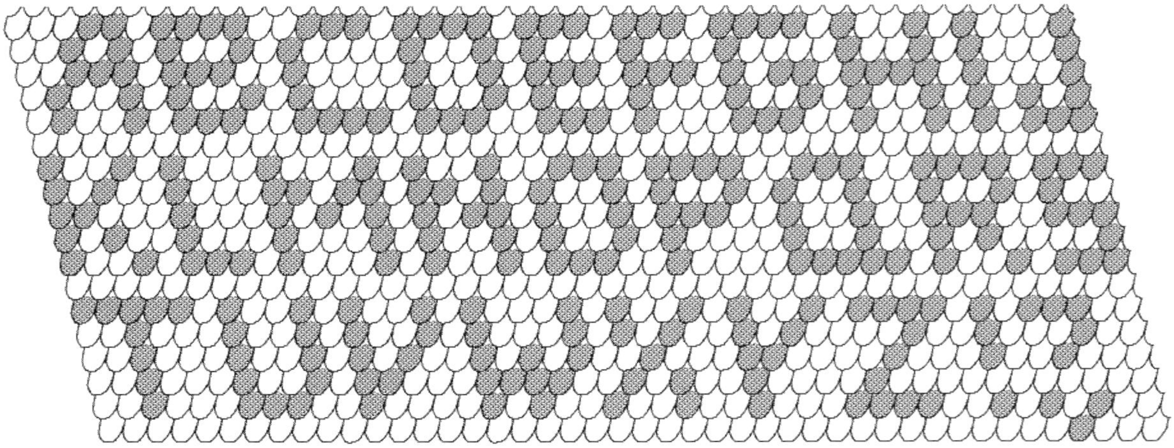

## Alphabet for Left-Handed Rounds

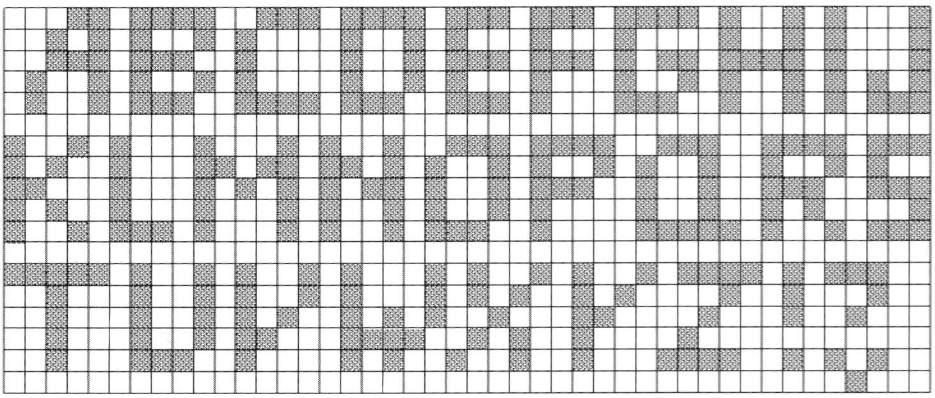

# Alphabet for Flat Pieces

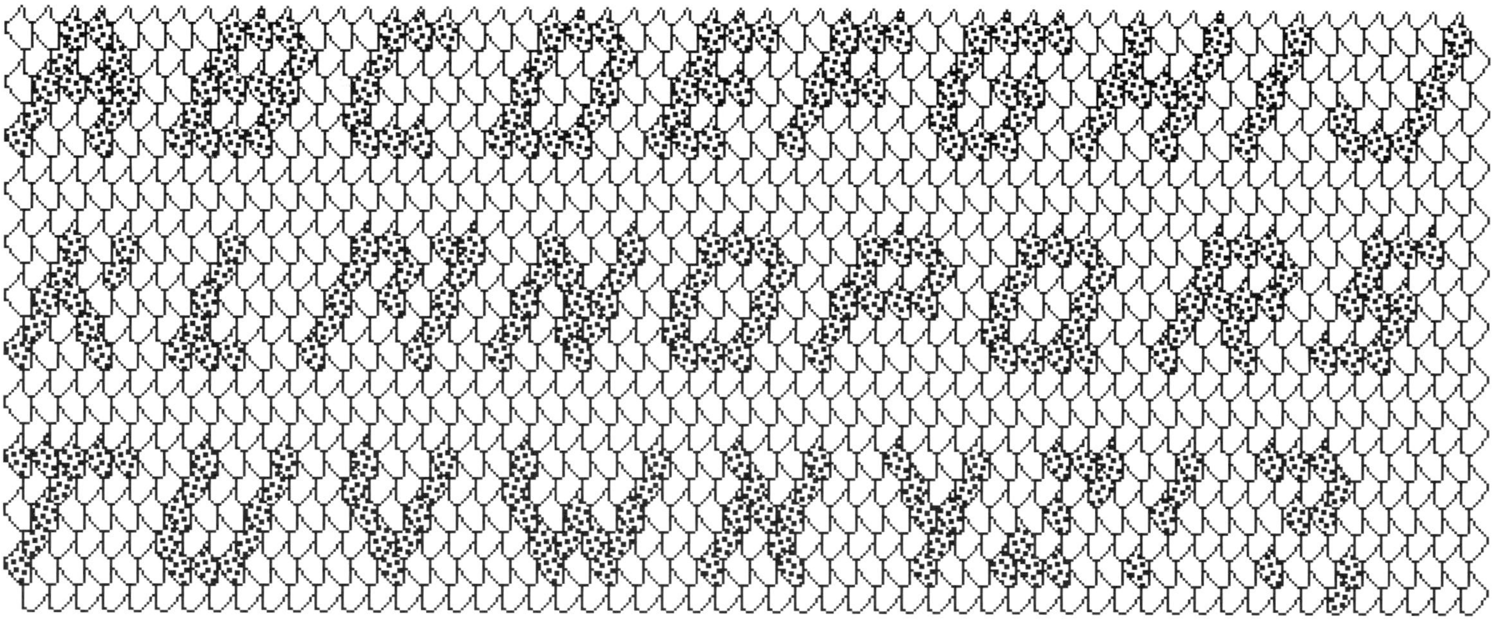

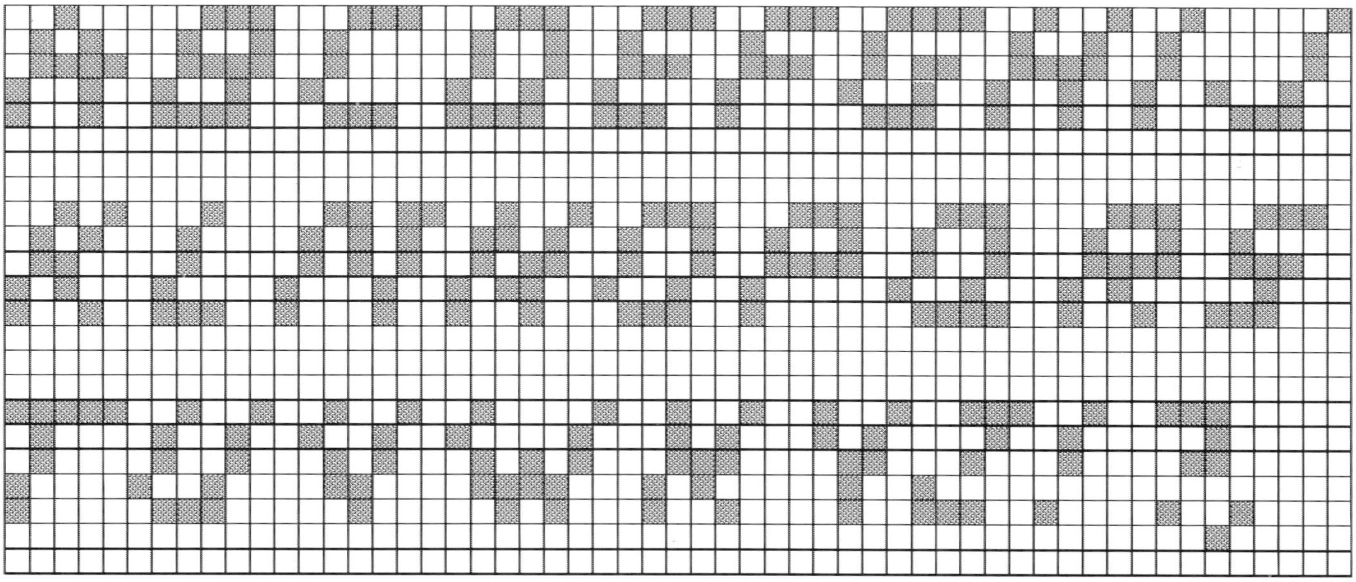

# 4 ROUNDS PROJECTS

## Amulet Pouches

These amulet pouches are a great beginning project because they are quick and they include most of the basic tapestry crochet techniques: the slip knot, chain stitch, single crochet worked in rounds, counting stitches, carrying a thread, and the tapestry crochet stitch. You will also interpret a graph paper design, check your gauge, cut the yarn flush, finish off, and work in the end.

The amulet pouches begin at the bottom. A base is crocheted first, then since the diameter of the base is not increased, the edges of the spiral move upwards to form the walls. The striped motif is five stitches wide, so the total number of stitches in the base is a multiple of five. It is possible to make a variety of sizes with the same design motif simply by increasing or decreasing the size of the base by five stitches. Feel free to substitute another motif, just be sure that the total number of stitches in the base is a multiple of the number of stitches in your motif.

### Hook

Steel crochet hook size 5 (1.90 mm.) or the size that will give an acceptable gauge

### Gauge

10 stitches equals 1 inch
8 rows equals 1 inch

# Small Pouch

### Size

1" wide by 1 3/4" high (not including the strap)

### Materials

Two (40 meters each) of color 6107 Kreinik Silk Mori (6 ply spun silk) and one color 042 Kreinik Heavy (#32) Metallic Braid;
Safety pin or a piece of thread of a contrasting color for counting the rounds.

# Medium Pouch

### Size

1 5/8" wide by 2" high (not including the strap)

### Materials

Three (40 meters each) of color 8000 Kreinik Silk Mori (6 ply spun silk) and one color 033 Kreinik Heavy (#32) Metallic Braid;
Safety pin or a piece of thread of a contrasting color for counting the rounds.

# Large Pouch

### Size

2" wide by 2 3/4" high (not including the strap)

### Materials

Four (40 meters each) of color 1114 Kreinik Silk Mori (6 ply spun silk) and two color 238 Kreinik Heavy (#32) Metallic Braid;
Safety pin or a piece of thread of a contrasting color for counting the rounds.

**Round 1:** Kreinik Silk Mori is sold in skeins. You can either open the skein and wind the silk around a spool or insert your hand into the center of the skein and wear it on your wrist while you crochet. Starting with the silk thread, make a slip knot (leaving a two-inch tail), then chain 10 for the small pouch, [15 for the medium pouch], (or 20 for the large pouch). Increase in multiples of 5 chain stitches at this point to make a wider pouch. Starting with the second chain, single crochet 8 [13] (18) stitches. Single crochet 3 stitches into the last chain for a total of 11 [16] (21) stitches. Continue to single crochet using the new top of the chain until you come around to the first stitch, carrying the "tail" as you go. Single crochet 2 stitches into the last stitch. This first round should have a total of 20 [30] (40) stitches. This piece is worked as a spiral, not in concentric rings, so it is difficult to tell where each round ends. To keep track of where each round ends, slip a safety pin into the top of the last stitch of the round or lay a two inch piece of thread of a contrasting color across the path of the last stitch. You will remove the safety pin from the last stitch as you come to it again and slip it into the new last stitch or cross the path of the last stitch with the end of the counting thread at the end of each round.
**Round 2:** Cut the silk tail flush and then start to carry the metallic thread. Single crochet around without any increases, carrying the metallic thread. The pouch should still have 20 [30] (40) stitches when you finish this round.

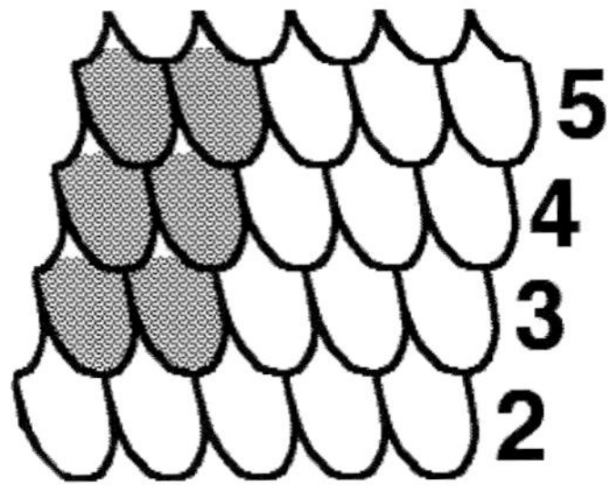


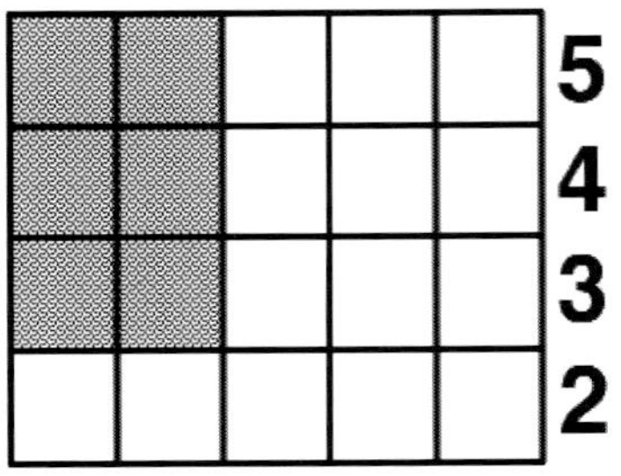


***The graphs on the left are for right-handed crocheters. Left-handed crocheters should look at the reversed image of the graphs in a mirror.***

**Round 3:** You will begin to tapestry crochet the motif in this round. Remember, that to do a tapestry crochet stitch, colors are switched while 2 loops are still on the hook; yarn over with the next color and pull it through the loops to prepare for the tapestry crochet stitch. Rounds 2 through 5 correspond to the illustrated stripe motif (read from right to left and bottom to top). Start the stripe pattern as follows: tapestry crochet 3 stitches with the silk thread, then 2 stitches with the metallic thread. Repeat this sequence 3 [5] (7) more times. Turn the pouch inside out (to make it right side out). As you tapestry crochet each stitch, the hook should point toward the inside of the pouch. Every once in a while, untwist the threads by holding the pouch up in the air with one of the threads while pulling on the other thread. Let the piece spin around in the air so that the threads untangle.

**Next Rounds:** Continue to tapestry crochet the pattern, 3 silk, then 2 metallic stitches, until the pouch is almost as tall as you want it to be. Notice that the stripe is slightly diagonal. This is normal, since tapestry crochet stitches are not exactly on top of the ones immediately below. Before you run out of thread, start to carry the new thread five or more stitches before it is needed, instead of tying on a new piece. Switch to the new thread, then carry the tail of the old thread five or more stitches to secure it before snipping it off.

**Last Rounds:** Crochet 2 plain rounds with the silk thread. Continue to carry the metallic thread. Cut the metallic thread flush at the end of the second round.

**To Finish:** Without cutting off the silk thread, crochet a chain as long as you want the necklace to be. Slip stitch the chain to the other side of the top of the pouch, then cut the thread (leaving a 6 inch tail), yarn over and pull it all the way through the loop. Work in the end for 1 inch to secure it, then trim it off. DO NOT STEAM BLOCK the finished piece because metallic thread and silk do not like steam and intense heat. Instead, set the iron on *silk,* cover the piece with a towel, then iron it with dry heat.

## Metallic Threads

Metallic thread was used in many parts of the pre-historic world, but was prohibited in the New World during colonial times. The use of gold and silver threads in Native American textiles came to an abrupt halt on October 25, 1563, when a royal warrant ordered “that no person, man or woman, be allowed to wear any textile that was brocaded . . . nor one that had gold or silver in its weaving . . . even if these threads were false imitation . . . as also it was prohibited that silver or gold should be used for the cloths that were used on horses and mules (Osborne 1975:23 from *Prontuario de cédulas reales*, p. 160).” We are lucky today, since we have access to a wide variety of metallic threads.

# Silk

Silk is the strongest natural fiber. Silkworm cocoons were collected from trees more than five thousand years ago in China. For centuries, only the Chinese nobility could wear silk clothing and the knowledge of sericulture was kept a closely guarded secret. Silk fabrics were carried over caravan routes extending from central China to Europe. The secret of sericulture was smuggled into Japan in the third century. In 552, two monks smuggled the secret of silk production to the West. They hid silkworm eggs and mulberry seeds inside their hollow bamboo canes.

The life span of the silk moth is around six weeks. After hatching, silkworms are fed mulberry leaves six times a day. The silkworm grows from less than 1/8 inch to 3 inches long the first thirty two days. It takes three days to spin a cocoon from a double filament of silk that may be up to seven hundred yards long. The filament is wrapped layer by layer around the insect's body in a series of figure-eights and cemented by a gelatinous protein called sericin. After around two weeks the chrysalis breaks through the cocoon filament and emerges as a moth. Female moths lay three to four hundred eggs before they die. Spun silk, which has a deep, creamy finish, is made from shorter lengths of silk from cocoons that have been pierced by adult silk moths as they emerge.

Filament silk has an unbroken sheen. To make filament silk, the worm is killed before maturity so that it doesn't break through the cocoon (breaking the filament in the process). Filament silk is wound right off the cocoon and may be as long as three thousand yards. Filaments from five to ten cocoons are wound together and twisted into a single fiber, glued together by the melted sericin. Since it is still too thin to used, it is plied together with other silk fibers. Silk is dyed after the sericin has been boiled off.

**This young woman is feeding mulberry leaves to silkworms in Japan. The silkworms are kept on trays, which can be seen stacked in the background (ca. 1900, Keystone View Company).**

**Two types of silkworm cocoons are commercially produced. The more common cultivated silkworm moth, the Bombyx mori, produces white cocoons (shown actual size in the upper left). The less common beige cocoons on the lower right were made by the semi-domestic Muga-Antherea Assama, who eat outside, then make their cocoon, emerge, mate, lay eggs and hatch indoors.**

# Eyeglass Case

This project is similar to the Amulet Pouch project, except that this eyeglass case is larger and features a more complex motif. Like the previous project, this case begins at the bottom. A base is crocheted first, then since the diameter of the base is not increased, the edges of the spiral move upwards to form the walls. The motif is 10 stitches wide, so the total number of stitches in the base is a multiple of 10. It is possible to make a variety of sizes with the same design motif simply by increasing or decreasing the size of the base by 10 stitches. Feel free to substitute another motif, just be sure that the total number of stitches in the base is a multiple of the number of stitches in your motif.

## Hook

Steel crochet hook size 4 (2.00 mm.) or the size that will give an acceptable gauge

## Gauge

9 stitches equals 1 inch
7 1/2 rows equals 1 inch

## Size

3" wide by 7" high

## Materials

One skein of Variegated (color 43) and one skein of White (color 101) Reynolds Sedona Four Ply Mercerized Egyptian cotton (or a similar substitute);
Safety pin or a piece of thread of a contrasting color for counting the rounds.

**Round 1:** Starting with the color thread, make a slip knot (leaving a six-inch tail), then chain 25 stitches. Increase in multiples of 5 chain stitches at this point to make a wider eyeglass case. Starting with the second chain, single crochet 23 stitches. Single crochet 3 stitches into the last chain for a total of 26 stitches. Continue to single crochet using the new top of the chain until you come around to the first stitch, carrying the "tail" as you go. Single crochet 2 stitches into the last stitch. This first round should have a total of 50 stitches. This piece is worked as a spiral, not in concentric rings, so it is difficult to tell where each round ends. To keep track of where each round ends, slip a safety pin into the top of the last stitch of the round or lay a two inch piece of thread of a contrasting color across the path of the last stitch. You will remove the safety pin from the last stitch as you come to it again and slip it into the new last stitch or cross the path of the last stitch with the end of the counting thread at the end of each round.

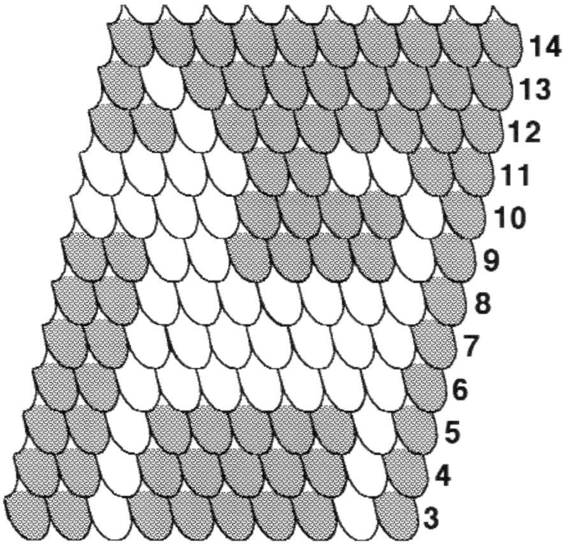


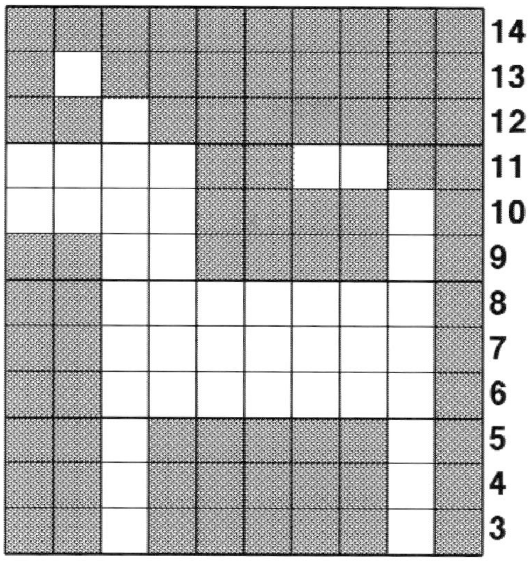


***The graphs on the left are for right-handed crocheters. Left-handed crocheters should look at the reversed image of the graphs in a mirror.***

**Round 2:** Cut the color tail flush and then start to carry the white thread. Crochet around without any increases, carrying the white thread. The case should still have 50 stitches when you finish this round.
**Round 3:** You will begin to tapestry crochet the motif in this round. Remember, that to do a tapestry crochet stitch, colors are switched while 2 loops are still on the hook; yarn over with the next color and pull it through the loops to prepare for the tapestry crochet stitch. Rounds 3 through 14 correspond to the illustrated motif (read from right to left and bottom to top). Start the motif as follows: tapestry crochet 1 color stitch, 1 white stitch, 5 color, 1 white, and then 2 color stitches. Repeat this sequence 4 more times. Turn the case inside out (to make it right side out). As you tapestry crochet each stitch, the hook should point toward the inside of the case. Every once in a while, untwist the threads by holding the case up in the air with one of the threads while pulling on the other thread. Let the piece spin around in the air so that the threads untangle.
**Round 4:** Tapestry crochet 1 color, 1 white, 5 color, 1 white, then 2 color stitches. Repeat this sequence 4 more times.
**Round 5:** Tapestry crochet 1 color, 1 white, 5 color, 1 white, then 2 color stitches. Repeat this sequence 4 more times.
**Round 6:** Tapestry crochet 1 color, 7 white, then 2 color stitches. Repeat this sequence 4 more times.
**Round 7:** Tapestry crochet 1 color, 7 white, then 2 color stitches. Repeat this sequence 4 more times.
**Round 8:** Tapestry crochet 1 color, 7 white, then 2 color stitches. Repeat this sequence 4 more times.
**Round 9:** Tapestry crochet 1 color, 1 white, 4 color, 2 white, then 2 color stitches. Repeat this sequence 4 more times.
**Round 10:** Tapestry crochet 1 color, 1 white, 4 color, then 4 white stitches. Repeat this sequence 4 more times.
**Round 11:** Tapestry crochet 2 color, 2 white, 2 color, then 4 white stitches. Repeat this sequence 4 more times.
**Round 12:** Tapestry crochet 7 color, 1 white, then 2 color stitches. Repeat this sequence 4 more times.
**Round 13:** Tapestry crochet 8 color, 1 white, then 1 color stitch. Repeat this sequence 4 more times.
**Round 14:** Tapestry crochet a round with color, while carrying the white thread.

***Repeat rounds 3 through 14 three more times.***

**Last Round:** Tapestry crochet a round with color, while carrying the white thread.

**To Finish:** Crochet 13 color stitches, then cut the white thread flush. Slip stitch with color, cut it (leaving a 6 inch tail) then yarn over and pull it all the way through the loop. Work in the end for 1 inch to secure it, then trim it off. Block the eyeglass case.

# Change Purse

This change purse begins at the bottom. A base is crocheted first, then since the diameter of the base is not increased, the edges of the spiral move upwards to form the walls. The pig motif is 22 stitches wide, so the total number of stitches in the base is a multiple of 22. It is possible to make a variety of sizes with the same design motif simply by increasing or decreasing the size of the base by 22 stitches. Feel free to substitute another motif, just be sure that the total number of stitches in the base is a multiple of the number of stitches in your motif. This project will teach you how to sew in a zipper.

## Hook

Steel crochet hook size 4 (2.00 mm.) or the size that will give an acceptable gauge.

## Gauge

8 stitches equals 1 inch
7 rows equals 1 inch

## Size

5 1/2" wide by 5" high

## Materials

One ball (100 yards) of Forest Green (color 449) and one ball of Orchid Pink (color 0401) size 3 J. & P. Coats Speed-Cro-Sheen 100% mercerized cotton, article C-45 (or a similar substitute);
4" nylon zipper or a longer one which may be cut down;
Invisible thread;
Safety pin or a piece of thread of a contrasting color for counting the rounds.

**Round 1:** Starting with the green thread, make a slip knot (leaving a six-inch tail), then chain 44 stitches. Increase or decrease in multiples of 11 chain stitches at this point to make a wider or narrower change purse. Starting with the second chain, single crochet 42 stitches. Single crochet 3 stitches into the last chain for a total of 45 stitches. Continue to single crochet using the new top of the chain until you come around to the first stitch, carrying the "tail" as you go. Single crochet 2 stitches into the last stitch. This first round should have a total of 88 stitches. This piece is worked as a spiral, not in concentric rings, so it is difficult to tell where each round ends. To keep track of where each round ends, slip a safety pin into the top of the last stitch of the round or lay a two inch piece of thread of a contrasting color across the path of the last stitch. You will remove the safety pin from the last stitch as you come to it again and slip it into the new last stitch or cross the path of the last stitch with the end of the counting thread at the end of each round.
**Round 2:** Cut the green tail flush and then start to carry the pink thread. Single crochet around without any increases, carrying the pink thread. The change purse should still have 88 stitches when you finish this round.

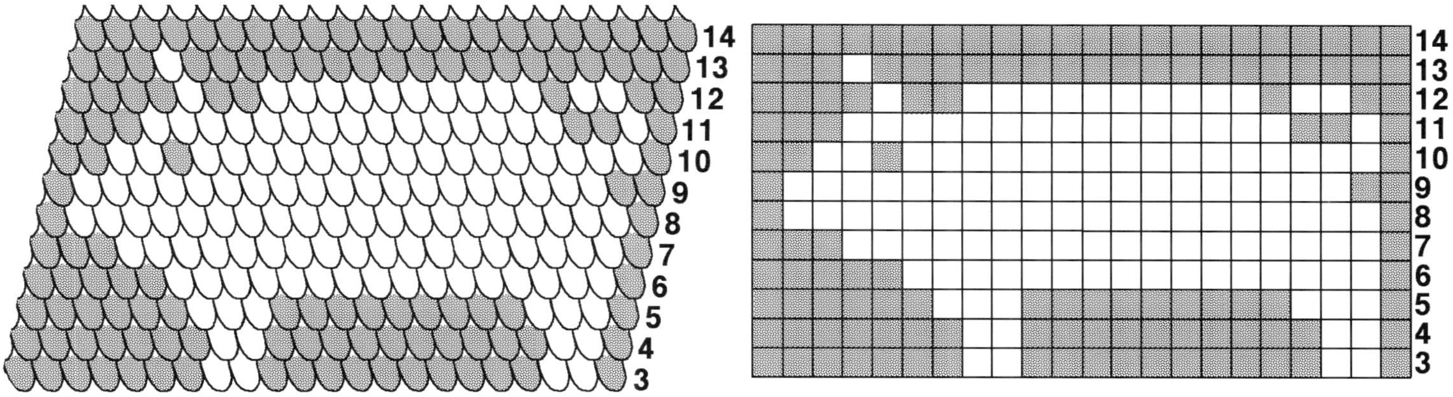


***The above graphs are for right-handed crocheters.***
***Left-handed crocheters should look at the reversed image of the graphs in a mirror.***

**Round 3:** You will begin to tapestry crochet the motif in this round. Remember, that to do a tapestry crochet stitch, colors are switched while 2 loops are still on the hook; yarn over with the next color and pull it through the loops to prepare for the tapestry crochet stitch. Rounds 3 through 14 correspond to the illustrated pig motif (read from right to left and bottom to top). Start the motif as follows: tapestry crochet 1 green stitch, 2 pink stitches, 10 green, 2 pink, and then 7 green stitches. Repeat this sequence 3 more times. Turn the change purse inside out (to make it right side out). As you tapestry crochet each stitch, the hook should point toward the inside of the change purse. Every once in a while, untwist the threads by holding the change purse up in the air with one of the threads while pulling on the other thread. Let the piece spin around in the air so that the threads untangle.
**Round 4:** Tapestry crochet 1 green, 2 pink, 10 green, 2 pink, then 7 green stitches. Repeat this sequence 3 more times.
**Round 5:** Tapestry crochet 1 green, 3 pink, 9 green, 3 pink, then 6 green stitches. Repeat this sequence 3 more times.
**Round 6:** Tapestry crochet 1 green, 16 pink, then 5 green stitches. Repeat this sequence 3 more times.
**Round 7:** Tapestry crochet 1 green, 18 pink, then 3 green stitches. Repeat this sequence 3 more times.
**Round 8:** Tapestry crochet 1 green, 20 pink, then 1 green stitch. Repeat this sequence 3 more times.
**Round 9:** Tapestry crochet 2 green, 19 pink, then 1 green stitch. Repeat this sequence 3 more times.
**Round 10:** Tapestry crochet 1 green, 16 pink, 1 green, 2 pink, then 2 green stitches. Repeat this sequence 3 more times.
**Round 11:** Tapestry crochet 1 green, 1 pink, 2 green, 15 pink, then 3 green stitches. Repeat this sequence 3 more times.
**Round 12:** Tapestry crochet 2 green, 2 pink, 1 green, 10 pink, 2 green, 1 pink, then 4 green stitches. Repeat this sequence 3 more times.

**Round 13:** Tapestry crochet 18 green, 1 pink, then 3 green stitches. Repeat this sequence 3 more times.
**Round 14:** Tapestry crochet a round with green, while carrying the pink thread. Notice that the motif is slightly diagonal. This is normal, since tapestry crochet stitches are not exactly on top of the ones immediately below.
**Last Round:** Tapestry crochet a round with green, while carrying the pink thread.

**To Finish:** Crochet 4 green stitches, then cut the pink thread flush. Slip stitch with green, cut it (leaving a 6 inch tail) then yarn over and pull it all the way through the loop. Work in the end for 1 inch to secure it, then trim it off. Block the change purse.

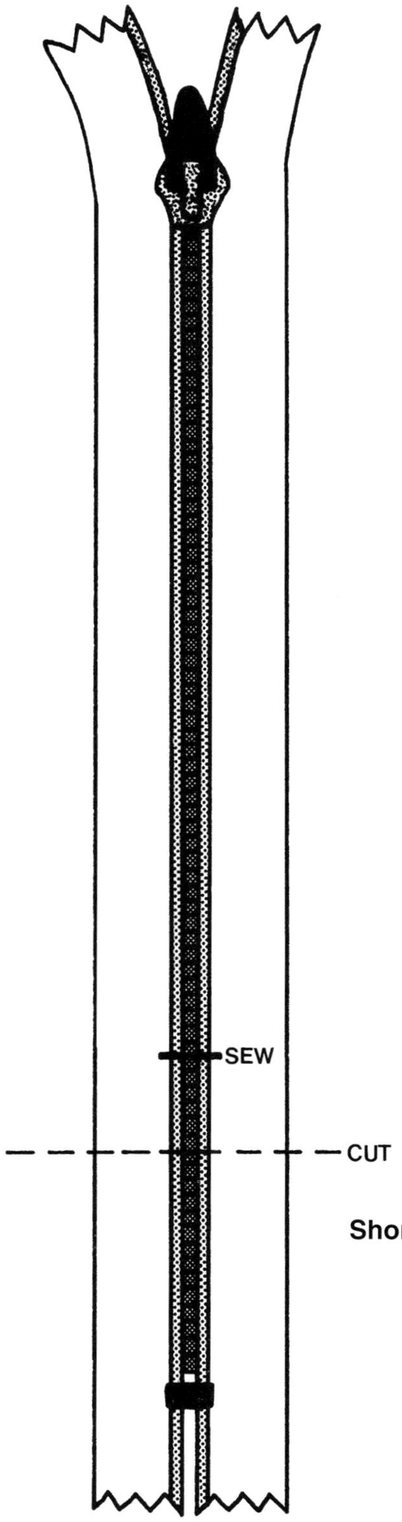


Shortening the zipper.

***Sew in the zipper as follows:***

1) If the zipper is too long, measure from the top of the zipper down to as long as you need it to be. Sew back and forth to create a "lock" as illustrated on the left. Cut off the lower portion of the zipper, leaving 3/4" piece below the sewn lock.

2) Open the zipper, and baste (hand sew with large stitches) the zipper into the change purse.

3) With invisible thread, either hand sew with small stitches or machine sew the zipper into the change purse.

4) Remove the basting.

5) Block the change purse again.

# Fishy Pillow

What could be more attractive than a tapestry crochet pillow? This project was crocheted with a loose tapestry crochet stitch in order to make the surface of the pillow soft. The pillow begins at the bottom (which becomes the side when the pillow is turned ninety degrees). The base is crocheted first, then since the diameter of the base is not increased, the edges of the spiral move upwards to form the sides. The fish motif is eight stitches wide, so the total number of stitches in the base is a multiple of eight. It is possible to make a variety of sizes with the same design motif simply by increasing or decreasing the size of the base by eight stitches. Feel free to substitute another motif, just be sure that the total number of stitches in the base is a multiple of the number of stitches in your motif.

## Hook
Steel crochet hook size G/6 (4.25 mm.) or the size that will give an acceptable gauge

## Gauge
5 1/2 stitches equals 1 inch
5 rows equals 1 inch

## Size
13" wide by 12 1/2" high (without pillow insert)

## Materials
Two balls (50 grams/1 3/4 oz./114 yards each) of white (color 0010) and three balls of light blue (color 5727) Kolibri mercerized cotton thread (or a similar substitute);
Safety pin or a piece of thread of a contrasting color for counting the rounds;
14" pillow insert;
Tapestry sewing needle.

**Round 1:** Starting with the color thread, make a slip knot (leaving a fourteen-inch tail), then chain 72 stitches. Increase or decrease in multiples of 4 chain stitches at this point to make a wider or narrower pillow. Starting with the second chain, single crochet 70 stitches. Single crochet 3 stitches into the last chain for a total of 73 stitches. Continue to single crochet using the new top of the chain until you come around to the first stitch, carrying the "tail" as you go. Single crochet 2 stitches into the last stitch. This first round should have a total of 144 stitches. This piece is worked as a spiral, not in concentric rings, so it is difficult to tell where each round ends. To keep track of where each round ends, slip a safety pin into the top of the last stitch of the round or lay a two inch piece of thread of a contrasting color across the path of the last stitch. You will remove the safety pin from the last stitch as you come to it again and slip it into the new last stitch or cross the path of the last stitch with the end of the counting thread at the end of each round.

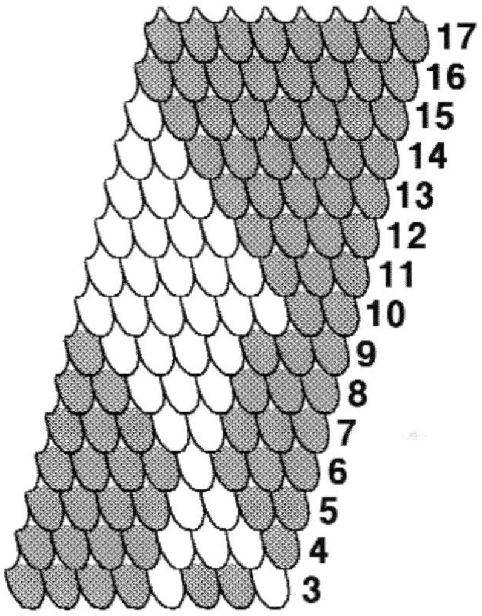


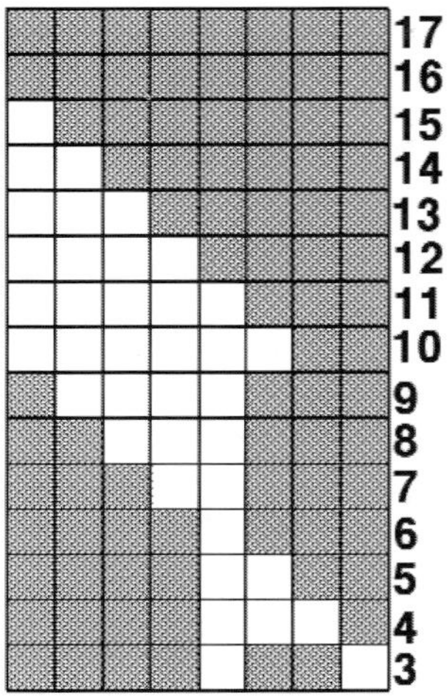

***The above graphs are for right-handed crocheters. Left-handed crocheters should look at the reversed image of the graphs in a mirror.***

**Round 2:** Cut the tail flush and then start to carry the white thread. Crochet around without any increases, carrying the white thread. The pillow should still have 144 stitches when you finish this round.

**Round 3:** You will begin to tapestry crochet the motif in this round. Remember, that to do a tapestry crochet stitch, threads are switched while 2 loops are still on the hook; yarn over with the other thread and pull it through the loops to prepare for the tapestry crochet stitch. Rounds 3 through 17 correspond to the illustrated fish motif (read from right to left and bottom to top). Start the fish motif as follows: tapestry crochet 1 white, 2 color, 1 white, then 4 color stitches. Repeat this sequence 17 more times. Turn the pillow inside out (to make it right side out). As you tapestry crochet each stitch, the hook should point toward the inside of the pouch. Every once in a while, untwist the threads by holding the pillow up in the air with one of the threads while pulling on the other thread. Let the piece spin around in the air so that the threads untangle.

**Round 4:** Tapestry crochet 1 color, 3 white, then 4 color stitches. Repeat this sequence 17 more times.

**Round 5:** Tapestry crochet 2 color, 2 white, then 4 color stitches. Repeat this sequence 17 more times.

**Round 6:** Tapestry crochet 3 color, 1 white, then 4 color stitches. Repeat this sequence 17 more times.

**Round 7:** Tapestry crochet 3 color, 2 white, then 3 color stitches. Repeat this sequence 17 more times.

**Round 8:** Tapestry crochet 3 color, 3 white, then 2 color stitches. Repeat this sequence 17 more times.

**Round 9:** Tapestry crochet 3 color, 4 white, then 1 color stitch. Repeat this sequence 17 more times.

**Round 10:** Tapestry crochet 2 color, then 6 white stitches. Repeat this sequence 17 more times.

**Round 11:** Tapestry crochet 3 color, then 5 white stitches. Repeat this sequence 17 more times.

**Round 12:** Tapestry crochet 4 color, then 4 white stitches. Repeat this sequence 17 more times.

**Round 13:** Tapestry crochet 5 color, then 3 white stitches. Repeat this sequence 17 more times.

**Round 14:** Tapestry crochet 6 color, then 2 white stitches. Repeat this sequence 17 more times.

**Round 15:** Tapestry crochet 7 color, then 1 white stitch. Repeat this sequence 17 more times.

**Round 16:** Tapestry crochet a round with color, while carrying the white thread.

**Round 17:** Tapestry crochet a round with color, while carrying the white thread. Notice that the motif is slightly diagonal. This is normal, since tapestry crochet stitches are not exactly on top of the ones immediately below. Before you run out of thread, start to carry the new thread five or more stitches before it is needed, instead of tying on a new piece. Switch to the new thread, then carry the tail of the old thread five or more stitches to secure it before snipping it off.

***Repeat rounds 3 through 17 three more times.***

**To Finish:** Crochet 16 blue stitches, then cut the white thread flush. Slip stitch with blue, cut it (leaving a 48 inch tail) then yarn over and pull it all the way through the loop. Block the project.

Insert a pillow.

Thread the 48 inch tail of blue thread through a tapestry needle.

From front to back, insert the needle into the top 2 loops of the next single crochet stitches of each side. Pull the thread through.

Repeat this stitch until you have sewn across the opening of the pillow.

Sew a couple of stitches into the last stitch.

Insert the needle under the last six stitches and then pull the thread through. Cut the thread flush.

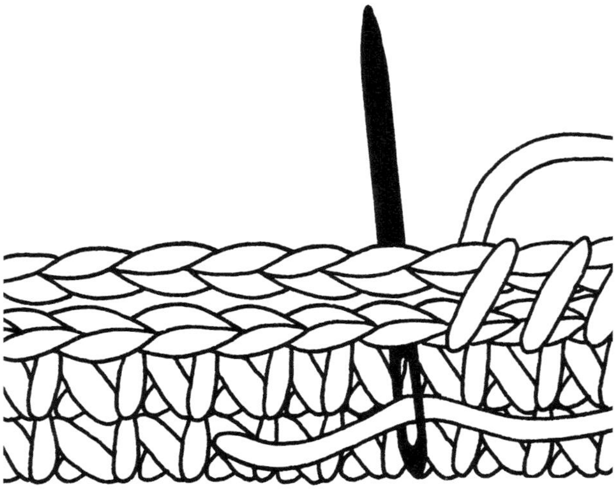

**The pillow seam.**

# Rectangular Shoulder Bag

This rectangular shoulder bag, inspired by its Guatemalan counterparts, is worked in a manner similar to the pillow project. Although the finished piece includes three colors, only two threads are worked at the same time. The base is crocheted first, then since the diameter of the base is not increased, the edges of the spiral move upwards to form the sides. The figure motif is ten stitches wide, so the total number of stitches in the base is a multiple of ten. It is possible to make a variety of sizes with the same design motif simply by increasing or decreasing the size of the base by ten stitches. Feel free to substitute another motif, just be sure that the total number of stitches in the base is a multiple of the number of stitches in your motif. This project will teach you how to alternate the background color and how to crochet a shoulder strap.

## Hook

Steel crochet hook size 4 (2.00 mm.) or the size that will give an acceptable gauge

## Gauge

8 stitches equals 1 inch
7 rows equals 1 inch

## Size

11" wide by 11 5/8" high (without strap)

## Materials

Four Spanish Red (color 126), two Navy (color 486), and two Purple (color 458) balls (100 yards each) size 3 J. & P. Coats Speed-Cro-Sheen 100% mercerized cotton, article C-45 (or a similar substitute);
Safety pin or a piece of thread of a contrasting color for counting the rounds.

**Round 1:** Starting with the red thread, make a slip knot (leaving a fourteen-inch tail), then chain 90 stitches. Increase or decrease in multiples of 5 chain stitches at this point to make a wider or narrower shoulder bag. Starting with the second chain, single crochet 88 stitches. Single crochet 3 stitches into the last chain for a total of 91 stitches. Continue to single crochet using the new top of the chain until you come around to the first stitch, carrying the "tail" as you go. Single crochet 2 stitches into the last stitch. This first round should have a total of 180 stitches. This piece is worked as a spiral, not in concentric rings, so it is difficult to tell where each round ends. To keep track of where each round ends, slip a safety pin into the top of the last stitch of the round or lay a two inch piece of thread of a contrasting color across the path of the last stitch. You will remove the safety pin from the last stitch as you come to it again and slip it into the new last stitch or cross the path of the last stitch with the end of the counting thread at the end of each round.

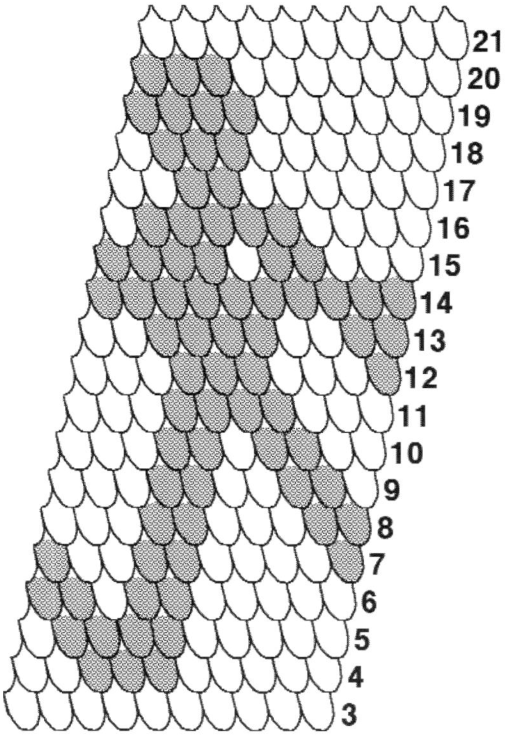


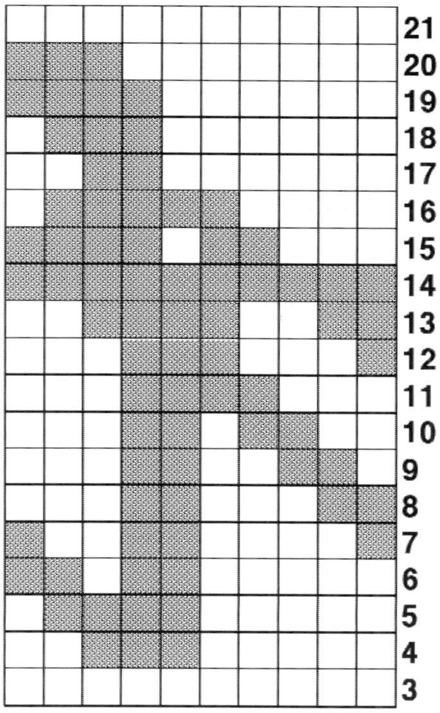


***The graphs on the left are for right-handed crocheters. Left-handed crocheters should look at the reversed image of the graphs in a mirror.***

**Round 2:** Cut the tail flush and then start to carry the navy thread. Single crochet around without any increases, carrying the navy thread. From now on, the shoulder bag should always have 180 stitches at the end of every round.

**Round 3:** Rounds 3 through 21 correspond to the illustrated motif (read from right to left and bottom to top). Crochet around with red, carrying the other thread.

**Round 4:** You will begin to tapestry crochet the figure motif in this round. Remember, that to do a tapestry crochet stitch, threads are switched while 2 loops are still on the hook; yarn over with the other thread and pull it through the loops to prepare for the tapestry crochet stitch. Start the figure motif as follows: tapestry crochet 5 red, 3 figure (navy or purple), then 2 red stitches. Repeat this sequence 17 more times. Turn the shoulder bag inside out (to make it right side out). As you tapestry crochet each stitch, the hook should point toward the inside of the shoulder bag. Every once in a while, untwist the threads by holding the shoulder bag up in the air with one of the threads while pulling on the other thread. Let the piece spin around in the air so that the threads untangle.

**Round 5:** Tapestry crochet 5 red, 4 figure, then 1 red stitch. Repeat this sequence 17 more times.

**Round 6:** Tapestry crochet 5 red, 2 figure, 1 red, then 2 figure stitches. Repeat this sequence 17 more times.

**Round 7:** Tapestry crochet 1 figure, 4 red, 2 figure, 2 red, then 1 figure stitch. Repeat this sequence 17 more times.

**Round 8:** Tapestry crochet 2 figure, 3 red, 2 figure, then 3 red figure stitches. Repeat this sequence 17 more times.

**Round 9:** Tapestry crochet 1 red, 2 figure, 2 red, 2 figure, then 3 red stitches. Repeat this sequence 17 more times.

**Round 10:** Tapestry crochet 2 red, 2 figure, 1 red, 2 figure, then 3 red stitches. Repeat this sequence 17 more times.
**Round 11:** Tapestry crochet 3 red, 4 figure, then 3 red stitches. Repeat this sequence 17 more times.
**Round 12:** Tapestry crochet 1 figure, 3 red, 3 figure, then 3 red stitches. Repeat this sequence 17 more times.
**Round 13:** Tapestry crochet 2 figure, 2 red, 4 figure, then 2 red stitches. Repeat this sequence 17 more times.
**Round 14:** Crochet around with the figure thread while carrying the red thread.
**Round 15:** Tapestry crochet 3 red, 2 figure, 1 red, then 4 figure stitches. Repeat this sequence 17 more times.
**Round 16:** Tapestry crochet 4 red, 5 figure, then 1 red stitch. Repeat this sequence 17 more times.
**Round 17:** Tapestry crochet 6 red, 2 figure, then 2 red stitches. Repeat this sequence 17 more times.
**Round 18:** Tapestry crochet 6 red, 3 figure, then 1 red stitch. Repeat this sequence 17 more times.
**Round 19:** Tapestry crochet 6 red, then 4 figure stitches. Repeat this sequence 17 more times.
**Round 20:** Tapestry crochet 7 red, then 3 figure stitches. Repeat this sequence 17 more times.
**Round 21:** Crochet around with the red thread while carrying the figure thread. Notice that the motif is slightly diagonal. This is normal, since tapestry crochet stitches are not exactly on top of the ones immediately below. Drop the figure thread and start to carry a new figure thread for the last 10 stitches of this round (use this same technique when a thread runs out and a new one must be used). Crochet 10 red stitches, then cut the previous figure thread flush.

***Repeat rounds 3 through 21 three more times.***

**Finishing:**
**Round A:** Crochet 20 red stitches. Do not cut the red thread, but do cut the carried thread flush. Chain 175 stitches with the red thread (that is still attached to the shoulder bag). If you would like a longer or shorter shoulder strap, increase or decrease at this point. Insert the hook into the 90th stitch away from the base of the chain, connecting the end of the chain to the other side of the top of the shoulder bag with a crochet stitch. Make sure that the chain is not twisted.
**Round B:** Start to carry the navy thread. Crochet 90 stitches across the top of the bag with the red thread. Continue to single crochet onto the chain. You should have 265 stitches when you finish this round.
**Round C:** Crochet 265 stitches around with the navy thread, while carrying the red thread.
**Round D:** Crochet 265 stitches around with the navy thread, while carrying the red thread.

**Detail of shoulder strap.**

**Round E:** Crochet 265 stitches around with the navy thread, while carrying the red thread, then at the end of the round cut the red thread flush. Slip stitch with navy, cut it (leaving a 6 inch tail) then yarn over and pull it all the way through the loop. Work in the end for 1 inch to secure it, then trim it off.
**Round F:** Turn over the shoulder bag. Have the side facing you with only one row of red over the motif. Insert the hook into the stitch in the upper right hand corner of the bag next to the shoulder strap. Pull through a loop of red thread, leaving a 2" piece hanging out of the back. Chain 1 with red, then crochet 1 stitch into the same stitch. Start to carry the navy thread along with the 2" piece of red thread. Crochet 89 more stitches across the top of the shoulder bag. Continue to crochet onto the shoulder strap, inserting the hook into the bottom loops of the original chain.
**Round G:** Repeat Round C.
**Round G:** Repeat Round D.
**Round H:** Repeat Round E, then block the finished shoulder bag.

# ROUNDS PROJECTS

# SPIRAL

# PROJECTS

# TUBE PROJECTS

# SQUARE SPIRAL PROJECT

# FLAT PROJECTS

# CIRCULAR SPIRAL PROJECTS 5

## Baby Blanket/Throw

The same instructions are followed for both pieces. The large blanket was crocheted with a large hook, which resulted in larger stitches and a bigger blanket. The blankets begin in the center, and spiral outward. The giraffe motif is twelve stitches wide at the bottom, so the total number of stitches in each round is a multiple of twelve. Since the number of stitches of every round is a multiple of twelve, you can start the motif at any point and it will still work out perfectly. Feel free to substitute another motif, just be sure that the total number of stitches of each round is a multiple of the number of stitches in your motif.

## Small Blanket/Throw

### Hook
Crochet hook size K/10 1/2 (6.50 mm.) or the size that will give an acceptable gauge

### Gauge
3 1/2 stitches equals 1 inch
3 rows equals 1 inch

### Size
34" diameter

### Materials
Four 4 ounce balls (113 grams/189 yards/172 meters each ball) of Sherbert Swirl (color 298) and two 5 ounce balls (142 grams/236 yards/215 meters) of White (color 100), Lion Brand Art. No. 760 four ply worsted weight Kitchen Cotton (or a similar substitute);
Safety pin or a piece of thread of a contrasting color for counting the rounds.

Detail of the Large Blanket/Throw

## Large Blanket/Throw

### Hook

Crochet hook size N (9.00 mm.) or the size that will give an acceptable gauge

### Gauge

3 stitches equals 1 inch
2 1/2 rows equals 1 inch

### Size

42" diameter

### Materials

Four 4 ounce balls (113 grams/189 yards/172 meters each ball) of Wedgewood (color 208) and two 5 ounce balls (142 grams/236 yards/215 meters) of Poppy Red (color 112), Lion Brand Art. No. 760 four ply worsted weight Kitchen Cotton (or a similar substitute);
Safety pin or a piece of thread of a contrasting color for counting the rounds.

**Round 1:** Starting with the variegated thread, make a slip knot (leaving an eight-inch tail), then chain 4 stitches. Join the ends together to form a ring by working a slip stitch into the first chain stitch. Single crochet 6 stitches loosely into the ring (while carrying the tail of the thread). The blanket should have a total of 6 stitches when you finish this round. This piece is worked as a spiral, not in concentric rings, so it is difficult to tell where each round ends. To keep track of where each round ends, slip a safety pin into the top of the last stitch of the round or lay a two inch piece of thread of a contrasting color across the path of the last stitch. You will remove the safety pin from the last stitch as you come to it again and slip it into the new last stitch or cross the path of the last stitch with the end of the counting thread at the end of each round. Pull a little on the counting thread as it runs out to make it longer.
**Round 2:** Continue to carry the tail. Increase by crocheting 2 stitches into each stitch. The blanket should have a total of 12 stitches when you finish this round.
**Round 3:** Cut the tail flush, then start to carry the other thread. Increase again in every stitch. The blanket should have 24 stitches when you finish this round.
**Round 4:** Increase in every second stitch. The blanket should have 36 stitches when you finish this round.
**Round 5:** Crochet one round without any increases.
**Round 6:** Increase in every third stitch. The blanket should have 48 stitches when you finish this round.
**Round 7:** Crochet one round without any increases.
**Round 8:** Increase in every fourth stitch. The blanket should have 60 stitches when you finish this round.
**Round 9:** Increase in every fifth stitch. The blanket should have 72 stitches when you finish this round.
**Round 10:** Crochet one round without any increases.
**Round 11:** Increase in every sixth stitch, The blanket should have 84 stitches when you finish this round.
**Round 12:** Increase in every seventh stitch. The blanket should have 96 stitches when you finish this round.
**Round 13:** Increase in every eighth stitch. The blanket should have 108 stitches when you finish this round.
**Round 14:** Crochet one round without any increases.
**Round 15:** Increase in every ninth stitch. The blanket should have 120 stitches when you finish this round.
**Round 16:** Increase in every tenth stitch. The blanket should have 132 stitches when you finish this round.
**Round 17:** Crochet one round without any increases.

**Round 18:** Increase in every eleventh stitch. The blanket should have 144 stitches when you finish this round.
**Round 19:** Crochet one round without any increases.

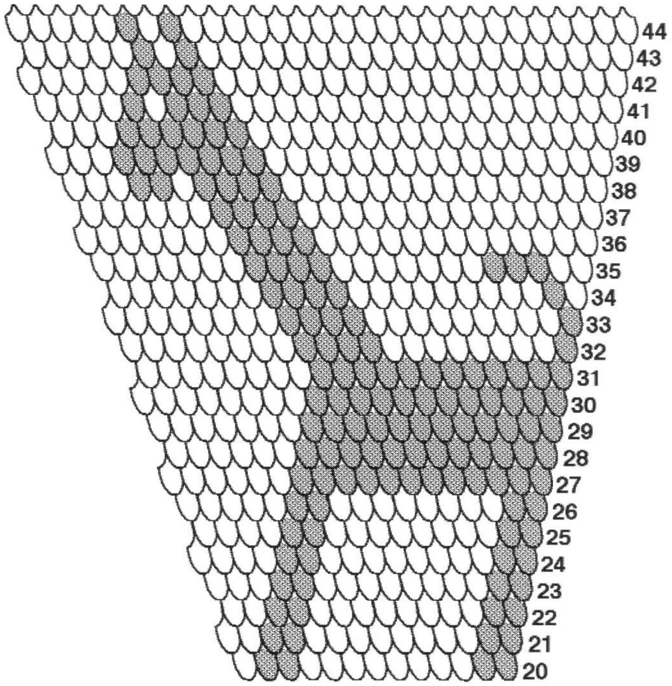

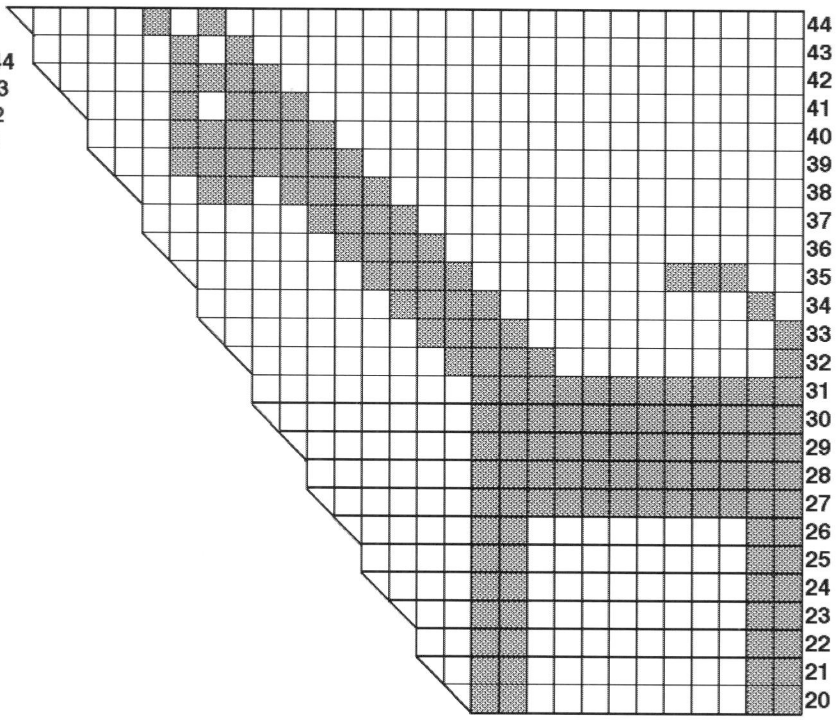

***The above graphs are for right-handed crocheters.***
***Left-handed crocheters should look at the reversed image of the graphs in a mirror.***

***Begin motif:***
**Round 20:** Rounds 20 through 44 correspond to the illustrated giraffe motif (read from right to left and bottom to top). To begin the tapestry crochet stitch, you will have to pull your hook out of the last loop you made at the end of the previous round, pull out the loop, insert your hook into the two remaining loops, switch threads and then yarn over and pull through a loop with the carried thread. Tapestry crochet 2 giraffe color, 8 background color, 2 giraffe, and then increase in the last stitch by tapestry crocheting 1 more background color stitch into the last stitch. Repeat around. Every once in a while, untwist the threads by holding the blanket up in the air with one of the threads while pulling on the other thread. Let the piece spin around in the air so that the threads untangle.
**Round 21:** Tapestry crochet 2 giraffe, 8 background, 2 giraffe, 1 background, and then increase in the last stitch by tapestry crocheting 1 more background color stitch into the last stitch. Repeat around.
**Round 22:** Tapestry crochet 2 giraffe, 8 background, 2 giraffe, and 2 background stitches. Repeat around.
**Round 23:** Tapestry crochet 2 giraffe, 8 background, 2 giraffe, 2 background, and then increase in the last stitch by tapestry crocheting 1 more background color stitch into the last stitch. Repeat around.
**Round 24:** Tapestry crochet 2 giraffe, 8 background, 2 giraffe, 3 background, and then increase in the last stitch by tapestry crocheting 1 more background color stitch into the last stitch. Repeat around.
**Round 25:** Tapestry crochet 2 giraffe, 8 background, 2 giraffe, and 4 background stitches. Repeat around.
**Round 26:** Tapestry crochet 2 giraffe, 8 background, 2 giraffe, 4 background, and then increase in the last stitch by tapestry crocheting 1 more background color stitch into the last stitch. Repeat around.
**Round 27:** Tapestry crochet 12 giraffe, 5 background, and then increase in the last stitch by tapestry crocheting 1 more background color stitch into the last stitch. Repeat around.
**Round 28:** Tapestry crochet 12 giraffe and 6 background stitches. Repeat around.
**Round 29:** Tapestry crochet 12 giraffe, 6 background, and then increase in the last stitch by tapestry crocheting 1 more background color stitch into the last stitch. Repeat around.

**Round 30:** Tapestry crochet 12 giraffe, 7 background, and then increase in the last stitch by tapestry crocheting 1 more background color stitch into the last stitch. Repeat around.
**Round 31:** Tapestry crochet 12 giraffe and 8 background stitches. Repeat around.
**Round 32:** Tapestry crochet 1 giraffe, 8 background, 4 giraffe, 7 background, and then increase in the last stitch by tapestry crocheting 1 more background color stitch into the last stitch. Repeat around.
**Round 33:** Tapestry crochet 1 giraffe, 9 background, 4 giraffe, 7 background, and then increase in the last stitch by tapestry crocheting 1 more background color stitch into the last stitch. Repeat around.
**Round 34:** Tapestry crochet 1 background, 1 giraffe, 9 background, 4 giraffe, and 7 background stitches. Repeat around.
**Round 35:** Tapestry crochet 2 background, 3 giraffe, 7 background, 4 giraffe, 6 background, and then increase in the last stitch by tapestry crocheting 1 more background color stitch into the last stitch. Repeat around.
**Round 36:** Tapestry crochet 13 background, 4 giraffe, 6 background, and then increase in the last stitch by tapestry crocheting 1 more background color stitch into the last stitch. Repeat around.
**Round 37:** Tapestry crochet 14 background, 4 giraffe, and 6 background stitches. Repeat around.
**Round 38:** Tapestry crochet 15 background, 4 giraffe, 1 background, 2 giraffe, 2 background, and then increase in the last stitch by tapestry crocheting 1 more background color stitch into the last stitch. Repeat around.
**Round 39:** Tapestry crochet 16 background, 7 giraffe, 2 background, and then increase in the last stitch by tapestry crocheting 1 more background color stitch into the last stitch. Repeat around.
**Round 40:** Tapestry crochet 17 background, 6 giraffe, and 3 background stitches. Repeat around.
**Round 41:** Tapestry crochet 18 background, 3 giraffe, 1 background, 1 giraffe, 3 background, and then increase in the last stitch by tapestry crocheting 1 more background color stitch into the last stitch. Repeat around.
**Round 42:** Tapestry crochet 19 background, 4 giraffe, 4 background, and then increase in the last stitch by tapestry crocheting 1 more background color stitch into the last stitch. Repeat around.
**Round 43:** Tapestry crochet 20 background, 1 giraffe, 1 background, 1 giraffe, and 5 background stitches. Repeat around.
**Round 44:** Tapestry crochet 21 background, 1 giraffe, 1 background, 1 giraffe, 4 background, and then increase in the last stitch by tapestry crocheting 1 more background color stitch into the last stitch. Repeat around.
**Round 45:** With background, increase in every twenty-ninth stitch.
**Round 46:** With background, crochet one round without any increases.
**Round 47:** With background, increase in every thirtieth stitch.
**Round 48:** With background, Increase in every thirty-first stitch.
**Round 49:** With giraffe, chain 10, then crochet 1 stitch. Repeat around, then cut the carried thread flush.

**To finish:** Slip stitch, cut the thread (leaving a 10 inch tail) then yarn over and pull it all the way through the loop. Work in the end for 6 inches to secure it, then trim it off. Block the body of the blanket/throw, but not the fringe.

# Hats/Baskets

This multipurpose project can serve as a hat or a basket, depending whether it is placed bottom up on a table or bottom down on someone's head! The hats/baskets begin in the center, and then work outward and upward. A flat spiral base is crocheted first, then when the diameter of the base is no longer increased, the edges of the spiral move upwards to form the sides. The zigzag motif is six stitches wide, so the total number of stitches in the base is a multiple of six. It is possible to make a variety of sizes with the same design motif simply by increasing or decreasing the size of the base by six stitches. Since the number of stitches of every round of the base is a multiple of six, you can start the sides at any point and the motif will still work out perfectly. Feel free to substitute another motif, just be sure that the total number of stitches in the base is a multiple of the number of stitches in your motif.

### Hook
Steel crochet hook size 4 (2.00 mm.) or size that will give an acceptable gauge

### Gauge
8 stitches equals 1 inch
7 rows equals 1 inch

## Medium Hat/Basket
### Size
5 3/4" diameter by 3 7/8" high (17" circumference)

### Materials
One ball (100 yards) each of Purple (color 458), White (color 001), Navy (color 486), Ecru (color 61), and Delft (color 0480) size 3 J. & P. Coats Speed-Cro-Sheen 100% mercerized cotton, article C-45 (or a similar substitute);
Safety pin or a piece of thread of a contrasting color for counting the rounds.

## Large Hat/Basket
### Size
7 3/4" diameter by 4" high (24" circumference)

### Materials
Two balls (100 yards each) of Hunter Green (color 48), and one ball (100 yards) each of Spanish Red (color 126), Canary Yellow (color 10A), 12 Black (color 12), and Pumpkin size 3 J. & P. Coats Speed-Cro-Sheen 100% mercerized cotton, article C-45 (or a similar substitute);
Safety pin or a piece of thread of a contrasting color for counting the rounds.

**Round 1:** Starting with the thread that you want to be on the top/base of the hat/basket, make a slip knot (leaving a six-inch tail), then chain 4 stitches. Join the ends together to form a ring by working a slip stitch into the first chain stitch. Single crochet 6 stitches loosely into the ring (while carrying the tail of the thread). The spiral should have a total of 6 stitches when you finish this round. This piece is worked as a spiral, not in concentric rings, so it is difficult to tell where each round ends. To keep track of where each round ends, slip a safety pin into the top of the last stitch of the round or lay a two inch piece of thread of a contrasting color across the path of the last stitch. You will remove the safety pin from the last stitch as you come to it again and slip it into the new last stitch or cross the path of the last stitch with the end of the counting thread at the end of each round. Pull a little on the counting thread as it runs out to make it longer.
**Round 2:** Continue to carry the tail. Increase by crocheting 2 stitches into each stitch. The spiral should have a total of 12 stitches when you finish this round.
**Round 3:** Cut the tail flush, then start to carry the other thread. Increase again in every stitch. The spiral should have 24 stitches when you finish this round.
**Round 4:** Increase in every second stitch. The spiral should have 36 stitches when you finish this round.
**Round 5:** Crochet one round without any increases.
**Round 6:** Increase in every third stitch. The spiral should have 48 stitches when you finish this round.
**Round 7:** Crochet one round without any increases.
**Round 8:** Increase in every fourth stitch. The spiral should have 60 stitches when you finish this round.
**Round 9:** Increase in every fifth stitch. The spiral should have 72 stitches when you finish this round.
**Round 10:** Crochet one round without any increases.
**Round 11:** Increase in every sixth stitch. The spiral should have 84 stitches when you finish this round.
**Round 12:** Increase in every seventh stitch. The spiral should have 96 stitches when you finish this round.
**Round 13:** Increase in every eighth stitch. The spiral should have 108 stitches when you finish this round.
**Round 14:** Crochet one round without any increases.
**Round 15:** Increase in every ninth stitch. The spiral should have 120 stitches when you finish this round.
**Round 16:** Increase in every tenth stitch. The spiral should have 132 stitches when you finish this round.
**Round 17:** Crochet one round without any increases.
**Round 18:** Increase in every eleventh stitch. The spiral should have 144 stitches when you finish this round.
**Round 19:** Crochet one round without any increases.

***For the medium hat, skip to round 26 and begin sides.***

**Round 20:** Increase in every twelfth stitch. The spiral should have 156 stitches when you finish this round.
**Round 21:** Increase in every thirteenth stitch. The spiral should have 168 stitches when you finish this round.
**Round 22:** Crochet one round without any increases.
**Round 23:** Increase in every fourteenth stitch. The spiral should have 180 stitches when you finish this round.
**Round 24:** Increase in every fifteenth stitch. The spiral should have 192 stitches when you finish this round.
**Round 25:** Crochet one round without any increases. The number of stitches will now remain constant from round to round.

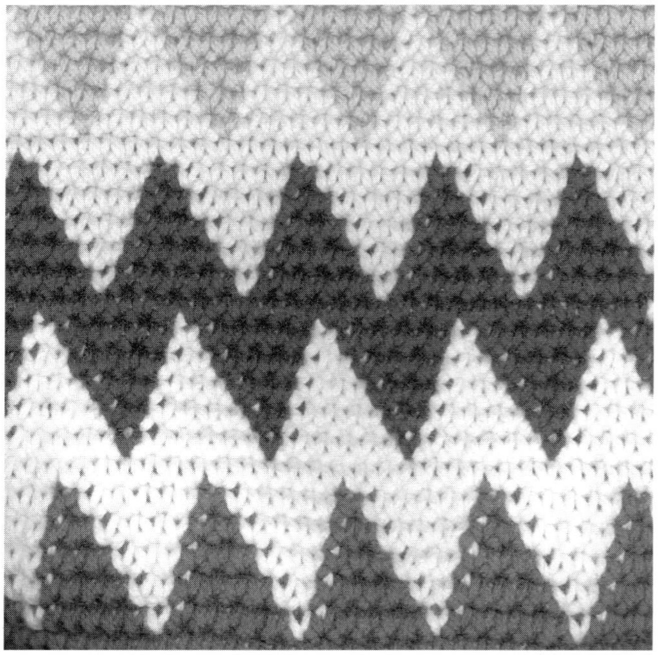

**Detail of the Hat/Basket.**

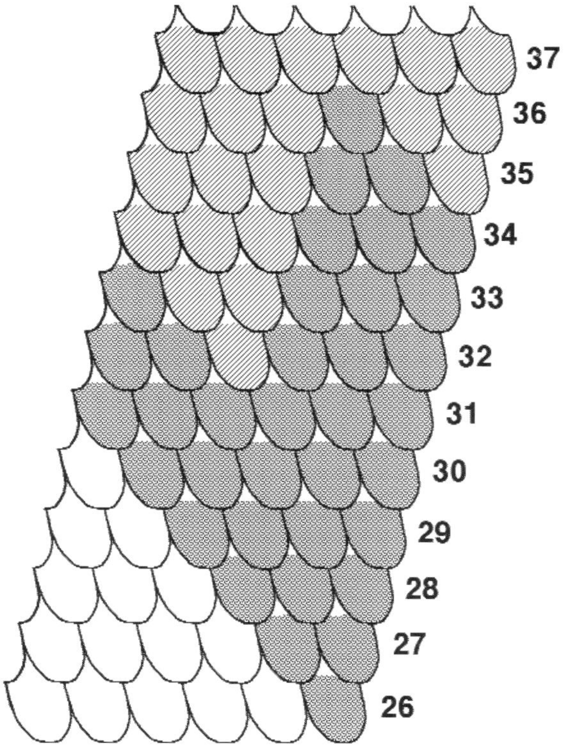


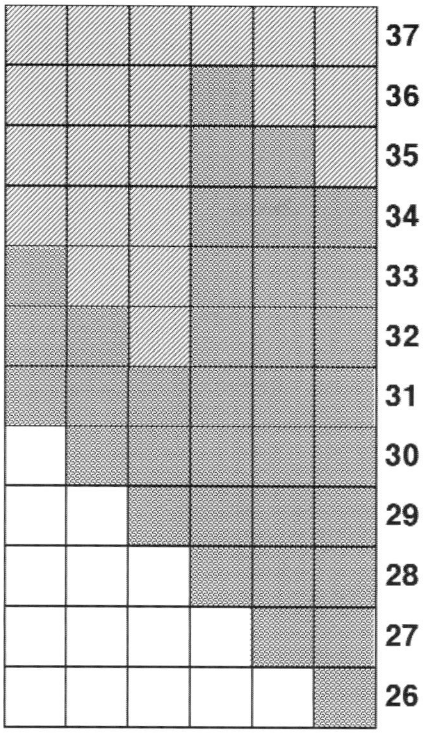


***The graphs on the left are for right-handed crocheters. Left-handed crocheters should look at the reversed image of the graphs in a mirror.***

*Begin sides and motif:*

**Round 26:** Rounds 26 through 37 correspond to the illustrated zigzag motif (read from right to left and bottom to top). To begin the tapestry crochet stitch, you will have to pull your hook out of the last loop you made at the end of the previous round, pull out the loop, insert your hook into the two remaining loops, switch threads and then yarn over and pull through a loop with the carried thread. Tapestry crochet 1 new color and 5 old color stitches. Repeat around. Every once in a while, untwist the threads by holding the hat/basket up in the air with one of the threads while pulling on the other thread. Let the piece spin around in the air so that the threads untangle.
**Round 27:** Tapestry crochet 2 new color and 4 old color stitches. Repeat around.
**Round 28:** Tapestry crochet 3 new color and 3 old color stitches. Repeat around.
**Round 29:** Tapestry crochet 4 new color and 2 old color stitches. Repeat around.
**Round 30:** Tapestry crochet 5 new color and 1 old color stitch. Repeat around. Turn the hat/basket inside out (to make it right side out). As you tapestry crochet each stitch, the hook should point toward the inside of the hat/basket.
**Round 31:** Crochet one round with the new color. Carry the old color thread for 6 stitches, then cut it and start to carry a different color thread (called latest color).
**Round 32:** Tapestry crochet 3 new color, 1 latest color, and 2 new color stitches. Repeat around.
**Round 33:** Tapestry crochet 3 new color, 2 latest color, and 1 new color stitch. Repeat around.
**Round 34:** Tapestry crochet 3 new color and 3 latest color stitches. Repeat around.
**Round 35:** Tapestry crochet 1 latest color, 2 new color and 3 latest color stitches (the beginning of this round will step in one stitch and break the diagonal line). Repeat around.
**Round 36:** Tapestry crochet 2 new color, 1 latest color and 3 new color stitches. Repeat around.
**Round 37:** Crochet one round with latest color. Carry the other color thread for 6 stitches, then cut it and start to carry a different color thread.

***Repeat rounds 26 through 37 as many times as you wish.***

**To finish:** Cut the carried thread flush. Slip stitch with the latest color, cut it (leaving a 6 inch tail) then yarn over and pull it all the way through the loop. Work in the end for 2 inches to secure it, then trim it off. Block the hat/basket.

# Cotton

Immature (upper left) and mature bolls of light brown cotton from Georgia.

Cotton is the most important vegetable fiber used for textiles today. Cotton has been cultivated in ancient Egypt, India, and China for thousands of years. White, brown, and yellow cotton have been cultivated in the Americas since 5800 BC. During the American Colonial period, Spaniards introduced a superior cotton variety from China. This new strain so improved the quality and quantity of production that cotton cultivation became one of the principle bases of the native economy during Colonial times. Today cotton is grown in more than seventy countries.

The cotton plant is usually three to six feet tall. Cotton fibers grow from the surface of the seeds in the boll. After the mature bolls burst open and the fluffy cotton fibers dry, they are ready for harvest and processing.

Although most cotton is harvested and processed into thread by machine, some people still hand pick, clean, and spin it on spindles or spinning wheels.

In 1984, this Mam Maya woman processed her own cotton. To prepare the cotton for spinning, she removed the seeds by hand, then beat it with forked sticks on a deerskin covered bundle. The beating separated the lumps of cotton fiber and married them into a fluffy, single mass. The cotton was then folded and shaped into a cylinder for spinning.

In Guatemala, cotton is spun on an upright spindle that rests in a small pine pitch-lined gourd bowl. The bowl keeps the spindle from wandering and the pitch is rubbed on the fingers to keep them dry. Dry fingers enable one to spin a fine, strong thread.

To start spinning the fiber, a bit of prepared cotton is twisted around a thread that is tied to the spindle. A comfortable amount of cotton is then drawn out. While holding the prepared cotton in the left hand, the spindle is rotated with the right hand. The cotton is then pulled upwards with the left hand and twisted into a uniform thread. After the thread is sufficiently spun, it is wrapped around the spindle and the procedure is repeated.

It's a real challenge to spin cotton on a spinning wheel, since the fibers are so short. Corinne has no problem though, spinning some home-grown brown cotton.

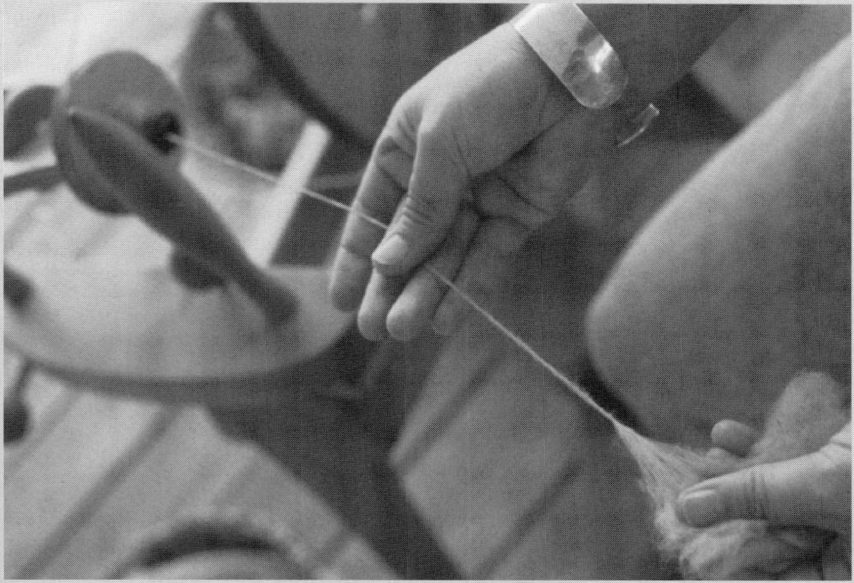

# Cat's Meow Purses

This project is simply a cylindrical basket with a strap. First, the flat spiral base is crocheted, then when the diameter of the base is no longer increased, the edges of the spiral move upwards to form the sides. The cat motif is twelve stitches wide, so the base of each purse is a multiple of twelve stitches. It is possible to make a variety of sizes with the same design motif simply by increasing or decreasing the number of stitches in the base. You could, of course, also substitute other motifs. The meow motif around the top was crocheted with the right hand, but separate graphs and instructions are included for left-handed crocheters.

### Hook
Steel crochet hook size 4 (2.00 mm.) or the size that will give an acceptable gauge

### Gauge
9 stitches equals 1 inch
8 rows equals 1 inch

## Small Purse
### Size
1 3/4" diameter by 4 1/4" high (without the strap)

### Materials
One skein (50 grams/111 yards) of Green (color 103) and one skein (50 grams/111 yards) of Variegated (color 61) Reynolds Sedona Four Ply Mercerized Egyptian cotton (or a similar substitute);
Safety pin or a piece of thread of a contrasting color for counting the rounds.

## Large Purse
### Size
5" diameter by 7 3/8" high (without the strap)

### Materials
Three skeins (150 grams) of Variegated (color 43) and three skeins (150 grams) of Ecru (color 102) Reynolds Sedona Four Ply Mercerized Egyptian cotton (or a similar substitute);
Safety pin or a piece of thread of a contrasting color for counting the rounds.

**Round 1:** This thread is sold in skeins, which must first be wound into a ball. To keep the skein from tangling while winding, wrap it around a new roll of paper towels. Starting with the thread that you want to be on the bottom of the purse, make a slip knot (leaving a six-inch tail), then chain 4 stitches. Join the ends together to form a ring by working a slip stitch into the first chain stitch. Single crochet 6 stitches loosely into the ring (while carrying the tail of the thread). The purse should have a total of 6 stitches when you finish this round. This piece is worked as a spiral, not in concentric rings, so it is difficult to tell where each round ends. To keep track of where each round ends, slip a safety pin into the top of the last stitch of the round or lay a two inch piece of thread of a contrasting color across the path of the last stitch. You will remove the safety pin from the last stitch as you come to it again and slip it into the new last stitch or cross the path of the last stitch with the end of the counting thread at the end of each round. Pull a little on the counting thread as it runs out to make it longer.

**Round 2:** Continue to carry the tail. Increase by crocheting 2 stitches into each stitch. The spiral should have a total of 12 stitches when you finish this round.
**Round 3:** Cut the tail flush and start to carry the other thread. Increase again in every stitch. The spiral should have 24 stitches when you finish this round.
**Round 4:** Increase in every second stitch. The spiral should have 36 stitches when you finish this round.
**Round 5:** Crochet one round without any increases.
**Round 6:** Increase in every third stitch. The spiral should have 48 stitches when you finish this round.
***If you are crocheting the Small Purse, stop the base here and go on to Round 20.***
**Round 7:** Crochet one round without any increases.
**Round 8:** Increase in every fourth stitch. The spiral should have 60 stitches when you finish this round.
**Round 9:** Increase in every fifth stitch. The spiral should have 72 stitches when you finish this round.
**Round 10:**Crochet one round without any increases.
**Round 11:** Increase in every sixth stitch. The spiral should have 84 stitches when you finish this round.
**Round 12:** Increase in every seventh stitch. The spiral should have 96 stitches when you finish this round.
**Round 13:** Increase in every eighth stitch. The spiral should have 108 stitches when you finish this round.
**Round 14:** Crochet one round without any increases.
**Round 15:** Increase in every ninth stitch. The spiral should have 120 stitches when you finish this round.
**Round 16:** Increase in every tenth stitch. The spiral should have 132 stitches when you finish this round.
**Round 17:** Crochet one round without any increases.
**Round 18:** Increase in every eleventh stitch. The spiral should have 144 stitches when you finish this round.
**Round 19:** Crochet one round without any increases.

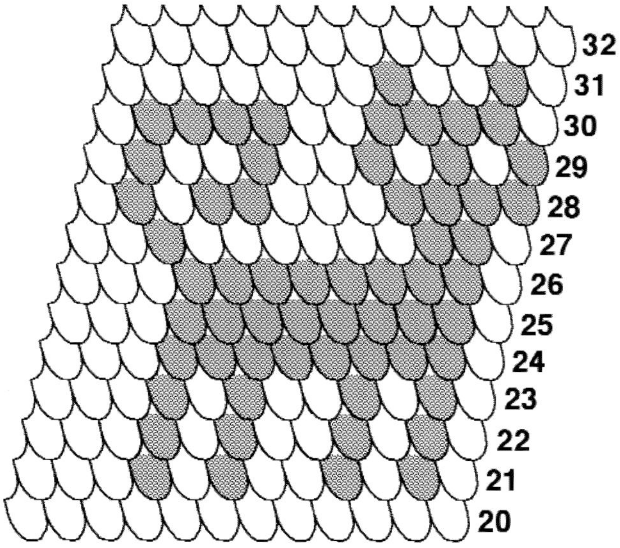


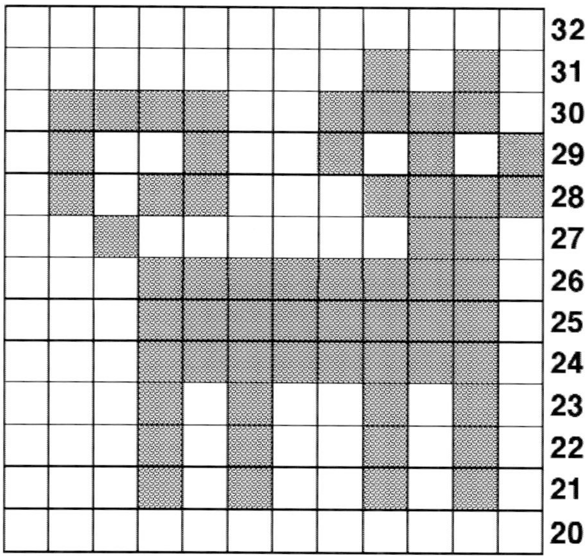


***The graphs on the left are for right-handed crocheters. Left-handed crocheters should look at the reversed image of the graphs in a mirror.***

***Begin sides and motif:***
**Round 20:** Rounds 20 through 32 correspond to the illustrated cat motif figure (read from right to left and bottom to top). Crochet one round with background thread. The number of stitches will now remain constant from round to round.
**Round 21:** You will now begin to tapestry crochet the cat motif. Remember, that to do a tapestry crochet stitch, colors are switched while 2 loops are still on the hook; yarn over with the next color and pull it through the loops to prepare for the tapestry crochet stitch. Tapestry crochet 1 background thread, 1 cat motif thread, 1 background, 1 cat, 2 background, 1 cat, 1 background, 1 cat, and 3 background stitches. Repeat around. Every once in a while, untwist the threads by suspending the purse in the air with one of the threads while pulling on the other thread. Let the piece spin around in the air so that the threads untangle.
**Round 22:** Tapestry crochet 1 background, 1 cat, 1 background, 1 cat, 2 background, 1 cat, 1 background, 1 cat, and 3 background stitches. Repeat around.
**Round 23:** Tapestry crochet 1 background, 1 cat, 1 background, 1 cat, 2 background, 1 cat, 1 background, 1 cat,

and 3 background stitches. Repeat around.
**Round 24:** Tapestry crochet 1 background, 8 cat, and 3 background stitches. Repeat around.
**Round 25:** Tapestry crochet 1 background, 8 cat, and 3 background stitches. Repeat around. Turn the purse inside out (to make it right side out). As you tapestry crochet each stitch, the hook should point toward the inside of the purse.
**Round 26:** Tapestry crochet 1 background, 8 cat, and 3 background stitches. Repeat around.
**Round 27:** Tapestry crochet 1 background, 2 cat, 6 background, 1 cat, and 2 background stitches. Repeat around.
**Round 28:** Tapestry crochet 4 cat, 3 background, 2 cat, 1 background, 1 cat, and 1 background stitches. Repeat around.
**Round 29:** Tapestry crochet 1 cat, 1 background, 1 cat, 1 background, 1 cat, 2 background, 1 cat, 2 background, 1 cat, and 1 background stitch. Repeat around.
**Round 30:** Tapestry crochet 1 background, 4 cat, 2 background, 4 cat, and 1 background stitch. Repeat around.
**Round 31:** Tapestry crochet 1 background, 1 cat, 2 background, 1 cat, and 7 background stitches. Repeat around.
**Round 32:** Finish the cat motif as follows: crochet one round with background. Switch threads so that the cat motif thread is now the background color thread.
***Repeat rounds 20 through 32 as many times as you wish.***

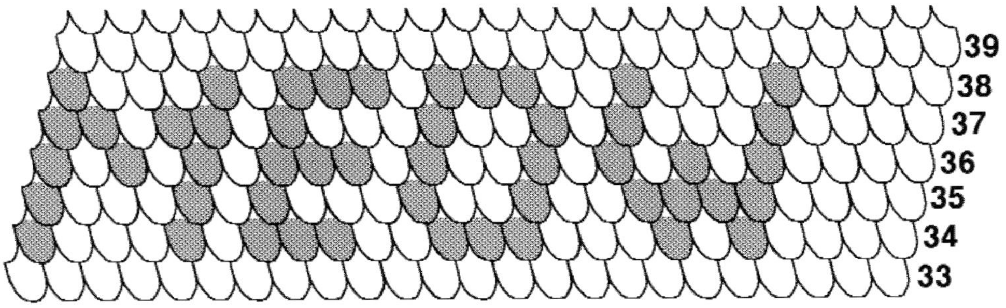


***The graphs on this page are for right-handed crocheters.***

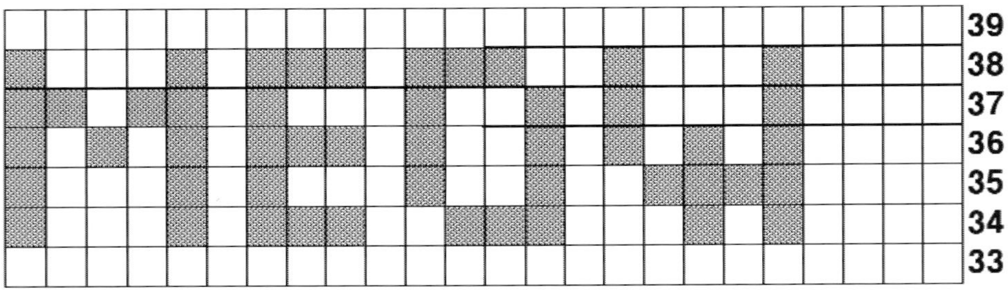


***For right-handed crocheters:***
**Round 33:** Rounds 33 through 39 correspond to the meow motif above (for right handed crocheters). Start the meow motif as follows: crochet one round with background thread.
**Round 34:** Tapestry crochet 4 background stitches, 1 meow stitch, 1 background, 1 meow, 3 background, 3 meow, 2 background, 3 meow, 1 background, 1 meow, 3 background, and 1 meow stitches. Repeat around.
**Round 35:** Tapestry crochet 4 background, 4 meow, 2 background, 1 meow, 2 background, 1 meow, 3 background, 1 meow, 1 background, 1 meow, 3 background, and 1 meow stitch. Repeat around.
**Round 36:** Tapestry crochet 4 background, 1 meow, 1 background, 1 meow, 1 background, 1 meow, 1 background, 1 meow, 2 background, 1 meow, 1 background, 3 meow, 1 background, 1 meow, 1 background, 1 meow, 1 background, and 1 meow stitch. Repeat around.
**Round 37:** Tapestry crochet 4 background, 1 meow, 3 background, 1 meow, 1 background, 1 meow, 2 background, 1 meow, 3 background, 1 meow, 1 background, 2 meow, 1 background, and 2 meow stitches. Repeat around.
**Round 38:** Tapestry crochet 4 background, 1 meow, 3 background, 1 meow, 2 background, 3 meow, 1 background, 3 meow, 1 background, 1 meow, 3 background, and 1 meow stitch. Repeat around.
**Round 39:** Finish the meow motif as follows: crochet one round with background.

# *Left-handed crocheters, please look at this page!*

***The graphs on this page are for left-handed crocheters.***

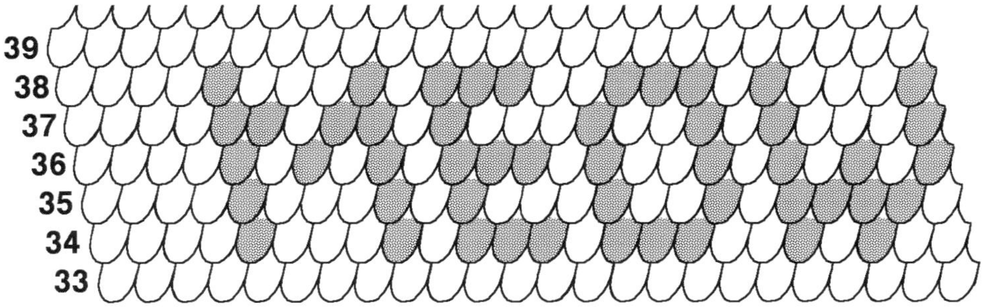


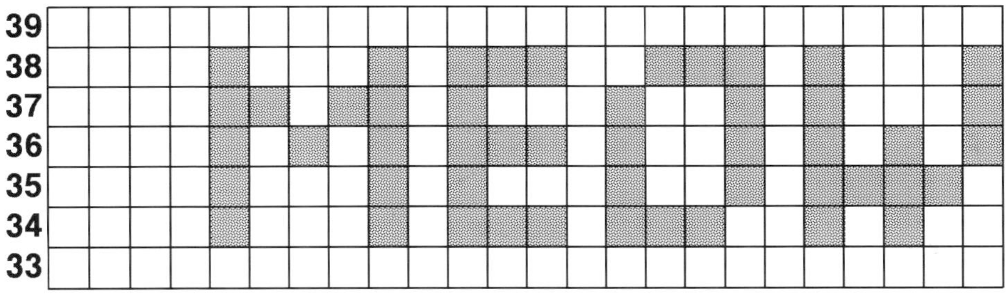


***For left-handed crocheters:***

**Round 33:** Rounds 33 through 39 correspond to the meow motif above for left-handed crocheters. Start the meow motif as follows: crochet one round with background thread.

**Round 34:** Tapestry crochet 4 background stitches, 1 meow stitch, 3 background, 1 meow, 1 background, 3 meow, 1 background, 3 meow, 2 background, 1 meow, 1 background, 1 meow, and 2 background stitches. Repeat around.

**Round 35:** Tapestry crochet 4 background, 1 meow, 3 background, 1 meow, 1 background, 1 meow, 3 background, 1 meow, 2 background, 1 meow, 1 background, 4 meow, and 1 background stitch. Repeat around.

**Round 36:** Tapestry crochet 4 background, 1 meow, 1 background, 1 meow, 1 background, 1 meow, 1 background, 3 meow, 1 background, 1 meow, 2 background, 1 meow, 1 background, 1 meow, 1 background, 1 meow, 1 background, and 1 meow stitch. Repeat around.

**Round 37:** Tapestry crochet 4 background, 2 meow, 1 background, 2 meow, 1 background, 1 meow, 3 background, 1 meow, 2 background, 1 meow, 1 background, 1 meow, 3 background, and 1 meow stitch. Repeat around.

**Round 38:** Tapestry crochet 4 background, 1 meow, 3 background, 1 meow, 1 background, 3 meow, 2 background, 3 meow, 1 background, 1 meow, 3 background, and 1 meow stitch. Repeat around.

**Round 39:** Finish the meow motif as follows: crochet one round with background.

***Strap:***

**First round:** From now on you will be crocheting with the background color thread while you carry the other thread. Without cutting off any of the threads, chain 150 for the small bag (or 180 for the large bag). Feel free to add or subtract chain stitches at this point to make the strap longer or shorter. Insert the hook into the next stitch (the chain will form a large loop) and crochet 20 stitches for the small bag (or 66 stitches for the large bag). To make an opening that the finished strap will pass through, chain 8 for the small bag (or 12 for the large bag). Insert the hook into the 9th stitch of the previous round for the small bag (or the 13th stitch for the large bag). Let the carried thread lay on the top of the previous round (you will crochet over it in the next round). Crochet 20 more stitches for the small bag (or 66 for the large bag).

**Second round:** Crochet around the strap and on the top of the bag with the background thread while carrying the other thread (170 stitches for the short bag or 246 for the large bag). When you get to the short chain, crochet over the chain and both carried threads, 8 stitches for the short bag (or 12 for the large bag). Crochet 20 more stitches for the short bag (or 66 for the large bag) until you reach the strap. Go to the "Last round" for the small bag (or "Next 2 rounds" for the large bag).

**Next 2 rounds** (for the large bag): Crochet around the strap and on the top of the bag with the background thread while carrying the other thread for 324 stitches. Repeat this round 1 more time.

**Last round:** Crochet 147 stitches of the strap for the short bag (or 177 for the large bag).

**To Finish:** Cut the carried thread flush. Do a slip stitch, cut the thread (leaving a 6 inch tail), then yarn over and pull it all the way through the loop. Work in the end for 2 inches to secure it, then cut it flush. Block the purse and strap.

**Detail of the strap.**

**Detail of the opening.**

# Beaded Basket

Traditional beaded items are usually crocheted with one thread, and all of the beads from a charted design need to be carefully loaded onto a single thread in the order that they will be needed. The beauty of tapestry crocheting with beads is that each thread can be loaded with one bead color and only the color that is needed at the time is crocheted to form a pattern while the other threads are carried. A decorative pattern is formed with or without adding a bead to each stitch since the colored threads also contribute to the design. This method offers fantastic design potential, since the motif does not have to be pre-planned. This basket is actually inside out. Since the bead falls to the back of the stitch, the back of the fabric is the front!

The flaring shape of this basket is achieved by increasing the stitches. The basket begins on the bottom. The motif is six stitches wide on the bottom, so the total number of stitches in the base is a multiple of six. Feel free to substitute different colors or another motif. Just be sure that the total number of stitches in the round is a multiple of the number of stitches in your motif.

## Hook

Steel crochet hook size 4 (2.00 mm.) or the size that will give an acceptable gauge

## Gauge

9 stitches equals 1 inch
7 rows equals 1 inch

## Size

8” diameter by 3 1/2” high

## Materials

Two balls (100 yards each) of Delft (color 0480) and two balls of Soft Yellow (color 0143) size 3 J. & P. Coats Speed-Cro-Sheen 100% mercerized cotton, article C-45 (or a similar substitute);
Two 1570 TL heavy beading needles;
108 white and 108 blue size 6/0 glass beads (or a similar substitute);
Safety pin or a piece of thread of a contrasting color for counting the rounds.

**Round 1:** (Do not load the beads onto the threads until round 39.) Make a slip knot with the yellow thread, then chain 4 stitches. Join the ends together to form a ring by working a slip stitch into the first chain stitch. Single crochet 6 stitches loosely into the ring while you carry the tail-end. The basket should have a total of 6 stitches when you finish this round. This basket is worked as a spiral, not in concentric rings, so it is difficult to tell where each round ends. To keep track of where each round ends, slip a safety pin into the top of the last stitch of the round or lay a two inch piece of thread of a contrasting color across the path of the last stitch. You will remove the safety pin from the last stitch as you come to it again and slip it into the new last stitch or cross the path of the last stitch with the end of the counting thread at the end of each round.
**Round 2:** Cut the tail-end piece and start to carry the delft thread. Increase in every stitch to 12 stitches.
**Round 3:** Increase in every stitch to 24 stitches.
**Round 4:** Increase in every second stitch to 36 stitches.
**Round 5:** Increase in every third stitch to 48 stitches.

**Round 6:** Crochet one round without any increases.
**Round 7:** Increase in every fourth stitch. The spiral should have 60 stitches when you finish this round.
**Round 8:** Increase in every fifth stitch. The spiral should have 72 stitches when you finish this round.
**Round 9:** Increase in every sixth stitch. The spiral should have 84 stitches when you finish this round.
**Round 10:** Crochet one round without any increases.
**Round 11:** Increase in every seventh stitch. The spiral should have 96 stitches when you finish this round.
**Round 12:** Increase in every eighth stitch. The spiral should have 108 stitches when you finish this round.

***Begin the sides:***

**Round 13:** Crochet one round without any increases.
**Round 14:** Crochet one round without any increases.
**Round 15:** Crochet one round without any increases.
**Round 16:** Crochet one round without any increases.
**Round 17:** Crochet one round without any increases.
**Round 18:** Crochet one round without any increases.
**Round 19:** Crochet one round without any increases.

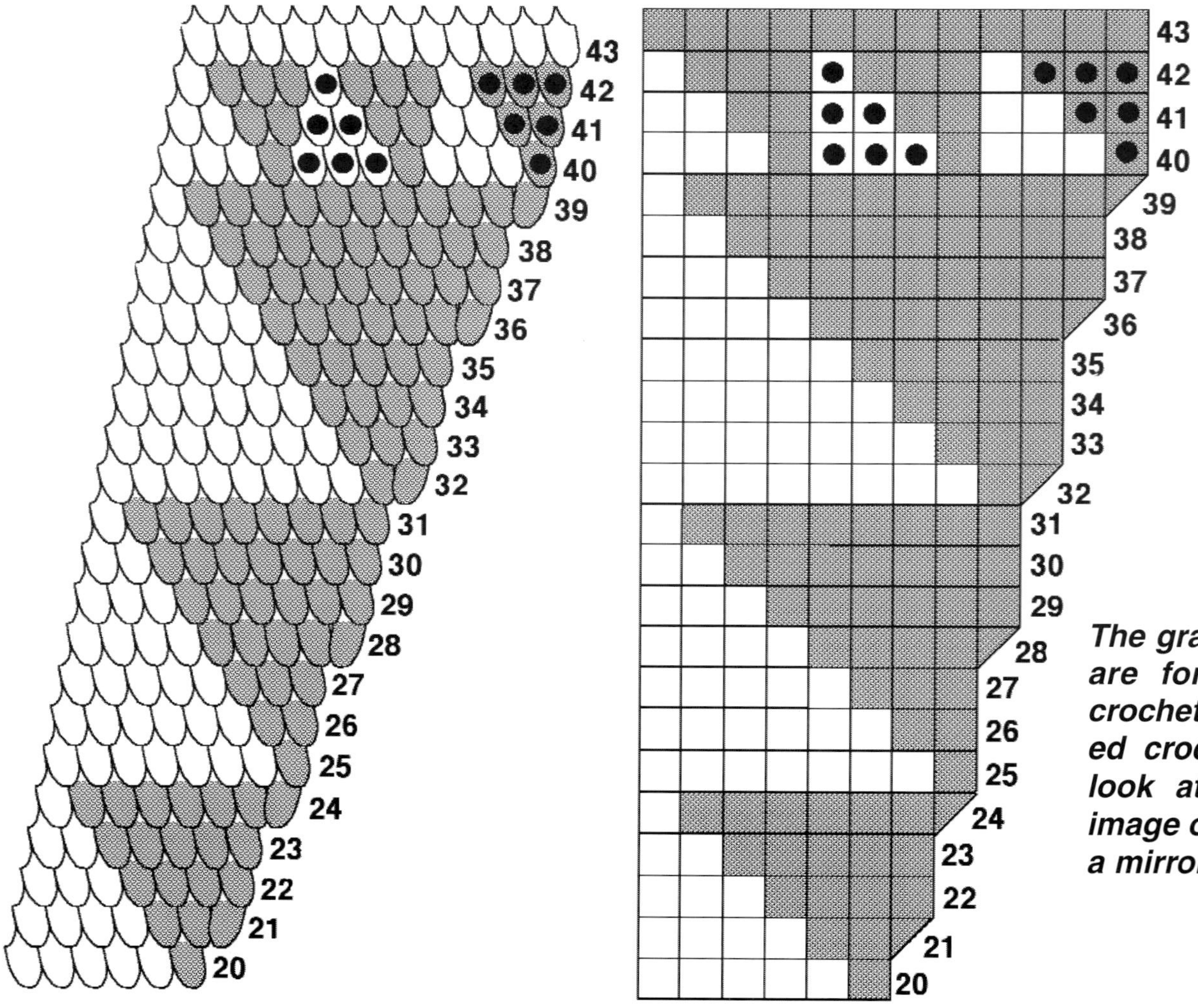


***The graphs on the left are for right-handed crocheters. Left-handed crocheters should look at the reversed image of the graphs in a mirror.***

***Begin the motif:***

**Round 20:** Rounds 20 through 43 correspond to the motif on the side of the basket (read from right to left and bottom to top). Remember, that to do a tapestry crochet stitch, colors are switched while 2 loops are still on the hook; yarn over with the other thread and pull it through the loops to prepare for the tapestry crochet stitch. Start the motif as follows: tapestry crochet 1 delft, then 5 yellow stitches. Repeat this sequence around. Every once in a while, untwist the threads by suspending the basket in the air with one of the threads while pulling on the other thread. Let the piece spin around in the air so that the threads untangle.

**Round 21:** Increase by tapestry crocheting 2 delft stitches into the first stitch, tapestry crochet 1 more delft stitch, then tapestry crochet 4 yellow stitches. Repeat around. The spiral should have 126 stitches when you finish this round.
**Round 22:** Tapestry crochet 4 delft, then 3 yellow stitches. Repeat around.
**Round 23:** Tapestry crochet 5 delft, then 2 yellow stitches. Repeat around.
**Round 24:** Increase in the first stitch with delft, tapestry crochet 5 more delft, then 1 yellow stitch. Repeat around. The spiral should have 144 stitches when you finish this round.
**Round 25:** Tapestry crochet 1 delft, then 7 yellow stitches. Repeat around.
**Round 26:** Tapestry crochet 2 delft, then 6 yellow stitches. Repeat around.
**Round 27:** Tapestry crochet 3 delft, then 5 yellow stitches. Repeat around.
**Round 28:** Increase in the first stitch with delft, tapestry crochet 3 more delft, then 4 yellow stitches. Repeat around. The spiral should have 162 stitches when you finish this round.
**Round 29:** Tapestry crochet 6 delft, then 3 yellow stitches. Repeat around.
**Round 30:** Tapestry crochet 7 delft, then 2 yellow stitches. Repeat around.
**Round 31:** Tapestry crochet 8 delft, then 1 yellow stitch. Repeat around.
**Round 32:** Increase in the first stitch with delft, then tapestry crochet 8 yellow stitches. Repeat around. The spiral should have 180 stitches when you finish this round.
**Round 33:** Tapestry crochet 3 delft, then 7 yellow stitches. Repeat around.
**Round 34:** Tapestry crochet 4 delft, then 6 yellow stitches. Repeat around.
**Round 35:** Tapestry crochet 5 delft, then 5 yellow stitches. Repeat around.
**Round 36:** Increase in the first stitch with delft, tapestry crochet 5 more delft, then 4 yellow stitches. Repeat around. The spiral should have 198 stitches when you finish this round.
**Round 37:** Tapestry crochet 8 delft, then 3 yellow stitches. Repeat around.
**Round 38:** Tapestry crochet 9 delft, then 2 yellow stitches. Repeat around.
**Round 39:** Increase in the first stitch with delft, tapestry crochet 9 more delft, then 1 yellow stitch. **Repeat only 16 times**. In order to prepare for the beaded stitches in the next round, cut the yellow and delft threads, leaving a 20" tail on each piece.

**Outside of basket.**

**Inside of basket.**

Load the white beads onto the yellow thread and the blue beads onto the delft thread with a beading needle. Push the beads down the thread, leaving a yard-long piece without beads on each thread. Resume tapestry crocheting the motif around with the tails while carrying the beaded yellow and delft beaded threads, then after the beaded threads have been anchored, crochet with the beaded threads while carrying the yellow and delft tails to finish the round. The spiral should have 216 stitches when you finish this round.

***Begin beaded stitches.***

**Round 40:** Tapestry crochet 1 beaded delft stitch (to crochet a beaded stitch, insert the hook into the next stitch, slide a bead next to the crochet hook, then continue crocheting the stitch, capturing the bead, which will fall to the back of the stitch, which is the inside of the basket), then tapestry crochet 3 yellow, 1 delft, 3 beaded yellow, 1 delft, and then 3 yellow stitches. Repeat around.

**Round 41:** Tapestry crochet 2 beaded delft, 2 yellow, 2 delft, 2 beaded yellow, 2 delft, and then 2 yellow stitches. Repeat around.

**Round 42:** Tapestry crochet 3 beaded delft, 1 yellow, 3 delft, 1 beaded yellow, 3 delft, and then 1 yellow stitch. Repeat around.

**Round 43:** Tapestry crochet a round of delft stitches while carrying the yellow thread.

**Finishing:** Cut the yellow thread flush. Do a slip stitch with delft, cut the delft thread (leaving a 6 inch tail), then yarn over and pull it all the way through the loop. Work in the end for one inch to secure it, then cut it flush. Cover the basket with a towel and carefully block the basket (too much heat might break the beads).

# Jewelry Basket

The shape of this basket is achieved by increasing and decreasing stitches. The basket begins on the bottom. The motif is twelve stitches wide, so the rounds are a multiple of twelve. Feel free to substitute different colors or another motif. Just be sure that the total number of stitches in the round is a multiple of the number of stitches in your motif.

## Hook
Steel crochet hook size 4 (2.00 mm.) or the size that will give an acceptable gauge

## Gauge
10 stitches equals 1 inch
9 rows equals 1 inch

## Size
6 3/4" wide by 4" high

## Materials
Two balls (136 yards each) of Champagne (color 60011) and one ball of Viola (color 60322) Patons Grace 100% mercerized cotton (or a similar substitute);
Safety pin or a piece of thread of a contrasting color for counting the rounds.

**Round 1:** Make a slip knot with the champagne thread, then chain 4 stitches. Join the ends together to form a ring by working a slip stitch into the first chain stitch. Single crochet 6 stitches loosely into the ring while you carry the tail-end. The basket should have a total of 6 stitches when you finish this round. This basket is worked as a spiral, not in concentric rings, so it is difficult to tell where each round ends. To keep track of where each round ends, slip a safety pin into the top of the last stitch of the round or lay a two inch piece of thread of a contrasting color across the path of the last stitch. You will remove the safety pin from the last stitch as you come to it again and slip it into the new last stitch or cross the path of the last stitch with the end of the counting thread at the end of each round.
**Round 2:** Cut the tail-end piece and start to carry the viola thread. Increase in every stitch to 12 stitches.
**Round 3:** Increase in every stitch to 24 stitches.
**Round 4:** Increase in every second stitch to 36 stitches.
**Round 5:** Increase in every third stitch to 48 stitches.
**Round 6:** Crochet one round without any increases.
**Round 7:** Increase in every fourth stitch. The spiral should have 60 stitches when you finish this round.
**Round 8:** Increase in every fifth stitch. The spiral should have 72 stitches when you finish this round.
**Round 9:** Crochet one round without any increases.
**Round 10:** Increase in every sixth stitch. The spiral should have 84 stitches when you finish this round.
**Round 11:** Crochet one round without any increases.

**Round 12:** Increase in every seventh stitch. The spiral should have 96 stitches when you finish this round.
**Round 13:** Crochet one round without any increases.
**Round 14:** Increase in every eighth stitch. The spiral should have 108 stitches when you finish this round.
**Round 15:** Crochet one round without any increases.
**Round 16:** Increase in every ninth stitch. The spiral should have 120 stitches when you finish this round.
**Round 17:** Crochet one round without any increases.
**Round 18:** Increase in every tenth stitch. The spiral should have 132 stitches when you finish this round.

***Begin the sides:***
**Round 19:** Crochet one round without any increases.
**Round 20:** Crochet one round without any increases.

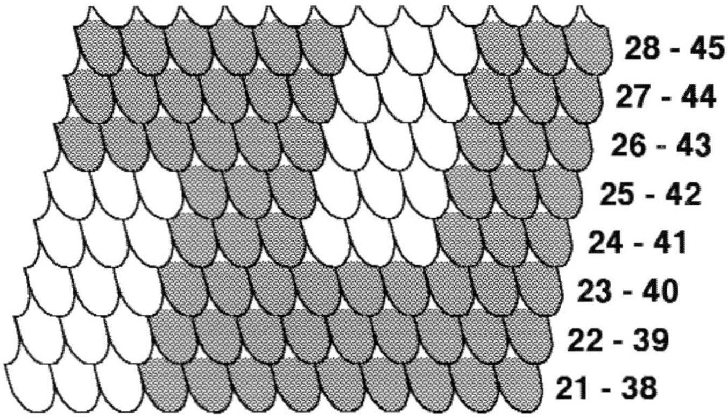


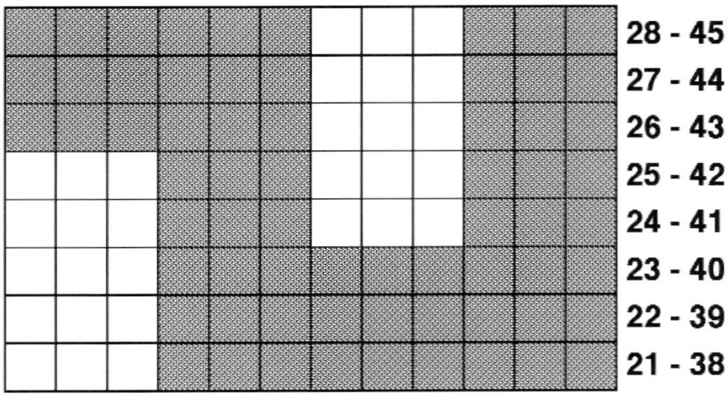


***The above graphs are for right-handed crocheters.***
***Left-handed crocheters should look at the reversed image of the graphs in a mirror.***

***Begin the first motif:***
**Round 21:** Rounds 21 through 28 correspond to the motif on the side of the basket (read from right to left and bottom to top). Remember, that to do a tapestry crochet stitch, colors are switched while 2 loops are still on the hook; yarn over with the other thread and pull it through the loops to prepare for the tapestry crochet stitch. Start the motif as follows: tapestry crochet 9 viola, then 3 champagne stitches. Repeat around. Every once in a while, untwist the threads by suspending the basket in the air with one of the threads while pulling on the other thread. Let the piece spin around in the air so that the threads untangle.
**Round 22:** Tapestry crochet 9 viola, then 3 champagne stitches. Repeat around.
**Round 23:** Tapestry crochet 9 viola, then 3 champagne stitches. Repeat around.
**Round 24:** Tapestry crochet 3 viola, 3 champagne, 3 viola, then 3 champagne stitches. Repeat around.
**Round 25:** Tapestry crochet 3 viola, 3 champagne, 3 viola, then 3 champagne stitches. Repeat around.
**Round 26:** Tapestry crochet 3 viola, 3 champagne, then 6 viola stitches. Repeat around.
**Round 27:** Tapestry crochet 3 viola, 3 champagne, then 6 viola stitches. Repeat around.
**Round 28:** Tapestry crochet 3 viola, 3 champagne, then 6 viola stitches. Repeat around.
**Round 29:** Increase in every sixth stitch with champagne. The spiral should have 154 stitches when you finish this round.
**Round 30:** Increase in every seventh stitch with champagne. The spiral should have 176 stitches when you finish this round.
**Round 31:** Crochet one round without any increases with champagne.
**Round 32:** With the viola thread, increase in every eighth stitch. The spiral should have 198 stitches when you finish this round.
**Round 33:** With the viola thread, increase in every ninth stitch. The spiral should have 220 stitches when you finish this round.

**Round 34:** Crochet one round without any increases with viola.
**Round 35:** With the champagne thread, increase in every tenth stitch. The spiral should have 242 stitches when you finish this round.
**Round 36:** With the champagne thread, increase in every eleventh stitch. The spiral should have 264 stitches when you finish this round.
**Round 37:** Crochet one round without any increases with champagne.
***Begin the second motif:***
**Round 38:** Rounds 38 through 45 correspond to the motif on the side of the basket. Tapestry crochet 9 viola, then 3 champagne stitches. Repeat around.
**Round 39:** Tapestry crochet 9 viola, then 3 champagne stitches. Repeat around.
**Round 40:** Tapestry crochet 9 viola, then 3 champagne stitches. Repeat around.
**Round 41:** Tapestry crochet 3 viola, 3 champagne, 3 viola, then 3 champagne stitches. Repeat around.
**Round 42:** Tapestry crochet 3 viola, 3 champagne, 3 viola, then 3 champagne stitches. Repeat around.
**Round 43:** Tapestry crochet 3 viola, 3 champagne, then 6 viola stitches. Repeat around.
**Round 44:** Tapestry crochet 3 viola, 3 champagne, then 6 viola stitches. Repeat around.
**Round 45:** Tapestry crochet 3 viola, 3 champagne, then 6 viola stitches. Repeat around.
**Round 46:** Increase in every twelfth stitch with champagne. The spiral should have 286 stitches when you finish this round.
**Round 47:** Increase in every thirteenth stitch with champagne. The spiral should have 308 stitches when you finish this round.
**Round 48:** Crochet one round without any increases with champagne.

***Begin ripple:***
**Round 49:** Continue to carry the champagne thread for the entire round. Crochet 3 viola, then chain 9 viola. Make the carried thread the same length as the chain (you will crochet over it in the next round). Skip 25 stitches before inserting the hook again. Repeat around.
**Round 50:** Continue to carry the champagne thread for the entire round. Crochet 3 viola, then crochet over the chain and the carried thread, 9 stitches. The spiral should have 132 stitches when you finish this round.
**Round 51:** Tapestry crochet one round without any increases or decreases with viola.
**Round 52:** Decrease in every fifth stitch with viola. The spiral should have 110 stitches when you finish this round.
**Round 53:** Decrease in every ninth stitch with champagne. The spiral should have 99 stitches when you finish this round.
**Round 54:** Tapestry crochet one round without any increases or decreases with champagne.
**Round 55:** Tapestry crochet one round without any increases or decreases with champagne.

**Finishing:**
Cut the viola thread flush. Do a slip stitch with champagne, cut the champagne thread (leaving a 6 inch tail), then yarn over and pull it all the way through the loop. Work in the end for one inch to secure it, then cut it flush. Stuff and cover the basket with a towel and block the basket.

# *Yarmulke/Kippah/*Skullcap

This traditional Jewish skullcap, *yarmulke* in Yiddish, and *kippah sruga* in Hebrew, is worn by orthodox Jewish men. (For interesting information about Jewish skullcaps, see Baizerman, Davis, and Yarhi, listed in the Bibliography). Although the caps are usually made by female friends and relatives of the wearer, they are also sold in shops. Besides the intricate tapestry crocheted caps, some are made of cloth that is plain, printed, or embroidered. In Israel, the tapestry crocheted caps are made of linen or mercerized cotton. The patterns on the caps include abstract geometric motifs, floral motifs, animals, Jewish symbols, words, and other figurative designs. The caps take a variety of forms. Although the size of the traditional skullcap may vary, it must be at least the width of four fingers.

I used a magnifying light to crochet this cap because the stitches were too small for me to see without magnification. It is possible to make a larger or smaller cap with the same design motif simply by increasing or decreasing the number of rounds. Feel free to substitute other motifs. To crochet a flatter cap with a larger diameter, eliminate some of the rounds without stitch increases (like rounds 7 and 17). If you would like to eliminate the rayed pattern that is formed by the regular increases, increase the stitches more randomly in each round.

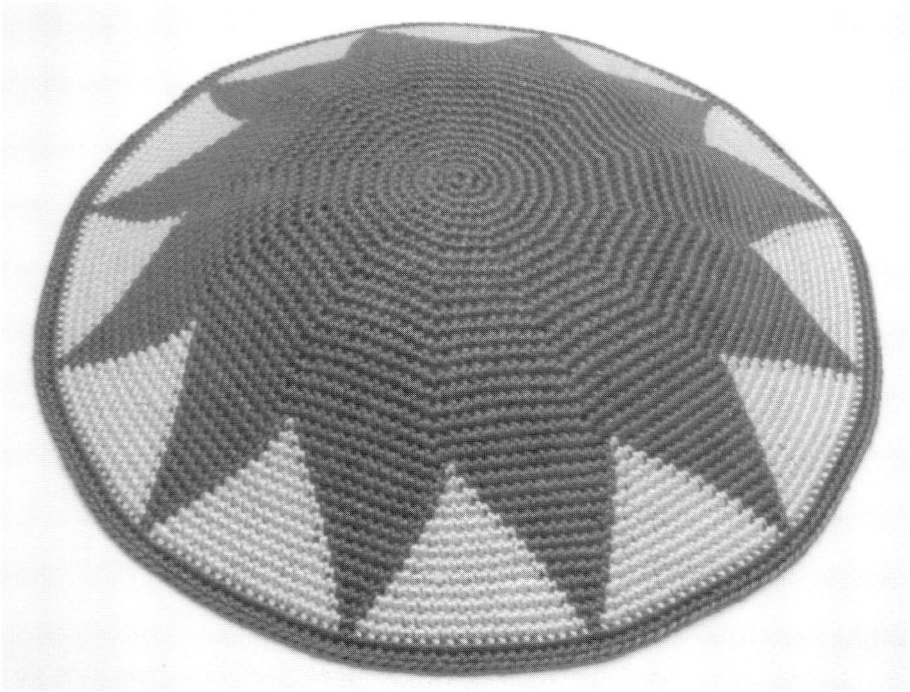

## Hook

steel crochet hook size 8 (1.50 mm.) or the size that will give an acceptable gauge

## Gauge

17 stitches equals 1 inch
14 rows equals 1 inch.

## Size

5" diameter by 7/8" high

## Materials

One ball (87 yards/80 meters/10 grams) of Ecru and one ball of Blue (color 322) of DMC, Size 8 two-ply Pearl Cotton, (or a similar substitute);
Safety pin or a piece of thread of a contrasting color for counting the rounds.

**Round 1:** Starting with the blue thread, make a slip knot (leaving a six-inch tail), then chain 4 stitches. Join the ends together to form a ring by working a slip stitch into the first chain stitch. Single crochet 6 stitches loosely into the ring (while carrying the tail of the thread). The spiral should have a total of 6 stitches when you finish this round. This piece is worked as a spiral, not in concentric rings, so it is difficult to tell where each round ends. To keep track of where each round ends, slip a safety pin into the top of the last stitch of the round or lay a two inch piece of thread of a contrasting color across the path of the last stitch. You will remove the safety pin from the last stitch as you come to it again and slip it into the new last stitch or cross the path of the last stitch with the end of the counting thread at the end of each round. Pull a little on the counting thread as it runs out to make it longer.
**Round 2:** Continue to carry the tail. Increase by crocheting 2 stitches into each stitch. The spiral should have a total of 12 stitches when you finish this round.
**Round 3:** Cut the tail flush, then start to carry the ecru thread. Increase again in every stitch. The spiral should have 24 stitches when you finish this round.

**Round 4:** Increase in every second stitch. The spiral should have 36 stitches when you finish this round.
**Round 5:** Crochet one round without any increases.
**Round 6:** Increase in every third stitch. The spiral should have 48 stitches when you finish this round.
**Round 7:** Crochet one round without any increases.
**Round 8:** Increase in every fourth stitch. The spiral should have 60 stitches when you finish this round.
**Round 9:** Increase in every fifth stitch. The spiral should have 72 stitches when you finish this round.
**Round 10:** Crochet one round without any increases.
**Round 11:** Increase in every sixth stitch, The spiral should have 84 stitches when you finish this round.
**Round 12:** Increase in every seventh stitch. The spiral should have 96 stitches when you finish this round.
**Round 13:** Increase in every eighth stitch. The spiral should have 108 stitches when you finish this round.
**Round 14:** Crochet one round without any increases.
**Round 15:** Increase in every ninth stitch. The spiral should have 120 stitches when you finish this round.
**Round 16:** Increase in every tenth stitch. The spiral should have 132 stitches when you finish this round.
**Round 17:** Crochet one round without any increases.
**Round 18:** Increase in every eleventh stitch. The spiral should have 144 stitches when you finish this round.
**Round 19:** Crochet one round without any increases.
**Round 20:** Increase in every twelfth stitch. The spiral should have 156 stitches when you finish this round.
**Round 21:** Increase in every thirteenth stitch. The spiral should have 168 stitches when you finish this round.

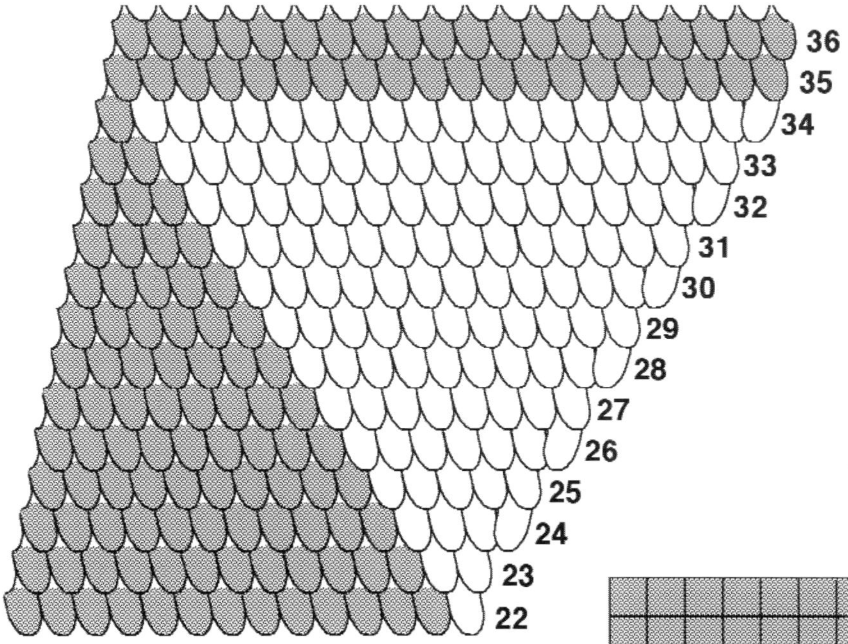


***These graphs are for right-handed crocheters. Left-handed crocheters should look at the reversed image of the graphs in a mirror.***

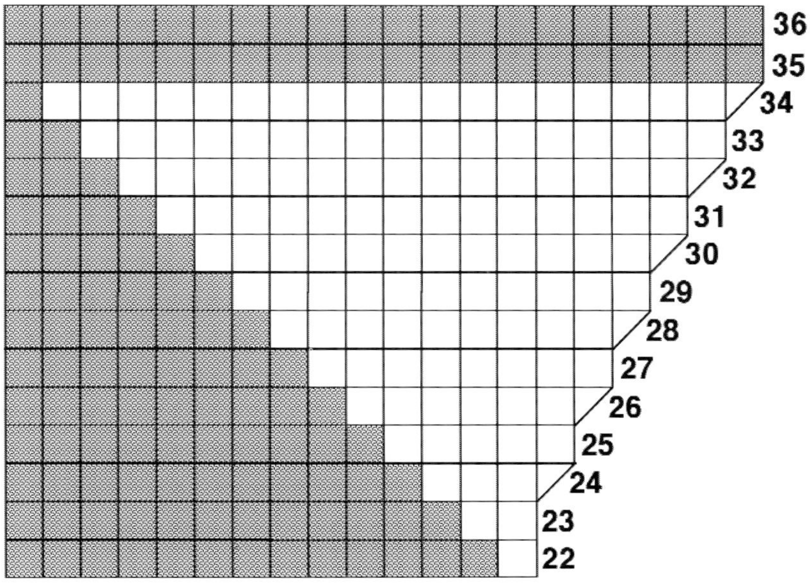


***Begin motif:***

**Round 22:** Rounds 22 through 36 correspond to the illustrated motif (read from right to left and bottom to top). Remember, that to do a tapestry crochet stitch, colors are switched while 2 loops are still on the hook; yarn over with the next color and pull it through the loops to prepare for the tapestry crochet stitch. Tapestry crochet 1 ecru, then 13 blue stitches. Repeat eleven more times around.

Every once in a while, untwist the threads by holding the cap up in the air with one of

the threads while pulling on the other thread. Let the piece spin around in the air so that the threads untangle.
**Round 23:** Tapestry crochet 2 ecru, then 12 blue stitches. Repeat eleven more times around.
**Round 24:** Increase by tapestry crocheting 2 ecru stitches into the first stitch, tapestry crochet 2 more ecru stitches, then tapestry crochet 11 blue stitches. Repeat eleven more times around.
**Round 25:** Tapestry crochet 5 ecru, then 10 blue stitches. Repeat eleven more times around.
**Round 26:** Increase by tapestry crocheting 2 ecru stitches into the first stitch, tapestry crochet 5 more ecru stitches, then tapestry crochet 9 blue stitches. Repeat eleven more times around.
**Round 27:** Tapestry crochet 8 ecru, then 8 blue stitches. Repeat eleven more times around.
**Round 28:** Increase by tapestry crocheting 2 ecru stitches into the first stitch, tapestry crochet 8 more ecru stitches, then tapestry crochet 7 blue stitches. Repeat eleven more times around.
**Round 29:** Tapestry crochet 11 ecru, then 6 blue stitches. Repeat eleven more times around.
**Round 30:** Increase by tapestry crocheting 2 ecru stitches into the first stitch, tapestry crochet 11 more ecru stitches, then tapestry crochet 5 blue stitches. Repeat eleven more times around.
**Round 31:** Tapestry crochet 14 ecru, then 4 blue stitches. Repeat eleven more times around.
**Round 32:** Increase by tapestry crocheting 2 ecru stitches into the first stitch, tapestry crochet 14 more ecru stitches, then tapestry crochet 3 blue stitches. Repeat eleven more times around.
**Round 33:** Tapestry crochet 17 ecru, then 2 blue stitches. Repeat eleven more times around.
**Round 34:** Increase by tapestry crocheting 2 ecru stitches into the first stitch, tapestry crochet 17 more ecru stitches, then tapestry crochet 1 blue stitch. Repeat eleven more times around.
**Round 35:** Crochet with blue (while carrying the ecru) and crochet one round without any increases.
**Round 36:** Crochet with blue (while carrying the ecru) and crochet one round without any increases.

**To finish:** Cut the ecru thread flush. Slip stitch with blue, cut it (leaving a 6 inch tail) then yarn over and pull it all the way through the loop. Work in the end for 1 inch to secure it, then trim it off. Block the cap.

# Ball/Hacky-Sack

Hacky-sacks are modern-day bean bags, but instead of beans, they are stuffed with beads, plastic pellets, or pebbles. Players keep the sack in the air with their feet. Although it can be played alone, it is more fun to play with other people, who use their feet to pass the sack from player to player. No matter what size or shape, these soft crocheted toys are great for people of all ages. Hacky-sack players prefer bright color combinations and they like the sacks to be soft and durable.

This project would be perfect for using up leftover thread. The spiral base is crocheted first, then when the diameter is no longer increased, the edges of the spiral move upwards to form the sides. The stitches are then gradually decreased to form the top. The zigzag motif is six stitches wide, so the total number of stitches in the base is a multiple of six. It is possible to make a variety of sizes with the same design motif simply by increasing or decreasing the size of the base by six stitches. Since the number of stitches of every round of the base is a multiple of six, you can start the sides at any point and the motif will still work out perfectly. Feel free to substitute another motif, just be sure that the total number of stitches in the base is a multiple of the number of stitches in your motif.

### Hook
Steel crochet hook size 00 or size that will give an acceptable gauge.

### Gauge
7 stitches equals 1 inch
6 rows equals 1 inch

## Larger Ball

### Size
4" diameter

### Materials
One partial ball (100 yards) each of Forest Green (color 449) and Mid Rose size 3 J. & P. Coats Speed-Cro-Sheen 100% mercerized cotton, article C-45 (or a similar substitute);
Safety pin or a piece of thread of a contrasting color for counting the rounds;
Fiber stuffing (or other filler);
Tapestry needle.

# Hacky-Sack

## Size

2 1/2" diameter

## Materials

One partial ball (100 yards) each of Spanish Red (color 126) and Canary Yellow (color 10A) size 3 J. & P. Coats Speed-Cro-Sheen 100% mercerized cotton, article C-45 (or a similar substitute);
Safety pin or a piece of thread of a contrasting color for counting the rounds;
6mm plastic beads or plastic pellets or fiber stuffing (or other filler);
Tapestry needle.

**Round 1:** Starting with the thread that you want to be on the bottom, make a slip knot (leaving a six-inch tail), then chain 4 stitches. Join the ends together to form a ring by working a slip stitch into the first chain stitch. Single crochet 6 stitches loosely into the ring (while carrying the tail of the thread). The spiral should have a total of 6 stitches when you finish this round. This piece is worked as a spiral, not in concentric rings, so it is difficult to tell where each round ends. To keep track of where each round ends, slip a safety pin into the top of the last stitch of the round or lay a two inch piece of thread of a contrasting color across the path of the last stitch. You will remove the safety pin from the last stitch as you come to it again and slip it into the new last stitch or cross the path of the last stitch with the end of the counting thread at the end of each round. Pull a little on the counting thread as it runs out to make it longer.
**Round 2:** Continue to carry the tail. Increase by crocheting 2 stitches into each stitch. The spiral should have a total of 12 stitches when you finish this round.
**Round 3:** Cut the tail flush and start to carry the other thread. Increase again in every stitch. The spiral should have 24 stitches when you finish this round.
**Round 4:** Increase in every second stitch. The spiral should have 36 stitches when you finish this round.
**Round 5:** Crochet one round without any increases.
**Round 6:** Increase in every third stitch. The spiral should have 48 stitches when you finish this round.
**Round 7:** Crochet one round without any increases.
**Round 8:** Increase in every fourth stitch. The spiral should have 60 stitches when you finish this round.

***If you are crocheting the hacky-sack, go to Round 13.***
**Round 9:** Crochet one round without any increases.
**Round 10:** Increase in every fifth stitch. The spiral should have 72 stitches when you finish this round.
**Round 11:** Crochet one round without any increases.
**Round 12:** Increase in every sixth stitch. The spiral should have 84 stitches when you finish this round.

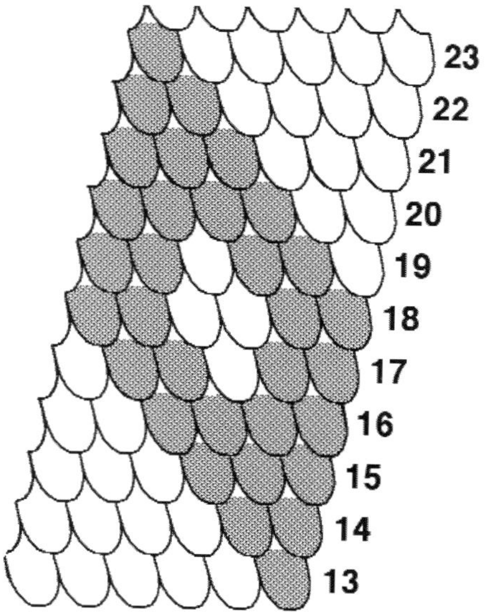


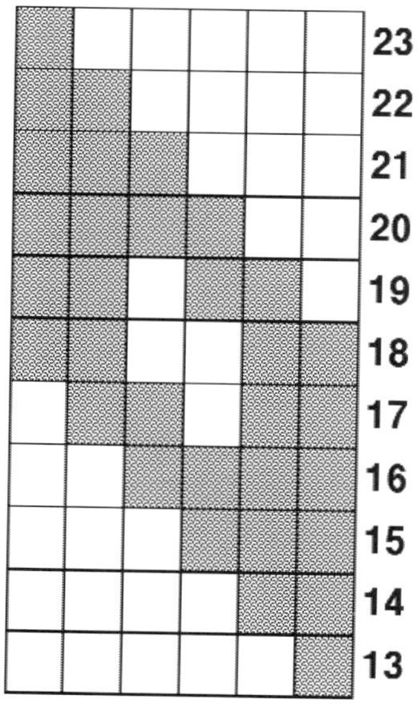


***The graphs on the left are for right-handed crocheters. Left-handed crocheters should look at the reversed image of the graphs in a mirror.***

***Begin the motif:***
**Round 13:** Rounds 13 through 23 correspond to the illustrated diamond motif (read from right to left and bottom to top). Start the motif as follows: (To begin the tapestry crochet stitch, you will have to pull your hook out of the last loop you made at the end of the previous round, pull out the loop, insert your hook into the two remaining loops, switch threads and then yarn over and pull through a loop with the carried thread) tapestry crochet 1 diamond color thread and 5 background stitches. Repeat around. Every once in a while, untwist the threads by holding the sack up in the air with one of the threads while pulling on the other thread. Let the piece spin around in the air so that the threads untangle.
**Round 14:** Tapestry crochet 2 diamond and 4 background stitches. Repeat around.
**Round 15:** Tapestry crochet 3 diamond and 3 background stitches. Repeat around. Turn the sack inside out (to make it right side out). As you tapestry crochet each stitch, the hook should point toward the inside of the sack.
**Round 16:** Tapestry crochet 4 diamond and 2 background stitches. Repeat around.
**Round 17:** Tapestry crochet 2 diamond, 1 background, 2 diamond, and 1 background stitch. Repeat around.
**Round 18:** Tapestry crochet 2 diamond, 2 background, and 2 diamond stitches. Repeat around.
**Round 19:** Tapestry crochet 1 background, 2 diamond stitches, 1 background, and 2 diamond stitches. Repeat around.
**Round 20:** Tapestry crochet 2 background and 4 diamond stitches. Repeat around.
**Round 21:** Tapestry crochet 3 background and 3 diamond stitches. Repeat around.
**Round 22:** Tapestry crochet 4 background and 2 diamond stitches. Repeat around.
**Round 23:** Tapestry crochet 5 background and 1 diamond stitches. Repeat around.
***If you are crocheting the hacky-sack, go to Round 28.***
**Round 24:** Decrease in every sixth stitch. The spiral should have 72 stitches when you finish this round. Pull the carried thread to make the opening a little smaller.
**Round 25:** Crochet one round without any decreases. Pull the carried thread to make the opening a little smaller.
**Round 26:** Decrease in every fifth stitch. The spiral should have 60 stitches when you finish this round. Pull the carried thread to make the opening a little smaller.
**Round 27:** Crochet one round without any decreases. Pull the carried thread to make the opening a little smaller.
**Round 28:** Decrease in every fourth stitch. The spiral should have 48 stitches when you finish this round. Pull the carried thread to make the opening a little smaller.
**Round 29:** Crochet one round without any decreases. Pull the carried thread to make the opening a little smaller.
**Round 30:** Decrease in every third stitch. The spiral should have 36 stitches when you finish this round. If you are crocheting the ball, stuff it now, then pull the carried thread to make the opening a little smaller.
**Round 31:** Crochet one round without any decreases. Pull the carried thread to make the opening a little smaller.
**Round 32:** Decrease in every second stitch. The spiral should have 24 stitches when you finish this round. Pull the carried thread to make the opening a little smaller.
**Round 33:** Decrease in every stitch. The spiral should have 12 stitches when you finish this round. If you are crocheting the hacky-sack, fill it 2/3 full (although most crocheted hacky-sacks are sold full, players prefer them to be only partially filled). Pull the carried thread to make the opening a little smaller.
**Round 34:** Decrease in every stitch. The spiral should have 6 stitches when you finish this round.

**To Finish:** Slip stitch with background color, cut it (leaving a 10 inch tail) then yarn over and pull it all the way through the loop. Pull the carried thread to make the opening as small as possible, tie together the two threads (a square knot is best), then cut the carried thread (leaving a 10 inch tail). Thread the tapestry needle with the carried thread, work in the end for an inch, cut it flush, then do the same thing with the other thread. Block the toy.

# 6 TUBE PROJECTS

## Scrunchies

Brighten up your pony tail or bun with one of these scrunchies! This project is a loosely crocheted tube that is sewn together end to end. The scrunchies begin at one end, which I will call the base. The base is crocheted first, then since the diameter of the base is not increased, the edges of the spiral move upwards to form the tube. The motif is five stitches wide, so the total number of stitches in the base is a multiple of five. A variety of sizes can be crocheted with the same motif by increasing or decreasing the base by five stitches. Feel free to substitute different colors or another motif. Just be sure that the total number of stitches in the base is a multiple of the number of stitches in your motif.

### Hook
Steel crochet hook size I/9 (5.50 mm.) or the size that will give an acceptable gauge

### Gauge
4 1/2 stitches equals 1 inch
4 rows equals 1 inch

### Size
1 3/4" wide by 24" long (before it is sewn together); 5" diameter sewn together

### Materials
Partial skein (50 grams/111 yards each skein) of Variegated (color 44) and of Pink (color 104) of Reynolds Sedona Four Ply Mercerized Egyptian cotton (or a similar substitute);
12" of black 1/4" wide braided elastic;
Safety pin or a piece of thread of a contrasting color for counting the rounds;
Tapestry sewing needle.

## Medium Scrunchie

### Size

2 1/4" wide by 19 1/4" long (before it is sewn together); 5 1/2" diameter sewn together

### Materials

Partial skein (50 grams/111 yards each skein) of Variegated (color 48) and of Teal (color 105) of Reynolds Sedona Four Ply Mercerized Egyptian cotton (or a similar substitute);
12" of black 1/4" wide braided elastic;
Safety pin or a piece of thread of a contrasting color for counting the rounds;
Tapestry sewing needle.

## Large Scrunchie

### Size

2 3/4" wide by 22" long (before it is sewn together); 6 3/4" diameter sewn together

### Materials

Partial skein (50 grams/111 yards each skein) of Variegated (color 30) and of White (color 101) of Reynolds Sedona Four Ply Mercerized Egyptian cotton (or a similar substitute);
12" of white 1/4" wide braided elastic;
Safety pin or a piece of thread of a contrasting color for counting the rounds;
Tapestry sewing needle.

**Round 1:** This thread is sold in skeins, which must first be wound into a ball. To keep the skein from tangling while winding, wrap it around a new roll of paper towels. With the light color thread, make a slip knot (leaving a two-inch tail), then chain 16 for the small scrunchie [or 21 for the medium scrunchie] (or 26 for the large scrunchie). Increase or decrease in multiples of 5 chain stitches at this point to make a narrower or wider tube. Join the ends together to form a ring by working a slip stitch into the first chain stitch. Single crochet 1 stitch into each stitch around, carrying the tail as you go along. Cut the tail flush at the end of this round. The scrunchie should have 15 [20] (25) stitches when you finish this round. This piece is worked as a spiral, not in concentric rings, so it is difficult to tell where each round ends. To keep track of where each round ends, slip a safety pin into the top of the last stitch of the round or lay a two inch piece of thread of a contrasting color across the path of the last stitch. You will remove the safety pin from the last stitch as you come to it again and slip it into the new last stitch or cross the path of the last stitch with the end of the counting yarn at the end of each round. Pull a little on the counting thread as it runs out to make it longer.
**Round 2:** Crochet around, carrying the dark color thread. The scrunchie should still have 15 [20] (25) stitches when you finish this round.
**Round 3:** Rounds 2 through 12 correspond to the illustrated diamond motif (read from right to left and bottom to top). Remember, that to do a tapestry crochet stitch, threads are switched while 2 loops are still on the hook, so to begin the tapestry crochet stitch, you will have to pull your hook out of the last loop you made at the end of the previous round, pull out the loop, insert your hook into the two remaining loops, switch threads and then yarn over and pull through a loop with the carried thread. Tapestry crochet 1 stitch with the dark color thread that you were carrying, then tapestry crochet 4 stitches with the light color thread. Repeat around. Every once in a while, untwist the threads by holding the project up in the air with one of the threads while pulling on the other thread. Let the piece spin around in the air so that the threads untangle.

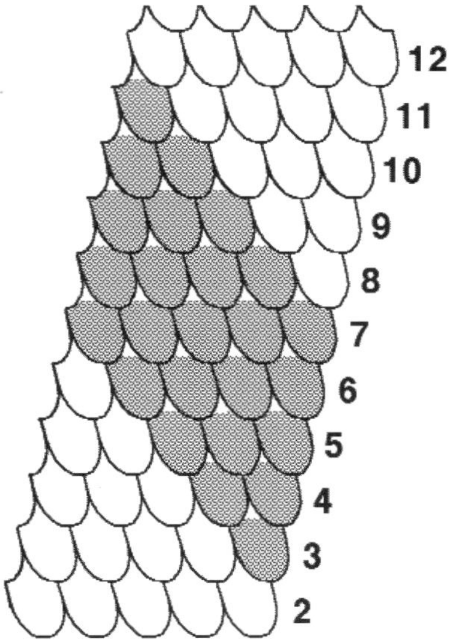


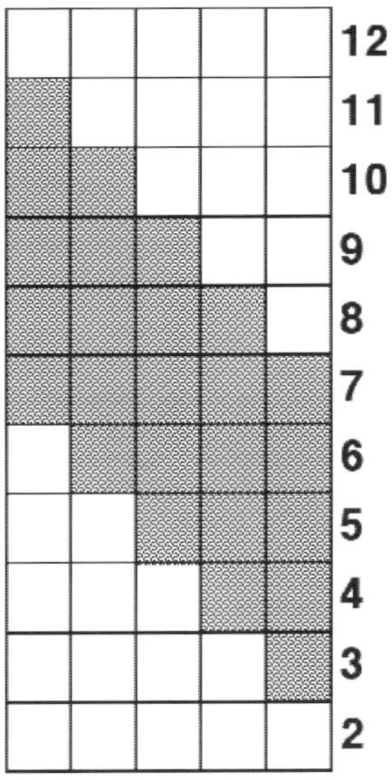


***The graphs on the left are for right-handed crocheters. Left-handed crocheters should look at the reversed image of the graphs in a mirror.***

**Round 4:** Tapestry crochet 2 dark, then 3 light stitches. Repeat around.
**Round 5:** Tapestry crochet 3 dark, then 2 light stitches. Repeat around.
**Round 6:** Tapestry crochet 4 dark, then 1 light stitch. Repeat around.
**Round 7:** Crochet around with dark.
**Round 8:** Tapestry crochet 1 light, then 4 dark stitches. Repeat around.
**Round 9:** Tapestry crochet 2 light, then 3 dark stitches. Repeat around.
**Round 10:** Tapestry crochet 3 light, then 2 dark stitches. Repeat around.
**Round 11:** Tapestry crochet 4 light, then 1 dark stitch. Repeat around.
**Round 12:** Crochet around with light.

***Repeat rounds 2 through 12 as many times as you wish. I repeated them 7 times for the small, 8 times for the medium, and 9 times for the large scrunchie.***

**Finishing:**
Cut the carried thread flush, slip stitch with light, cut it (leaving a 30" tail) then yarn over and pull it all the way through the loop. Cut off a 12" piece of 1/4" elastic, then hook a safety pin to one end. Insert the pinned elastic into one end of the crocheted tube and push it all the way through to the other end (while you hold the unpinned end). Remove the safety pin, then tie the ends of the elastic together with an overhand knot (to make an overhand knot, put both ends of the elastic next to each other, make a loop, then put the ends through the loop and pull, leaving two 1" long ends). Thread the tail through a tapestry needle, join the ends of the tubes to each other, then sew them together to create a doughnut shape. When you have finished, sew a couple of stitches into the last stitch. Insert the needle under the last six stitches and then pull the thread through the stitches to bury the tail. Cut the thread flush. You do not have to block this project.

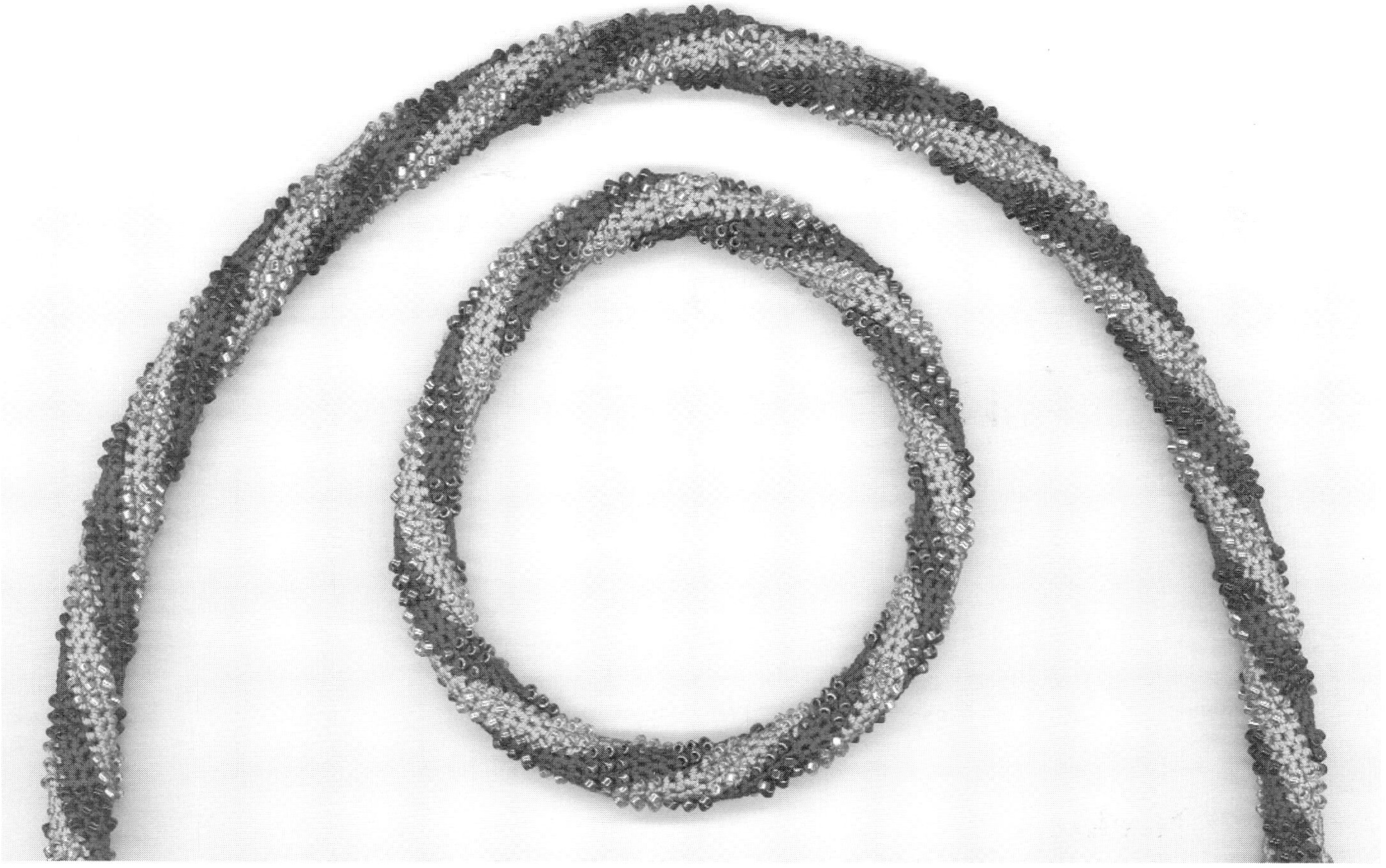

# Beaded Bracelet/Necklace

What could be more dramatic than a tapestry crocheted beaded bracelet and necklace? The beauty of tapestry crocheting with beads is that each thread can be loaded with one bead color and only the color that is needed at the time is crocheted to form a pattern while the other threads are carried. A decorative pattern is formed with or without adding a bead to each stitch since the colored threads also contribute to the design.

Two spools of silk thread are enough to make both this necklace and bracelet. This bracelet and necklace feature different beads to show off four color effects, but you could use the same beads for both projects or even pick totally different colors for your own bracelet and necklace.

This project was designed for people who have already crocheted with tiny beads. If you haven't crocheted with seed beads before, I suggest that you crochet the Beaded Basket project in this book, which uses larger thread and beads. I used a magnifying light to crochet these pieces because the stitches were too small for me to see without magnification.

The bracelet and necklace begin at one end, which I will call the base. The base is crocheted first, then since the diameter of the base is not increased, the edges of the spiral move upwards to form the tube. When crocheting with beads, the bead naturally slides to the back of the stitch, so the back of the stitch is on the outside of the tube. The crochet needle is inserted from the inside of the tube to the outside. The motif is six stitches wide, so the total number of stitches in the base is a multiple of six. It is possible to make a variety of sizes with the same design motif simply by increasing or decreasing the length of the chain by six stitches. Feel free to substitute different colors or another motif. Just be sure that the total number of stitches in the base is a multiple of the number of stitches in your motif.

### Hooks
Steel crochet hook size 8 (1.50 mm.) or the size that will give an acceptable gauge;
Steel crochet hook size 10 (1.30 mm.) for joining the ends together.

### Gauge
15 stitches equals 1 inch
13 rows equals 1 inch

## Bracelet

### Size
3/8" wide by 9 1/2" circumference

### Materials
Two 1570 TL heavy beading needles;
5 grams of 1106SB Ocean Blue and 5 grams of 1198SB Metallic Raspberry Iris Delica Beads;
One third of a spool of Red (color 1329TL) and one third of a spool of Royal Blue (color 1321TL) Gudebrod Silk Thread size FFF (equivalent to size 5 cotton thread);
A piece of thread of a contrasting color for counting the rounds.

## Necklace

### Size
3/8" wide by 26" circumference

### Materials
Two 1570 TL heavy beading needles;
10 grams of Silver Lined Cranberry (color 1300SB) and 10 grams of Silver Lined Blue (color 1318SB) Delica Beads;
Two thirds of a spool of Red (color 1329TL) and two thirds of a spool of Royal Blue (color 1321TL) Gudebrod Silk Thread size FFF (equivalent to size 5 cotton thread);
A piece of thread of a contrasting color for counting the rounds.

**Preparation:** First, load the red beads onto the red silk thread and the blue beads onto the blue silk thread with a beading needle. To load the beads, dump the red beads into one small bowl and the blue beads into another bowl. Thread a beading needle into each silk thread, leaving a 4 inch tail, then slightly curve the needle and push it into a mound of beads. Sometimes the needle will pick up one or more beads; sometimes nothing. This method is much easier than putting the beading needle through the hole of each bead one at a time.

After loading 19 inches (for the bracelet) or 50 inches [for the necklace] of beads onto the thread, push the beads down the thread, leaving a yard-long piece without beads. Tie the blue and red silk threads together, leaving 6 inch tails. Starting with the blue thread, make a slip knot next to the knot, then chain 13. Increase in multiples of 6 chain stitches at this point to make a wider tube.

Rounds 1 through 12 correspond to the illustrated motif (read from right to left and bottom to top).

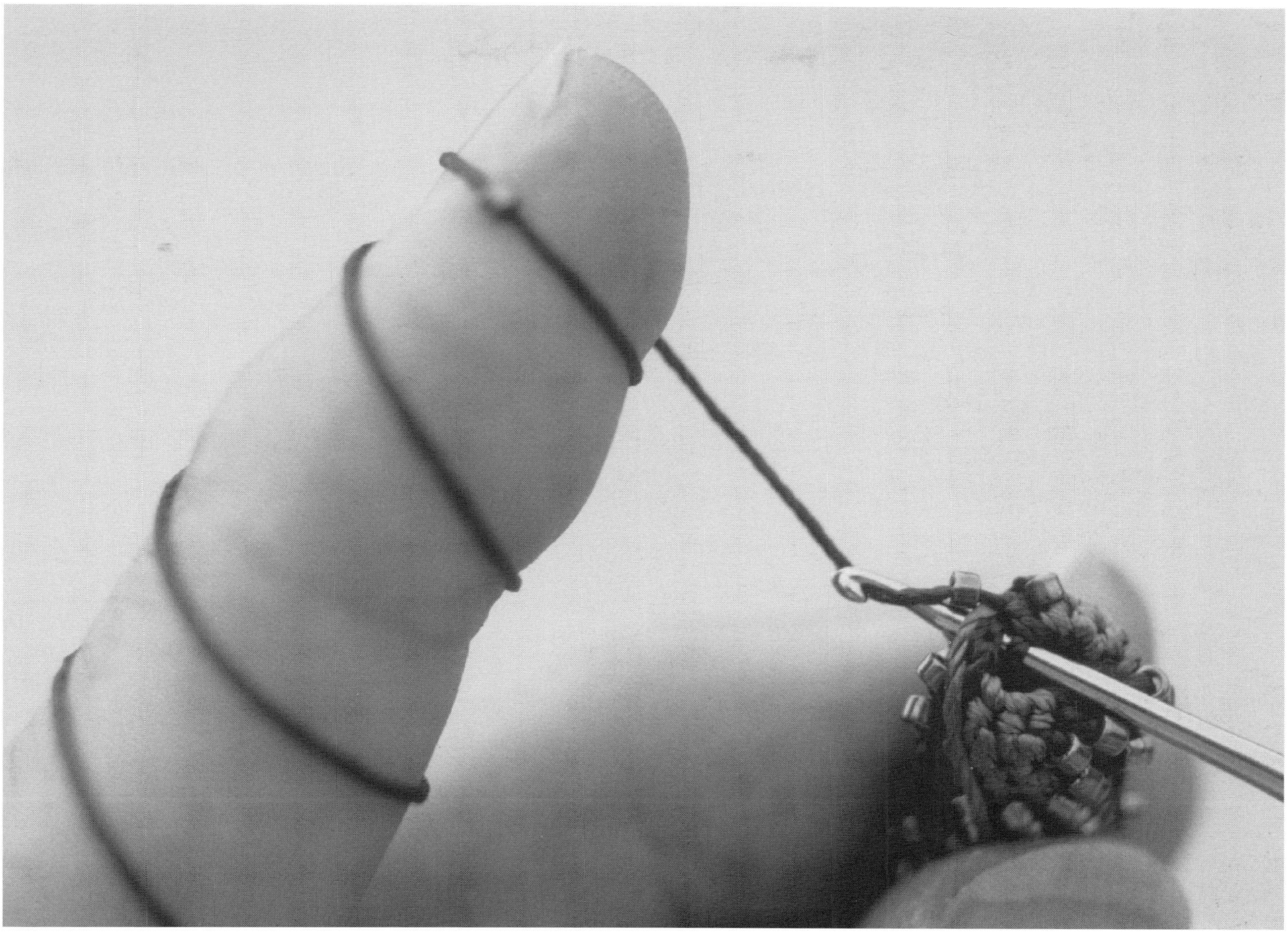

**The crochet needle is inserted from the inside of the tube to the outside.**

**Round 1:** Join the ends of the blue thread together to form a ring by working a slip stitch into the first chain stitch. Start to carry the red silk. Insert the hook into the first blue stitch, slide a blue bead next to the crochet hook, then tapestry crochet 1 blue stitch (capturing the blue bead, which will fall to the back of the stitch, which is the outside of the tube). Crochet another beaded blue stitch into the second stitch, then tapestry crochet 1 more beaded blue stitch into the third stitch (while carrying the red thread).

Remember, that to do a tapestry crochet stitch, colors are switched while 2 loops are still on the hook, so yarn over with red and pull it through the two blue loops of the third stitch to prepare for the red tapestry crochet stitch. Tapestry crochet 1 red stitch into each of the next 3 stitches (without beads this time). Repeat this sequence (crochet 3 beaded blue stitches, and then 3 red stitches) 1 more time. The tube should have 12 stitches when you finish this round.

This tube is worked as a spiral, not in concentric rings, so it is difficult to tell where each round ends. If you cannot tell where each round ends, lay a two inch piece of thread of a contrasting color across the path of the last stitch. Cross the path of the last stitch with the end of the counting thread at the end of each round. Pull a little on the counting thread as it runs out to make it longer.

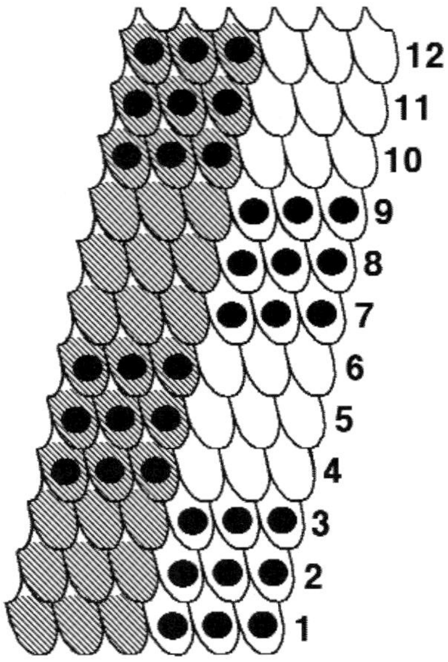


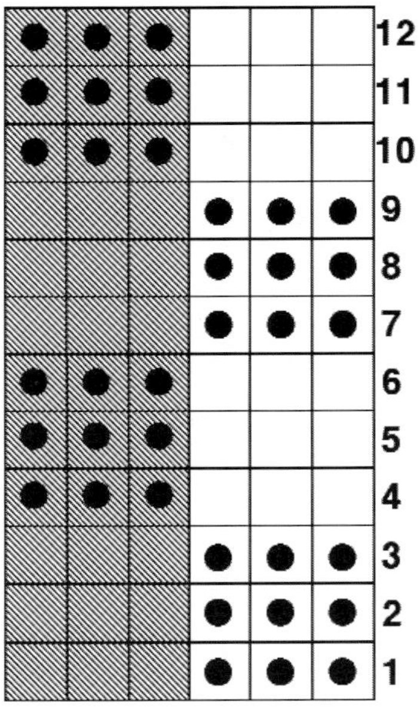


***The graphs on the left are for right-handed crocheters. Left-handed crocheters should look at the reversed image of the graphs in a mirror.***

**Round 2:** Tapestry crochet 3 beaded blue stitches, then 3 red stitches. Repeat around. The piece should still have 12 stitches when you finish this round. Every once in a while, untwist the threads by holding the piece up in the air with one of the threads while pulling on the other thread. Let the piece spin around in the air so that the threads untangle. The beads also have to be occasionally pushed down the thread.
**Round 3:** Tapestry crochet 3 beaded blue stitches, then 3 red stitches. Repeat around. The piece should still have 12 stitches when this round is finished. As each stitch is crocheted, the hook should point toward the outside of the pouch. Because of the way that the beads need to be worked, the back of the stitch will be seen on the outside of the project.
**Round 4:** In this round, the beading is done on the red instead of the blue thread. Tapestry crochet 3 blue stitches, then 3 beaded red stitches. Repeat around.
**Round 5:** Tapestry crochet 3 blue stitches, then 3 beaded red stitches. Repeat around.
**Round 6:** Tapestry crochet 3 blue stitches, then 3 beaded red stitches. Repeat around.
**Round 7:** In this round, the beading is done on the blue instead of the red thread. Tapestry crochet 3 beaded blue stitches, then 3 red stitches. Repeat around.
**Round 8:** Tapestry crochet 3 beaded blue stitches, then 3 red stitches. Repeat around.
**Round 9:** Tapestry crochet 3 beaded blue stitches, then 3 red stitches. Repeat around.
**Round 10:** In this round, the beading is done on the red instead of the blue thread. Tapestry crochet 3 blue stitches, then 3 beaded red stitches. Repeat around.
**Round 11:** Tapestry crochet 3 blue stitches, then 3 beaded red stitches. Repeat around.
**Round 12:** Tapestry crochet 3 blue stitches, then 3 beaded red stitches. Repeat around. Notice that the stripe is slightly diagonal. This is normal, since crochet stitches are not exactly on top of each other. If you run out of beads, start to carry a new beaded thread five or more stitches before it is needed. Switch to the new beaded thread, then carry the tail of the old thread five or more stitches to secure it before snipping it off. Occasionally, stretch the tube by pulling on both ends (it will shrink back quite a bit).

***Repeat rounds 7 through 12 eighteen times for the bracelet [or forty nine times for the necklace] or as many times as desired. Make sure that the bracelet will be large enough to fit over your hand and that the necklace will be large enough to fit over your head when they are finished.***

**Finishing:** Finish the last round with a red crochet stitch. Cut both threads (leaving 12" inch long tails), yarn over and pull the red silk all the way through the red loop.

These joining instructions will not produce an invisible seam, but the seam will camouflage itself into the pattern of the finished piece. Push the 6" tails from the beginning of the tube all the way into the bottom tube opening with the blunt end of your crochet hook.

Butt the ends of the tube together, with the first blue stitch next to the last stitch red stitch. The blue and red stripes should mate (blue to blue and red to red). The size 10 steel crochet hook will be used to join the blue and the red stripes together, using the blue thread for the blue stripes and the red thread for the red stripes.

Beginning with the red thread, slip the hook into the space next to the first red stitch at the side of the stripe at the bottom of the tube and pull through the red thread, then insert the hook through the corresponding stitch on the top end of the tube and pull through the red thread. Pull the stitch tight. Repeat this two more times with the red thread. Keep the blue thread out of the way behind the red stitches until it is needed. After three red stitches have been completed, do three blue stitches (some of the blue beads will end up out of place). Do 3 more red stitches, then 3 more blue stitches. Pull the threads tight, then work the red tail into the red stitches and the blue tail into the blue stitches to hide and secure them. Do not block this piece.

**Detail of the joined ends (middle of each photo) of the necklace (above) and bracelet (below).**

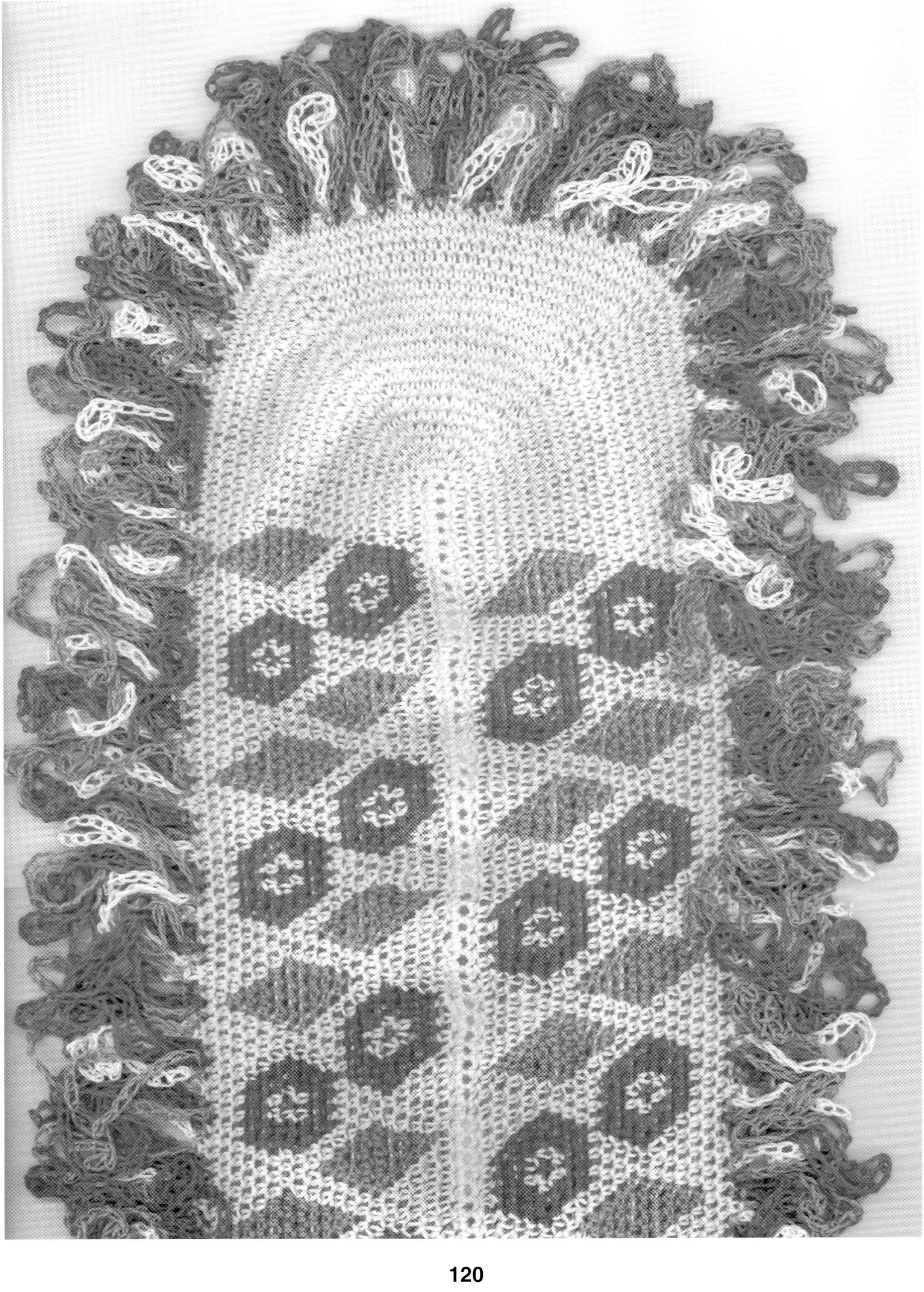

# OBLONG SPIRAL PROJECTS 7

## Scarf

This attractive scarf was crocheted loosely with linen. The motif is sixteen stitches wide. It is possible to make a variety of sizes with the same design motif simply by increasing or decreasing the size of the base by sixteen stitches. The increases at the ends of the scarf form a pattern as they build one on the other.

### Hooks
Steel crochet hook size 0 (3.25 mm.) or the size that will give an acceptable gauge, and a steel crochet hook size 1 (2.75 mm.) for finishing.

### Gauge
7 stitches equals 1 inch
8 rows equals 1 inch

### Size (with fringe)
8" wide by 48" long

### Materials
One tube (600 yards; 3 1/2 oz./100 grams) each of Green (color 589), Yellow (color 504), and Red (color 540) Klippan Berga 16/2 linen (or a similar substitute);
Safety pin or a piece of thread of a contrasting color for counting the rounds.

**Round 1:** Starting with the yellow linen, make a slip knot (leaving a ten-inch tail), then loosely chain 298 stitches. Increase or decrease in multiples of 8 chain stitches at this point to make a longer or shorter scarf. Starting with the second chain, single crochet 296 stitches. Single crochet 3 stitches into the last chain for a total of 299 stitches. Continue to single crochet using the new top of the chain until you come around to the first stitch, car rying the “tail” as you go (until it runs out). Single crochet 3 stitches into the last stitch of this round. This first round should have a total of 596 stitches. This piece is worked as a spiral, not in concentric rings, so it is difficult to tell where each round ends. To keep track of where each round ends, slip a safety pin into the top of the last stitch of the round or lay a two inch piece of thread of a contrasting color across the path of the last stitch. You will remove the safety pin from the last stitch as you come to it again and slip it into the new last stitch or cross the path of the last stitch with the end of the counting thread at the end of each round. Pull a little on the counting thread as it runs out to make it longer.

**Round 2:** Continue to crochet with yellow. Start to carry the red and green linen. To keep the scarf flat, you will increase each round by 8 stitches; 4 at each end. So begin this round by crocheting 2 stitches into the first stitch, 2 stitches into the next stitch, 294 stitches (one in each stitch), 2 stitches into each of the next 4 stitches, 294 stitches, 2 stitches into the next stitch, then 2 stitches into the last stitch of this round. The scarf should have 604 stitches when you finish this round.

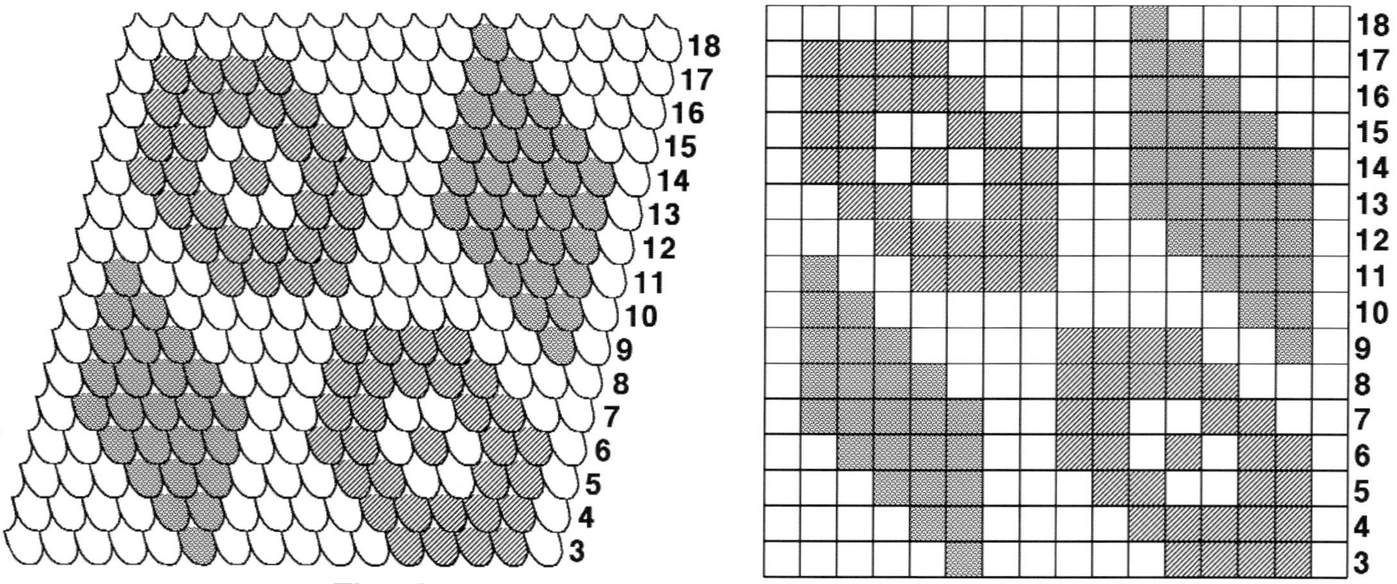


***The above graphs are for right-handed crocheters.***
***Left-handed crocheters should look at the reversed image of the graphs in a mirror.***

**Round 3:** Continue to crochet with yellow while you carry the red and green linen. Crochet 2 stitches into the first stitch, 1 stitch into the next stitch, 2 stitches into the next stitch, then 4 stitches (one in each stitch). You will begin to tapestry crochet the motif in this round. Remember, that to do a tapestry crochet stitch, colors are switched while 2 loops are still on the hook; yarn over with the next color and pull it through the loops to prepare for the tapestry crochet stitch. Rounds 3 through 18 correspond to the illustrated motif (read from right to left and bottom to top).

Tapestry crochet 1 yellow, 4 red, 5 yellow, 1 green, and 5 yellow stitches. Repeat this sequence 17 more times.

Every once in a while, untwist the carried threads. You can avoid twisted threads if you separate the three tubes. One way to separate them is to place one color to your right, another in your lap, and the third to your left. As you change colors, you will see a twist in the threads where they cross over one another. The twist will not show in the finished piece.

After the 18th motif has been completed, you will crochet around the end with yellow as follows: crochet 4 yellow stitches (one into each stitch), 2 yellow stitches into the next stitch, 1 yellow stitch into the next stitch, 2 yellow stitches into the next stitch, 2 yellow stitches into the next stitch, 1 yellow stitch into the next stitch, 2 yellow stitches into the next stitch, then 4 yellow stitches (one in each stitch).

Tapestry crochet 1 yellow, 4 red, 5 yellow, 1 green, and 5 yellow stitches. Repeat this sequence 17 more times.

Crochet 4 yellow stitches (one in each stitch), 2 yellow stitches into the next stitch, 1 yellow stitch into the next stitch, then 2 yellow stitches into the last stitch of this round. 612 total stitches.

**Round 4:** While carrying the other linen, crochet 1 yellow stitch into the first stitch, 2 yellow stitches into the next stitch, 1 yellow stitch into the next stitch, 2 yellow stitches into the next stitch, then 5 yellow stitches (one in each stitch).

Tapestry crochet 1 yellow, 5 red, 4 yellow, 2 green, and 4 yellow stitches. Repeat this sequence 17 more times.

After the 18th motif has been completed, crochet 5 yellow stitches (one into each stitch), 2 yellow stitches into the next stitch, 1 yellow stitch into the next stitch, 2 yellow stitches into the next stitch, 2 yellow stitches (one in each stitch), 2 yellow stitches into the next stitch, 1 yellow stitch into the next stitch, 2 yellow stitches into the next stitch, then 5 yellow stitches.

Tapestry crochet 1 yellow, 5 red, 4 yellow, 2 green, and 4 yellow stitches. Repeat this sequence 17 more times.

Crochet 5 yellow stitches, 2 yellow stitches into the next stitch, 1 yellow stitch into the next stitch, 2 yellow stitches into the next stitch, then 1 yellow stitch into the last stitch of this round. 620 total stitches.

**Round 5:** While carrying the other linen, crochet 2 yellow stitches (one in each stitch), 2 yellow stitches into the next stitch, 1 yellow stitch into the next stitch, 2 yellow stitches into the next stitch, then 6 yellow stitches (one in each stitch).

Tapestry crochet 1 yellow, 2 red, 2 yellow, 2 red, 3 yellow, 3 green, and 3 yellow stitches. Repeat this sequence 17 more times.

After the 18th motif has been completed, crochet 6 yellow stitches, 2 yellow stitches into the next stitch, 1 yellow stitch into the next stitch, 2 yellow stitches into the next stitch, 4 yellow stitches, 2 yellow stitches into the next stitch, 1 yellow stitch into the next stitch, 2 yellow stitches into the next stitch, then 6 yellow stitches.

Tapestry crochet 1 yellow, 2 red, 2 yellow, 2 red, 3 yellow, 3 green, and 3 yellow stitches. Repeat this sequence 17 more times.

Crochet 6 yellow stitches, 2 yellow stitches into the next stitch, 1 yellow stitch into the next stitch, 2 yellow stitches into the next stitch, then 2 yellow stitches (one in each stitch). 628 total stitches.

**Round 6:** While carrying the other linen, crochet 3 yellow stitches (one in each stitch), 2 yellow stitches into the next stitch, 1 yellow stitch into the next stitch, 2 yellow stitches into the next stitch, then 7 yellow stitches.

Tapestry crochet 1 yellow, 2 red, 1 yellow, 1 red, 1 yellow, 2 red, 2 yellow, 4 green, and 2 yellow stitches. Repeat this sequence 17 more times.

After the 18th motif has been completed, crochet 7 yellow stitches (one into each stitch), 2 yellow stitches into the next stitch, 1 yellow stitch into the next stitch, 2 yellow stitches into the next stitch, 6 yellow stitches, 2 yellow stitches into the next stitch, 1 yellow stitch into the next stitch, 2 yellow stitches into the next stitch, then 7 yellow stitches.

Tapestry crochet 1 yellow, 2 red, 1 yellow, 1 red, 1 yellow, 2 red, 2 yellow, 4 green, and 2 yellow stitches. Repeat this sequence 17 more times.

Crochet 7 yellow stitches, 2 yellow stitches into the next stitch, 1 yellow stitch into the next stitch, 2 yellow stitches into the next stitch, then 3 yellow stitches (one in each stitch). 636 total stitches.

**Round 7:** While carrying the other linen, crochet 4 yellow stitches, 2 yellow stitches into the next stitch, 1 yellow stitch into the next stitch, 2 yellow stitches into the next stitch, then 8 yellow stitches.

Tapestry crochet 2 yellow, 2 red, 2 yellow, 2 red, 2 yellow, 5 green, and 1 yellow stitch. Repeat this sequence 17 more times.

After the 18th motif has been completed, crochet 8 yellow stitches (one into each stitch), 2 yellow stitches into the next stitch, 1 yellow stitch into the next stitch, 2 yellow stitches into the next stitch, 8 yellow stitches, 2 yellow stitches into the next stitch, 1 yellow stitch into the next stitch, 2 yellow stitches into the next stitch, then 8 yellow stitches.

Tapestry crochet 2 yellow, 2 red, 2 yellow, 2 red, 2 yellow, 5 green, and 1 yellow stitch. Repeat this sequence 17 more times.

Crochet 8 yellow stitches, 2 yellow stitches into the next stitch, 1 yellow stitch into the next stitch, 2 yellow stitches into the next stitch, then 4 yellow stitches. 644 total stitches.

**Round 8:** While carrying the other linen, crochet 5 yellow stitches, 2 yellow stitches into the next stitch, 1 yellow stitch into the next stitch, 2 yellow stitches into the next stitch, then 9 yellow stitches.

Tapestry crochet 3 yellow, 5 red, 3 yellow, 4 green, and 1 yellow stitch. Repeat this sequence 17 more times.

After the 18th motif has been completed, crochet 9 yellow stitches (one into each stitch), 2 yellow stitches into the next stitch, 1 yellow stitch into the next stitch, 2 yellow stitches into the next stitch, 10 yellow stitches, 2 yellow stitches into the next stitch, 1 yellow stitch into the next stitch, 2 yellow stitches into the next stitch, then 9 yellow stitches.

Tapestry crochet 3 yellow, 5 red, 3 yellow, 4 green, and 1 yellow stitch. Repeat this sequence 17 more times.

Crochet 9 yellow stitches, 2 yellow stitches into the next stitch, 1 yellow stitch into the next stitch, 2 yellow stitches into the next stitch, then 5 yellow stitches. 652 total stitches.

**Round 9:** While carrying the other linen, crochet 6 yellow stitches, 2 yellow stitches into the next stitch, 1 yellow stitch into the next stitch, 2 yellow stitches into the next stitch, then 10 yellow stitches.

Tapestry crochet 1 yellow, 1 green, 2 yellow, 4 red, 4 yellow, 3 green, and 1 yellow stitch. Repeat this sequence 17 more times.

After the 18th motif has been completed, crochet 10 yellow stitches (one into each stitch), 2 yellow stitches into the next stitch, 1 yellow stitch into the next stitch, 2 yellow stitches into the next stitch, 12 yellow stitches, 2 yellow stitches into the next stitch, 1 yellow stitch into the next stitch, 2 yellow stitches into the next stitch, then 10 yellow stitches.

Tapestry crochet 1 yellow, 1 green, 2 yellow, 4 red, 4 yellow, 3 green, and 1 yellow stitch. Repeat this sequence 17 more times.

Crochet 10 yellow stitches, 2 yellow stitches into the next stitch, 1 yellow stitch into the next stitch, 2 yellow stitches into the next stitch, then 6 yellow stitches. 660 total stitches.

**Round 10:** While carrying the other linen, crochet 7 yellow stitches, 2 yellow stitches into the next stitch, 1 yellow stitch into the next stitch, 2 yellow stitches into the next stitch, then 11 yellow stitches.

Tapestry crochet 1 yellow, 2 green, 10 yellow, 2 green, and 1 yellow stitch. Repeat this sequence 17 more times.

After the 18th motif has been completed, crochet 11 yellow stitches (one into each stitch), 2 yellow stitches into the next stitch, 1 yellow stitch into the next stitch, 2 yellow stitches into the next stitch, 14 yellow stitches, 2 yellow stitches into the next stitch, 1 yellow stitch into the next stitch, 2 yellow stitches into the next stitch, then 11 yellow stitches.

Tapestry crochet 1 yellow, 2 green, 10 yellow, 2 green, and 1 yellow stitch. Repeat this sequence 17 more times.

Crochet 11 yellow stitches, 2 yellow stitches into the next stitch, 1 yellow stitch into the next stitch, 2 yellow stitches into the next stitch, then 7 yellow stitches. 668 total stitches.

**Round 11:** While carrying the other linen, crochet 8 yellow stitches, 2 yellow stitches into the next stitch, 1 yellow stitch into the next stitch, 2 yellow stitches into the next stitch, then 12 yellow stitches.

Tapestry crochet 1 yellow, 3 green, 4 yellow, 4 red, 2 yellow, 1 green, and 1 yellow stitch. Repeat this sequence 17 more times.

After the 18th motif has been completed, crochet 12 yellow stitches (one into each stitch), 2 yellow stitches into the next stitch, 1 yellow stitch into the next stitch, 2 yellow stitches into the next stitch, 16 yellow stitches, 2 yellow stitches into the next stitch, 1 yellow stitch into the next stitch, 2 yellow stitches into the next stitch, then 12 yellow stitches.

Tapestry crochet 1 yellow, 3 green, 4 yellow, 4 red, 2 yellow, 1 green, and 1 yellow stitch. Repeat this sequence 17 more times.

Crochet 12 yellow stitches, 2 yellow stitches into the next stitch, 1 yellow stitch into the next stitch, 2 yellow stitches into the next stitch, then 8 yellow stitches. 676 total stitches.

**Round 12:** While carrying the other linen, crochet 9 yellow stitches, 2 yellow stitches into the next stitch, 1 yellow stitch into the next stitch, 2 yellow stitches into the next stitch, then 13 yellow stitches.

Tapestry crochet 1 yellow, 4 green, 3 yellow, 5 red, and 3 yellow stitches. Repeat this sequence 17 more times.

After the 18th motif has been completed, crochet 13 yellow stitches (one into each stitch), 2 yellow stitches into the next stitch, 1 yellow stitch into the next stitch, 2 yellow stitches into the next stitch, 18 yellow stitches, 2 yellow stitches into the next stitch, 1 yellow stitch into the next stitch, 2 yellow stitches into the next stitch, then 13 yellow stitches.

Tapestry crochet 1 yellow, 4 green, 3 yellow, 5 red, and 3 yellow stitches. Repeat this sequence 17 more times.

Crochet 13 yellow stitches, 2 yellow stitches into the next stitch, 1 yellow stitch into the next stitch, 2 yellow stitches into the next stitch, then 9 yellow stitches. 684 total stitches.

**Round 13:** While carrying the other linen, crochet 10 yellow stitches, 2 yellow stitches into the next stitch, 1 yellow stitch into the next stitch, 2 yellow stitches into the next stitch, then 14 yellow stitches.

Tapestry crochet 1 yellow, 5 green, 2 yellow, 2 red, 2 yellow, 2 red, and 2 yellow stitches. Repeat this sequence 17 more times.

After the 18th motif has been completed, crochet 14 yellow stitches (one into each stitch), 2 yellow stitches into the next stitch, 1 yellow stitch into the next stitch, 2 yellow stitches into the next stitch, 20 yellow stitches, 2 yellow stitches into the next stitch, 1 yellow stitch into the next stitch, 2 yellow stitches into the next stitch, then 14 yellow stitches.

Tapestry crochet 1 yellow, 5 green, 2 yellow, 2 red, 2 yellow, 2 red, and 2 yellow stitches. Repeat this sequence 17 more times.

Crochet 14 yellow stitches, 2 yellow stitches into the next stitch, 1 yellow stitch into the next stitch, 2 yellow stitches into the next stitch, then 10 yellow stitches. 692 total stitches.

**Round 14:** While carrying the other linen, crochet 11 yellow stitches, 2 yellow stitches into the next stitch, 1 yellow stitch into the next stitch, 2 yellow stitches into the next stitch, then 15 yellow stitches.

Tapestry crochet 1 yellow, 5 green, 2 yellow, 2 red, 1 yellow, 1 red, 1 yellow, 2 red, and 1 yellow stitch. Repeat this sequence 17 more times.

After the 18th motif has been completed, crochet 15 yellow stitches (one into each stitch), 2 yellow stitches into the next stitch, 1 yellow stitch into the next stitch, 2 yellow stitches into the next stitch, 22 yellow stitches, 2 yellow stitches into the next stitch, 1 yellow stitch into the next stitch, 2 yellow stitches into the next stitch, then 15 yellow stitches.

Tapestry crochet 1 yellow, 5 green, 2 yellow, 2 red, 1 yellow, 1 red, 1 yellow, 2 red, and 1 yellow stitch. Repeat this sequence 17 more times.

Crochet 15 yellow stitches, 2 yellow stitches into the next stitch, 1 yellow stitch into the next stitch, 2 yellow stitches into the next stitch, then 11 yellow stitches. 700 total stitches.

**Round 15:** While carrying the other linen, crochet 12 yellow stitches, 2 yellow stitches into the next stitch, 1 yellow stitch into the next stitch, 2 yellow stitches into the next stitch, then 16 yellow stitches.

Tapestry crochet 2 yellow, 4 green, 3 yellow, 2 red, 2 yellow, 2 red, and 1 yellow stitch. Repeat this sequence 17 more times.

After the 18th motif has been completed, crochet 16 yellow stitches (one into each stitch), 2 yellow stitches into the next stitch, 1 yellow stitch into the next stitch, 2 yellow stitches into the next stitch, 24 yellow stitches, 2 yellow stitches into the next stitch, 1 yellow stitch into the next stitch, 2 yellow stitches into the next stitch, then 16 yellow stitches.

Tapestry crochet 2 yellow, 4 green, 3 yellow, 2 red, 2 yellow, 2 red, and 1 yellow stitch. Repeat this sequence 17 more times.

Crochet 16 yellow stitches, 2 yellow stitches into the next stitch, crochet 1 yellow stitch into the next stitch, 2 yellow stitches into the next stitch, then 12 yellow stitches. 708 total stitches.

**Round 16:** While carrying the other linen, crochet 13 yellow stitches, 2 yellow stitches into the next stitch, 1 yellow stitch into the next stitch, 2 yellow stitches into the next stitch, then 17 yellow stitches.

Tapestry crochet 3 yellow, 3 green, 4 yellow, 5 red, and 1 yellow stitch. Repeat this sequence 17 more times.

After the 18th motif has been completed, crochet 17 yellow stitches (one into each stitch), 2 yellow stitches into the next stitch, 1 yellow stitch into the next stitch, 2 yellow stitches into the next stitch, 26 yellow stitches, 2 yellow stitches into the next stitch, 1 yellow stitch into the next stitch, 2 yellow stitches into the next stitch, then 17 yellow stitches.

Tapestry crochet 3 yellow, 3 green, 4 yellow, 5 red, and 1 yellow stitch. Repeat this sequence 17 more times.

Crochet 17 yellow stitches, 2 yellow stitches into the next stitch, 1 yellow stitch into the next stitch, 2 yellow stitches into the next stitch, then 13 yellow stitches. 716 total stitches.

**Round 17:** While carrying the other linen, crochet 14 yellow stitches, 2 yellow stitches into the next stitch, 1 yellow stitch into the next stitch, 2 yellow stitches into the next stitch, then 18 yellow stitches.

Tapestry crochet 4 yellow, 2 green, 5 yellow, 4 red, and 1 yellow stitch. Repeat this sequence 17 more times.

After the 18th motif has been completed, crochet 18 yellow stitches (one into each stitch), 2 yellow stitches into the next stitch, 1 yellow stitch into the next stitch, 2 yellow stitches into the next stitch, 28 yellow stitches, 2 yellow stitches into the next stitch, 1 yellow stitch into the next stitch, 2 yellow stitches into the next stitch, then 18 yellow stitches.

Tapestry crochet 4 yellow, 2 green, 5 yellow, 4 red, and 1 yellow stitch. Repeat this sequence 17 more times.

Crochet 18 yellow stitches, 2 yellow stitches into the next stitch, 1 yellow stitch into the next stitch, 2 yellow stitches into the next stitch, then 14 yellow stitches. 724 total stitches.

**Round 18:** While carrying the other linen, crochet 15 yellow stitches, 2 yellow stitches into the next stitch, 1 yellow stitch into the next stitch, 2 yellow stitches into the next stitch, then 19 yellow stitches.

Tapestry crochet 5 yellow, 1 green, and 10 yellow stitches. Repeat this sequence 17 more times.

After the 18th motif has been completed, crochet 19 yellow stitches (one into each stitch), 2 yellow stitches into the next stitch, 1 yellow stitch into the next stitch, 2 yellow stitches into the next stitch, 30 yellow stitches, 2 yellow stitches into the next stitch, 1 yellow stitch into the next stitch, 2 yellow stitches into the next stitch, then 19 yellow stitches.

Tapestry crochet 5 yellow, 1 green, and 10 yellow stitches. Repeat this sequence 17 more times.

Crochet 19 yellow stitches, 2 yellow stitches into the next stitch, 1 yellow stitch into the next stitch, 2 yellow stitches into the next stitch, then 15 yellow stitches. 732 total stitches.

**Round 19:** While carrying the other linen, crochet 16 yellow stitches, 2 yellow stitches into the next stitch, 1 yellow stitch into the next stitch, 2 yellow stitches into the next stitch, 328 yellow stitches, 2 yellow stitches into the next stitch, 1 yellow stitch into the next stitch, 2 yellow stitches into the next stitch, 32 yellow stitches, 2 yellow stitches into the next stitch, 1 yellow stitch into the next stitch, 2 yellow stitches into the next stitch, 328 yellow stitches, 2 yellow stitches into the next stitch, 1 yellow stitch into the next stitch, 2 yellow stitches into the next stitch, then 16 yellow stitches. 740 total stitches.

**Round 20:** While carrying the other linen, crochet 17 yellow stitches, 2 yellow stitches into the next stitch, 1 yellow stitch into the next stitch, 2 yellow stitches into the next stitch, 330 yellow stitches, 2 yellow stitches into the next stitch, 1 yellow stitch into the next stitch, 2 yellow stitches into the next stitch, 34 yellow stitches, 2 yellow stitches into the next stitch, 1 yellow stitch into the next stitch, 2 yellow stitches into the next stitch, 330 yellow stitches, 2 yellow stitches into the next stitch, 1 yellow stitch into the next stitch, 2 yellow stitches into the next stitch, then 17 yellow stitches. 748 total stitches.

**Fringe:** Chain 20 yellow, then single crochet 1 yellow stitch into the next stitch; chain 25 green, then single crochet 1 green stitch into the next stitch; chain 30 red, then single crochet 1 red stitch into the next stitch; chain 25 green, then single crochet 1 green stitch into the next. Repeat this sequence 186 more times (all the way around the edge of the scarf).

**To finish:** Cut the yellow, green and red threads (leaving 6" tails). Yarn over with green and pull it all the way through the green loop on the hook. Turn the scarf over and with a size one crochet hook, work in the ends by pulling them through the last row of stitches for two inches. Cut the ends flush. Block the body of the scarf (but not the fringe).

# Linen

Fiber from the inner stem of the flax plant has been processed into linen for over 12,000 years, dating back to the Neolithic Age, making it one of the oldest natural fibers. It was used before cotton and is twice as strong as cotton. The word "linen" comes from the Celtic word *Llin* and the Latin word, *Linum.* Because of its strength, and because it wicks moisture and dries quickly, linen was very popular in ancient Egypt.

Flax has been cultivated for centuries. Today it is grown in the Americas, Northern Europe, and Russia. When Irish linen weavers emigrated to the United States, they brought flax seeds with them. Two types of flax plants are cultivated; a short one for seeds and a tall one for fiber. Blue flowers, on two to three feet long stems, produce round seed balls that contain two to seven seeds each. Flax seeds can be eaten or pressed into linseed oil.

**Unprocessed flax, a flax comb, paddle, *hackles,* and unspun processed flax.**

Flax that is raised for seed is allowed to grow to maturity. The mature fiber is of little value so the plants are harvested by a machine. Flax that is grown for its fiber is harvested by pulling the plants out of the ground when still green because some of the best fibers run down the stalk into the roots. Stems are tied in small bundles and hung to dry, then the seeds are *rippled* off with a comb. The flax is then *retted* with water for several days to dissolve the pectin and liberate the fibers. The flax can be laid down in a field where dew accumulates every night, or it can be *retted* in running water. After drying, the flax is ready to *break*, which separates the straw from the fiber. Next, the flax is *scutched* with a flat paddle and beat against a post to remove the cortex from the fiber bundles. The fibers are then pulled through the teeth of a *hackle,* also known as a *hetchel* or *heckle,* to separate and align the fibers, beginning with coarse teeth and working to smaller teeth. The shorter fibers that are left behind after *hackling* are used to make tow linen for rough fabric. The long fiber, called *line* or *line flax*, is placed on a distaff and spun into a strong thread, which is then used to weave fine linen cloth. Although some people still carry on this age-old labor intensive tradition, today most flax is processed by machine.

Heavy stones hold down the flax so that it doesn't float away in the Lys River in Belgium. On the far bank, bundles are waiting to be *retted* in the river. The flax is left in the water just long enough so that the outer surface of the stalk rots away (Keystone View Company and Underwood and Underwood, c. 1900).

Les Harding holds a flax seed pod (below). The wooded tool to the right is used to *ripple* off the seeds by pulling the bundle through the dowels.

Ann Harding *breaks* flax by raising and lowering the hinged break onto the stems. Notice the dried bundles of flax hanging behind her (on the left).

This photograph documents how flax was *hackled* in a linen mill in Belfast Ireland. (Underwood and Underwood, c. 1900).

Les Harding *scutches* the flax with a flat paddle (above) to remove the cortex from the fiber bundles. After *hackling*, Les transforms the flax into linen on a spinning wheel (right).

# "Opposites Attract" Shawl

This shawl was crocheted loosely with alpaca. The yarn is so soft that it was a sensual treat to feel the shawl as it evolved! The opposites attract motif is sixteen stitches wide. It is possible to make a variety of sizes with the same design motif simply by increasing or decreasing the length of the chain by sixteen stitches. The increases at both ends of the shawl are somewhat random to avoid an obvious pattern.

## Hooks

Aluminum crochet hook size I/9 (5.50 mm.) or the size that will give an acceptable gauge, and a steel crochet hook size 1 (2.75 mm.) for finishing.

## Gauge

4 1/2 stitches equals 1 inch
4 1/2 rows equals 1 inch

## Size (with fringe)

3' wide by 7' long

## Materials

15 balls (1 3/4 ounces/50 grams/100 yards each) of gray (color 11) and 21 balls of white (color 3) of item 117 Four-Ply Knitting Worsted Indiecita Peruvian Alpaca (or a similar substitute);
Safety pin or a piece of yarn of a contrasting color for counting the rounds.

**Round 1:** Starting with the white alpaca, make a slip knot (leaving a ten-inch tail), then loosely chain 216 stitches. Increase or decrease in multiples of 8 chain stitches at this point to make a longer or shorter shawl. Starting with the second chain, single crochet 214 stitches. Single crochet 3 stitches into the last chain for a total of 217 stitches. Continue to single crochet using the new top of the chain until you come around to the first stitch, carrying the "tail" as you go (until it runs out). Single crochet 2 stitches into the last stitch of this round. This first round should have a total of 432 stitches. This piece is worked as a spiral, not in concentric rings, so it is difficult to tell where each round ends. To keep track of where each round ends, slip a safety pin into the top of the last stitch of the round or lay a two inch piece of yarn of a contrasting color across the path of the last stitch. You will remove the safety pin from the last stitch as you come to it again and slip it into the new last stitch or cross the path of the last stitch with the end of the counting yarn at the end of each round. Pull a little on the counting thread as it runs out to make it longer.

**Round 2:** Continue to crochet with white. Start to carry the gray. To keep the shawl flat, you will increase each round by 8 stitches; 4 at each end. Crochet 2 stitches into the first stitch, 2 stitches into the next stitch, 212 stitches, 2 stitches into each of the next 4 stitches, 212 stitches, then 2 stitches into each of the last two stitches of this round. The shawl should have 440 stitches when you finish this round.
**Round 3:** Continue to crochet with white while you carry the gray. Crochet 2 stitches into the first stitch, 1 stitch into the next stitch, 2 stitches into the next stitch, 214 stitches, 2 stitches into the next stitch, 1 stitch into the next stitch, 2 stitches into each of the next two stitches, 1 stitch into the next stitch, 2 stitches into the next stitch, 214 stitches, 2 stitches into the next stitch, 1 stitch into the next stitch, then 2 stitches into the last stitch of this round. The shawl should have 448 stitches when you finish this round.
**Round 4:** Continue to crochet with white while you carry the gray. Crochet 2 stitches into the first stitch, 1 stitch into the next stitch, 2 stitches into the next stitch, 218 stitches, 2 stitches into the next stitch, 1 stitch into the next stitch, 2 stitches into each of the next two stitches, 1 stitch into the next stitch, 2 stitches into the next stitch, 218 stitches, 2 stitches into the next stitch, 1 stitch into the next stitch, then 2 stitches into the last stitch of this round. 456 total stitches.

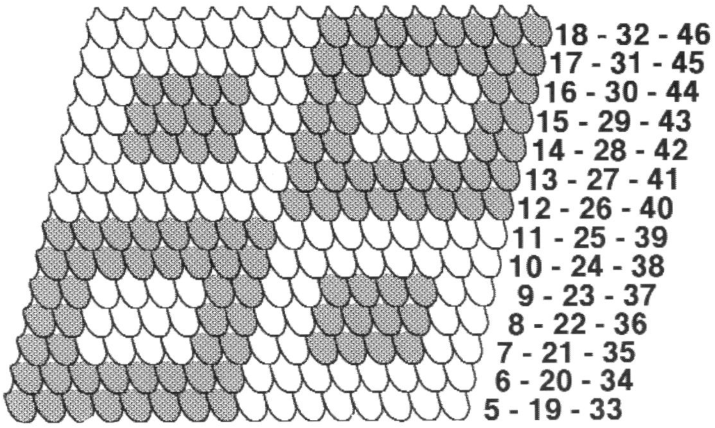


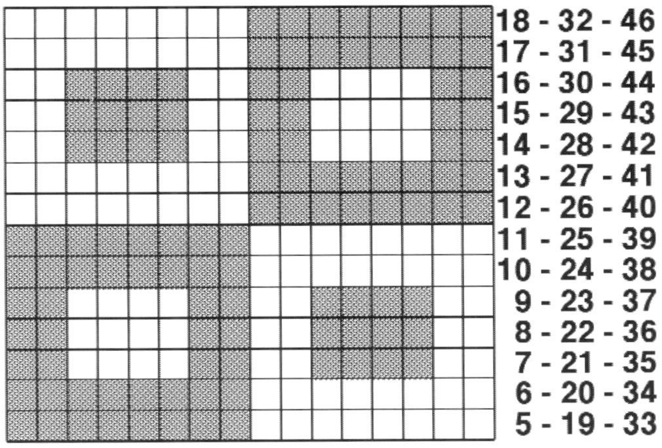


***The above graphs are for right-handed crocheters.***
***Left-handed crocheters should look at the reversed image of the graphs in a mirror.***

**Round 5:** Rounds 5 through 18 correspond to the illustrated motif (read from right to left and bottom to top). Continue to crochet with white while you carry the gray. Crochet 2 stitches into the first stitch then crochet 2 stitches into the next stitch. You will now begin the tapestry crochet motif. Remember, that to do a tapestry crochet stitch, colors are switched while 2 loops are still on the hook; yarn over with the next color and pull it through the loops to prepare for the tapestry crochet stitch.

Tapestry crochet 8 white and then 8 gray stitches. Repeat this sequence 13 more times.

After the 14th motif has been completed, crochet 2 white stitches into each of the next four stitches.
Tapestry crochet 8 white and then 8 gray stitches. Repeat this sequence 13 more times.
Crochet 2 white stitches into the next stitch, then 2 white stitches into the last stitch of this round. 464 total stitches.

Every once in a while, untwist the carried yarns. You can avoid twisted yarns if you separate the two yarns. One way to separate them is to place one color to your right and the other to your left. As you change colors, you will see a twist in the yarns where they cross over one another. The twist will not show in the finished piece.
**Round 6:** Crochet 2 white stitches into the first stitch, 1 white into the next stitch, 2 white into the next stitch, then 1 white into the next stitch.

Tapestry crochet 8 white and then 8 gray stitches. Repeat this sequence 13 more times.
After the 14th motif has been completed, crochet 1 white stitch into the next stitch, 2 white into the next stitch, 1 white into the next stitch, 2 white into each of the next 2 stitches, 1 white into the next stitch, 2 white into the next stitch, and then 1 white into the next stitch.

Tapestry crochet 8 white and then 8 gray stitches. Repeat this sequence 13 more times.

Crochet 1 white stitch into the next stitch, 2 white into the next stitch, 1 white into the next stitch, then 2 white into the last stitch of this round. 472 total stitches.

**Round 7:** Crochet 1 white stitch into the first stitch, 2 white into the next stitch, 1 white into each of the next 2 stitches, 2 white into the next stitch, then 1 white into the next stitch.

Tapestry crochet 2 white, 4 gray, 2 white, 2 gray, 4 white, and then 2 gray stitches. Repeat this sequence 13 more times.

After the 14th motif has been completed, crochet 1 white stitch into the next stitch, 2 white into the next stitch, 1 white into each of the next 2 stitches, 2 white into the next stitch, 1 white into each of the next 2 stitches, 2 white into the next stitch, 1 white into each of the next 2 stitches, 2 white into the next stitch, then 1 white into the next stitch.

Tapestry crochet 2 white, 4 gray, 2 white, 2 gray, 4 white, and then 2 gray stitches. Repeat this sequence 13 more times.

Crochet 1 white stitch into the next stitch, 2 white into the next stitch, 1 white into each of the next 2 stitches, 2 white into the next stitch, then 1 white into the last stitch of this round. 480 total stitches.

**Round 8:** Crochet 2 white into the first stitch, 1 white into each of the next 6 stitches, then 2 white into the next stitch.

Tapestry crochet 2 white, 4 gray, 2 white, 2 gray, 4 white, and then 2 gray stitches. Repeat this sequence 13 more times.

After the 14th motif has been completed, crochet 2 white into the next stitch, 1 white into each of the next 6 stitches, then 2 white into each of the next 2 stitches, 1 white into each of the next 6 stitches, then 2 white into the next stitch.

Tapestry crochet 2 white, 4 gray, 2 white, 2 gray, 4 white, and then 2 gray stitches. Repeat this sequence 13 more times.

Crochet 2 white into the next stitch, 1 white into each of the next 6 stitches, then 2 white into the last stitch of this round. 488 total stitches.

**Round 9:** Crochet 1 white into each of the first 4 stitches, 2 white into the next stitch, 1 white into each of the next 2 stitches, 2 white into the next stitch, then 1 white into each of the next 2 stitches.

Tapestry crochet 2 white, 4 gray, 2 white, 2 gray, 4 white, and then 2 gray stitches. Repeat this sequence 13 more times.

After the 14th motif has been completed, crochet 1 white into each of the next 2 stitches, 2 white into the next stitch, 1 white into each of the next 2 stitches, 2 white into the next stitch, 1 white into each of the next 8 stitches, 2 white into the next stitch, 1 white into each of the next 2 stitches, 2 white into the next stitch, then 1 white into each of the next 2 stitches.

Tapestry crochet 2 white, 4 gray, 2 white, 2 gray, 4 white, and then 2 gray stitches. Repeat this sequence 13 more times.

Crochet 1 white into each of the next 2 stitches, 2 white into the next stitch, 1 white into each of the next 2 stitches, 2 white into the next stitch, then 1 white into each of the last 4 stitches of this round. 496 total stitches.

**Round 10:** Crochet 1 white into the first stitch, 2 white into the next stitch, 1 white into each of the next 5 stitches, 2 white into the next stitch, then 1 white into each of the next 4 stitches.

Tapestry crochet 8 white and then 8 gray stitches. Repeat this sequence 13 more times.

After the 14th motif has been completed, crochet 1 white into each of the next 4 stitches, 2 white into the next stitch, 1 white into each of the next 5 stitches, 2 white into the next stitch, 1 white into each of the next 2 stitches, 2 white into the next stitch, 1 white into each of the next 5 stitches, 2 white into the next stitch, then 1 white into each of the next 4 stitches.

Tapestry crochet 8 white and then 8 gray stitches. Repeat this sequence 13 more times.

Crochet 1 white into each of the next 4 stitches, 2 white into the next stitch, 1 white into each of the next 5 stitches, 2 white into the next stitch, then 1 white into the last stitch of this round. 504 total stitches.

**Round 11:** Crochet 1 white into each of the first 5 stitches, 2 white into the next stitch, 1 white into each of the next 6 stitches, 2 white into the next stitch, then 1 white into the next stitch.

Tapestry crochet 8 white and then 8 gray stitches. Repeat this sequence 13 more times.

After the 14th motif has been completed, crochet 1 white into the next stitch, 2 white into the next stitch, 1 white into each of the next 6 stitches, 2 white into the next stitch, 1 white into each of the next 10 stitches, 2 white into the next stitch, 1 white into each of the next 6 stitches, 2 white into the next stitch, then 1 white into the next stitch.

Tapestry crochet 8 white and then 8 gray stitches. Repeat this sequence 13 more times.

Crochet 1 white into the next stitch, 2 white into the next stitch, 1 white into each of the next 6 stitches, 2 white into the next stitch, then 1 white into the each of the last 5 stitches of this round. 512 total stitches.

**Round 12:** Crochet 1 white into each of the first 3 stitches, 2 white into the next stitch, 1 white into each of the next 6 stitches, 2 white into the next stitch, then 1 white into each of the next 5 stitches.

Tapestry crochet 8 gray and then 8 white stitches. Repeat this sequence 13 more times.

After the 14th motif has been completed, crochet 1 white into each of the next 5 stitches, 2 white into the next stitch, 1 white into each of the next 6 stitches, 2 white into the next stitch, 1 white into each of the next 6 stitches, 2 white into the next stitch, 1 white into each of the next 6 stitches, 2 white into the next stitch, then 1 white into each of the next 5 stitches.

Tapestry crochet 8 gray and then 8 white stitches. Repeat this sequence 13 more times.

Crochet 1 white into each of the next 5 stitches, 2 white into the next stitch, 1 white into each of the next 6 stitches, 2 white into the next stitch, then 1 white into the each of the last 3 stitches of this round. 520 total stitches.

**Round 13:** Crochet 2 white into the first stitch, 1 white into each of the next 7 stitches, 2 white into the next stitch, then 1 white into each of the next 9 stitches.

Tapestry crochet 8 gray and then 8 white stitches. Repeat this sequence 13 more times.

After the 14th motif has been completed, crochet 1 white into each of the next 9 stitches, 2 white into the next stitch, 1 white into each of the next 7 stitches, 2 white into each of the next 2 stitches, 1 white into each of the next 7 stitches, 2 white into the next stitch, then 1 white into each of the next 9 stitches.

Tapestry crochet 8 gray and then 8 white stitches. Repeat this sequence 13 more times.

Crochet 1 white into each of the next 9 stitches, 2 white into the next stitch, 1 white into each of the next 7 stitches, 2 white into the last stitch of this round. 528 total stitches.

**Round 14:** Crochet 1 white into each of the first 5 stitches, 2 white into the next stitch, 1 white into each of the next 8 stitches, 2 white into the next stitch, then 1 white into each of the next 5 stitches.

Tapestry crochet 2 gray, 4 white, 2 gray, 2 white, 4 gray, and then 2 white stitches. Repeat this sequence 13 more times.

After the 14th motif has been completed, crochet 1 white into each of the next 5 stitches, 2 white into the next stitch, 1 white into each of the next 8 stitches, 2 white into the next stitch, 1 white into each of the next 10 stitches, 2 white into the next stitch, 1 white into each of the next 8 stitches, 2 white into the next stitch, and then 1 white into each of the next 5 stitches.

Tapestry crochet 2 gray, 4 white, 2 gray, 2 white, 4 gray, and then 2 white stitches. Repeat this sequence 13 more times.

Crochet 1 white into each of the next 5 stitches, 2 white into the next stitch, 1 white into each of the next 8 stitches, 2 white into the next stitch, then 1 white into each of the last 5 stitches of this round. 536 total stitches.

**Round 15:** Crochet 1 white into each of the first 3 stitches, 2 white into the next stitch, 1 white into each of the next 14 stitches, 2 white into the next stitch, then 1 white into each of the next 3 stitches.

Tapestry crochet 2 gray, 4 white, 2 gray, 2 white, 4 gray, and then 2 white stitches. Repeat this sequence 13 more times.

After the 14th motif has been completed, crochet 1 white into each of the next 3 stitches, 2 white into the next stitch, 1 white into each of the next 14 stitches, 2 white into the next stitch, 1 white into each of the next 6 stitches, 2 white into the next stitch, 1 white into each of the next 14 stitches, 2 white into the next stitch, and then 1 white into each of the next 3 stitches.

Tapestry crochet 2 gray, 4 white, 2 gray, 2 white, 4 gray, and then 2 white stitches. Repeat this sequence 13 more times.

Crochet 1 white into each of the next 3 stitches, 2 white into the next stitch, 1 white into each of the next 14 stitches, 2 white into the next stitch, then 1 white into each of the last 3 stitches of this round. 544 total stitches.

**Round 16:** Crochet 1 white into each of the first 9 stitches, 2 white into the next stitch, 1 white into each of the next 4 stitches, 2 white into the next stitch, then 1 white into each of the next 9 stitches.

Tapestry crochet 2 gray, 4 white, 2 gray, 2 white, 4 gray, and then 2 white stitches. Repeat this sequence 13 more times.

After the 14th motif has been completed, crochet 1 white into each of the next 9 stitches, 2 white into the next stitch, 1 white into each of the next 4 stitches, 2 white into the next stitch, 1 white into each of the next 18 stitches, 2 white into the next stitch, 1 white into each of the next 4 stitches, 2 white into the next stitch, and then 1 white into each of the next 9 stitches.

Tapestry crochet 2 gray, 4 white, 2 gray, 2 white, 4 gray, and then 2 white stitches. Repeat this sequence 13 more times.

Crochet 1 white into each of the next 9 stitches, 2 white into the next stitch, 1 white into each of the next 4 stitches, 2 white into the next stitch, then 1 white into each of the last 9 stitches of this round. 552 total stitches.

**Round 17:** Crochet 1 white into each of the first 7 stitches, 2 white into the next stitch, 1 white into each of the next 10 stitches, 2 white into the next stitch, then 1 white into each of the next 7 stitches.

Tapestry crochet 8 gray and then 8 white stitches. Repeat this sequence 13 more times.

After the 14th motif has been completed, crochet 1 white into each of the next 7 stitches, 2 white into the next stitch, 1 white into each of the next 10 stitches, 2 white into the next stitch, 1 white into each of the next 14 stitches, 2 white into the next stitch, 1 white into each of the next 10 stitches, 2 white into the next stitch, and then 1 white into each of the next 7 stitches.

Tapestry crochet 8 gray and then 8 white stitches. Repeat this sequence 13 more times.

Crochet 1 white into each of the next 7 stitches, 2 white into the next stitch, 1 white into each of the next 10 stitches, 2 white into the next stitch, then 1 white into each of the last 7 stitches of this round. 560 total stitches.

**Round 18:** Crochet 1 white into each of the first 4 stitches, 2 white into the next stitch, 1 white into each of the next 18 stitches, 2 white into the next stitch, then 1 white into each of the next 4 stitches.

Tapestry crochet 8 gray and then 8 white stitches. Repeat this sequence 13 more times.

After the 14th motif has been completed, crochet 1 white into each of the next 4 stitches, 2 white into the next stitch, 1 white into each of the next 18 stitches, 2 white into the next stitch, 1 white into each of the next 8 stitches, 2 white into the next stitch, 1 white into each of the next 18 stitches, 2 white into the next stitch, and then 1 white into each of the next 4 stitches.

Tapestry crochet 8 gray and then 8 white stitches. Repeat this sequence 13 more times.

Crochet 1 white into each of the next 4 stitches, 2 white into the next stitch, 1 white into each of the next 18 stitches, 2 white into the next stitch, then 1 white into each of the last 4 stitches of this round. 568 total stitches.

**Round 19:** In this round you will begin the motif again, but you will begin it 16 stitches earlier and finish it 16 stitches later, so you will have 16 motifs instead of 14 motifs per side. Crochet 1 white into each of the first 3 stitches, 2 white into the next stitch, 1 white into each of the next 6 stitches, 2 white into the next stitch, then 1 white into each of the next 3 stitches.

Tapestry crochet 8 white and then 8 gray stitches. Repeat this sequence 15 more times.

After the 16th motif has been completed, crochet 1 white into each of the next 3 stitches, 2 white into the next stitch, 1 white into each of the next 6 stitches, 2 white into the next stitch, 1 white into each of the next 6 stitches, 2 white into the next stitch, 1 white into each of the next 6 stitches, 2 white into the next stitch, and then 1 white into each of the next 3 stitches.

Tapestry crochet 8 white and then 8 gray stitches. Repeat this sequence 15 more times.

Crochet 1 white into each of the next 3 stitches, 2 white into the next stitch, 1 white into each of the next 6 stitches, 2 white into the next stitch, then 1 white into each of the last 3 stitches of this round. 576 total stitches.

**Round 20:** Crochet 1 white into the first stitch, 2 white into the next stitch, 1 white into each of the next 12 stitches, 2 white into the next stitch, then 1 white into the next stitch.

Tapestry crochet 8 white and then 8 gray stitches. Repeat this sequence 15 more times.

After the 16th motif has been completed, crochet 1 white into the next stitch, 2 white into the next stitch, 1 white into each of the next 12 stitches, 2 white into the next stitch, 1 white into each of the next 2 stitches, 2 white into the next stitch, 1 white into each of the next 12 stitches, 2 white into the next stitch, and then 1 white into the next stitch.

Tapestry crochet 8 white and then 8 gray stitches. Repeat this sequence 15 more times.

Crochet 1 white into the next stitch, 2 white into the next stitch, 1 white into each of the next 12 stitches, 2 white into the next stitch, then 1 white into the last stitch of this round. 584 total stitches.

**Round 21:** Crochet 1 white into each of the first 5 stitches, 2 white into the next stitch, 1 white into each of the next 6 stitches, 2 white into the next stitch, then 1 white into each of the next 5 stitches.

Tapestry crochet 2 white, 4 gray, 2 white, 2 gray, 4 white, and then 2 gray stitches. Repeat this sequence 15 more times.

After the 16th motif has been completed, crochet 1 white into each of the next 5 stitches, 2 white into the next stitch, 1 white into each of the next 6 stitches, 2 white into the next stitch, 1 white into each of the next 10 stitches, 2 white into the next stitch, 1 white into each of the next 6 stitches, 2 white into the next stitch, and then 1 white into each of the next 5 stitches.

Tapestry crochet 2 white, 4 gray, 2 white, 2 gray, 4 white, and then 2 gray stitches. Repeat this sequence 15 more times.

Crochet 1 white into each of the next 5 stitches, 2 white into the next stitch, 1 white into each of the next 6 stitches, 2 white into the next stitch, then 1 white into each of the last 5 stitches of this round. 592 total stitches.

**Round 22:** Crochet 1 white into each of the first 3 stitches, 2 white into the next stitch, 1 white into each of the next 8 stitches, 2 white into the next stitch, then 1 white into each of the next 7 stitches.

Tapestry crochet 2 white, 4 gray, 2 white, 2 gray, 4 white, and then 2 gray stitches. Repeat this sequence 15 more times.

After the 16th motif has been completed, crochet 1 white into each of the next 7 stitches, 2 white into the next stitch, 1 white into each of the next 8 stitches, 2 white into the next stitch, 1 white into each of the next 6 stitches, 2 white into the next stitch, 1 white into each of the next 8 stitches, 2 white into the next stitch, and then 1 white into each of the next 7 stitches.

Tapestry crochet 2 white, 4 gray, 2 white, 2 gray, 4 white, and then 2 gray stitches. Repeat this sequence 15 more times.

Crochet 1 white into each of the next 7 stitches, 2 white into the next stitch, 1 white into each of the next 8 stitches, 2 white into the next stitch, then 1 white into each of the last 3 stitches of this round. 600 total stitches.

**Round 23:** Crochet 1 white into each of the first 6 stitches, 2 white into the next stitch, 1 white into each of the next 8 stitches, 2 white into the next stitch, then 1 white into each of the next 6 stitches.

Tapestry crochet 2 white, 4 gray, 2 white, 2 gray, 4 white, and then 2 gray stitches. Repeat this sequence 15 more times.

After the 16th motif has been completed, crochet 1 white into each of the next 6 stitches, 2 white into the next stitch, 1 white into each of the next 8 stitches, 2 white into the next stitch, 1 white into each of the next 12 stitches, 2 white into the next stitch, 1 white into each of the next 8 stitches, 2 white into the next stitch, and then 1 white into each of the next 6 stitches.

Tapestry crochet 2 white, 4 gray, 2 white, 2 gray, 4 white, and then 2 gray stitches. Repeat this sequence 15 more times.

Crochet 1 white into each of the next 6 stitches, 2 white into the next stitch, 1 white into each of the next 8 stitches, 2 white into the next stitch, then 1 white into each of the last 6 stitches of this round. 608 total stitches.

**Round 24:** Crochet 1 white into each of the first 4 stitches, 2 white into the next stitch, 1 white into each of the next 14 stitches, 2 white into the next stitch, then 1 white into each of the next 4 stitches.

Tapestry crochet 8 white and then 8 gray stitches. Repeat this sequence 15 more times.

After the 16th motif has been completed, crochet 1 white into each of the next 4 stitches, 2 white into the next stitch, 1 white into each of the next 14 stitches, 2 white into the next stitch, 1 white into each of the next 8 stitches, 2 white into the next stitch, 1 white into each of the next 14 stitches, 2 white into the next stitch, and then 1 white into each of the next 4 stitches.

Tapestry crochet 8 white and then 8 gray stitches. Repeat this sequence 15 more times.

Crochet 1 white into each of the next 4 stitches, 2 white into the next stitch, 1 white into each of the next 14 stitches, 2 white into the next stitch, then 1 white into each of the last 4 stitches of this round. 616 total stitches.

**Round 25:** Crochet 1 white into each of the first 8 stitches, 2 white into the next stitch, 1 white into each of the next 8 stitches, 2 white into the next stitch, then 1 white into each of the next 8 stitches.

Tapestry crochet 8 white and then 8 gray stitches. Repeat this sequence 15 more times.

After the 16th motif has been completed, crochet 1 white into each of the next 8 stitches, 2 white into the next stitch, 1 white into each of the next 8 stitches, 2 white into the next stitch, 1 white into each of the next 16 stitches, 2 white into the next stitch, 1 white into each of the next 8 stitches, 2 white into the next stitch, and then 1 white into each of the next 8 stitches.

Tapestry crochet 8 white and then 8 gray stitches. Repeat this sequence 15 more times.

Crochet 1 white into each of the next 8 stitches, 2 white into the next stitch, 1 white into each of the next 8 stitches, 2 white into the next stitch, then 1 white into each of the last 8 stitches of this round. 624 total stitches.

**Round 26:** Crochet 1 white into each of the first 11 stitches, 2 white into the next stitch, 1 white into each of the next 4 stitches, 2 white into the next stitch, then 1 white into each of the next 11 stitches.

Tapestry crochet 8 gray and then 8 white stitches. Repeat this sequence 15 more times.

After the 16th motif has been completed, crochet 1 white into each of the next 11 stitches, 2 white into the next stitch, 1 white into each of the next 4 stitches, 2 white into the next stitch, 1 white into each of the next 22 stitches, 2 white into the next stitch, 1 white into each of the next 4 stitches, 2 white into the next stitch, and then 1 white into each of the next 11 stitches.

Tapestry crochet 8 gray and then 8 white stitches. Repeat this sequence 15 more times.

Crochet 1 white into each of the next 11 stitches, 2 white into the next stitch, 1 white into each of the next 4 stitches, 2 white into the next stitch, then 1 white into each of the last 11 stitches of this round. 632 total stitches.

**Round 27:** Crochet 1 white into each of the first 7 stitches, 2 white into the next stitch, 1 white into each of the next 14 stitches, 2 white into the next stitch, then 1 white into each of the next 7 stitches.

Tapestry crochet 8 gray and then 8 white stitches. Repeat this sequence 15 more times.

After the 16th motif has been completed, crochet 1 white into each of the next 7 stitches, 2 white into the next stitch, 1 white into each of the next 14 stitches, 2 white into the next stitch, 1 white into each of the next 14 stitches, 2 white into the next stitch, 1 white into each of the next 14 stitches, 2 white into the next stitch, and then 1 white into each of the next 7 stitches.

Tapestry crochet 8 gray and then 8 white stitches. Repeat this sequence 15 more times.

Crochet 1 white into each of the next 7 stitches, 2 white into the next stitch, 1 white into each of the next 14 stitches, 2 white into the next stitch, then 1 white into each of the last 7 stitches of this round. 640 total stitches.

**Round 28:** Crochet 1 white into each of the first 12 stitches, 2 white into the next stitch, 1 white into each of the next 6 stitches, 2 white into the next stitch, then 1 white into each of the next 12 stitches.

Tapestry crochet 2 gray, 4 white, 2 gray, 2 white, 4 gray, and then 2 white stitches. Repeat this sequence 15 more times.

After the 16th motif has been completed, crochet 1 white into each of the next 12 stitches, 2 white into the next stitch, 1 white into each of the next 6 stitches, 2 white into the next stitch, 1 white into each of the next 24 stitches, 2 white into the next stitch, 1 white into each of the next 6 stitches, 2 white into the next stitch, and then 1 white into each of the next 12 stitches.

Tapestry crochet 2 gray, 4 white, 2 gray, 2 white, 4 gray, and then 2 white stitches. Repeat this sequence 15 more times.

Crochet 1 white into each of the next 12 stitches, 2 white into the next stitch, 1 white into each of the next 6 stitches, 2 white into the next stitch, then 1 white into each of the last 12 stitches of this round. 648 total stitches.

**Round 29:** Crochet 1 white into each of the first 5 stitches, 2 white into the next stitch, 1 white into each of the next 22 stitches, 2 white into the next stitch, then 1 white into each of the next 5 stitches.

Tapestry crochet 2 gray, 4 white, 2 gray, 2 white, 4 gray, and then 2 white stitches. Repeat this sequence 15 more times.

After the 16th motif has been completed, crochet 1 white into each of the next 5 stitches, 2 white into the next stitch, 1 white into each of the next 22 stitches, 2 white into the next stitch, 1 white into each of the next 10 stitches, 2 white into the next stitch, 1 white into each of the next 22 stitches, 2 white into the next stitch, and then 1 white into each of the next 5 stitches.

Tapestry crochet 2 gray, 4 white, 2 gray, 2 white, 4 gray, and then 2 white stitches. Repeat this sequence 15 more times.

Crochet 1 white into each of the next 5 stitches, 2 white into the next stitch, 1 white into each of the next 22 stitches, 2 white into the next stitch, then 1 white into each of the last 5 stitches of this round. 656 total stitches.

**Round 30:** Crochet 1 white into each of the first 10 stitches, 2 white into the next stitch, 1 white into each of the next 14 stitches, 2 white into the next stitch, then 1 white into each of the next 10 stitches.

Tapestry crochet 2 gray, 4 white, 2 gray, 2 white, 4 gray, and then 2 white stitches. Repeat this sequence 15 more times.

After the 16th motif has been completed, crochet 1 white into each of the next 10 stitches, 2 white into the next stitch, 1 white into each of the next 14 stitches, 2 white into the next stitch, 1 white into each of the next 20 stitches, 2 white into the next stitch, 1 white into each of the next 14 stitches, 2 white into the next stitch, and then 1 white into each of the next 10 stitches.

Tapestry crochet 2 gray, 4 white, 2 gray, 2 white, 4 gray, and then 2 white stitches. Repeat this sequence 15 more times.

Crochet 1 white into each of the next 10 stitches, 2 white into the next stitch, 1 white into each of the next 14 stitches, 2 white into the next stitch, then 1 white into each of the last 10 stitches of this round. 664 total stitches.

**Round 31:** Crochet 1 white into each of the first 16 stitches, 2 white into the next stitch, 1 white into each of the next 4 stitches, 2 white into the next stitch, then 1 white into each of the next 16 stitches.

Tapestry crochet 8 gray and then 8 white stitches. Repeat this sequence 15 more times.

After the 16th motif has been completed, crochet 1 white into each of the next 16 stitches, 2 white into the next stitch, 1 white into each of the next 4 stitches, 2 white into the next stitch, 1 white into each of the next 32 stitches, 2 white into the next stitch, 1 white into each of the next 4 stitches, 2 white into the next stitch, and then 1 white into each of the next 16 stitches.

Tapestry crochet 8 gray and then 8 white stitches. Repeat this sequence 15 more times.

Crochet 1 white into each of the next 16 stitches, 2 white into the next stitch, 1 white into each of the next 4 stitches, 2 white into the next stitch, then 1 white into each of the last 16 stitches of this round. 672 total stitches.

**Round 32:**Crochet 1 white into each of the first 8 stitches, 2 white into the next stitch, 1 white into each of the next 22 stitches, 2 white into the next stitch, then 1 white into each of the next 8 stitches.

Tapestry crochet 8 gray and then 8 white stitches. Repeat this sequence 15 more times.

After the 16th motif has been completed, crochet 1 white into each of the next 8 stitches, 2 white into the next stitch, 1 white into each of the next 22 stitches, 2 white into the next stitch, 1 white into each of the next 16 stitches, 2 white into the next stitch, 1 white into each of the next 22 stitches, 2 white into the next stitch, and then 1 white into each of the next 8 stitches.

Tapestry crochet 8 gray and then 8 white stitches. Repeat this sequence 15 more times.

Crochet 1 white into each of the next 8 stitches, 2 white into the next stitch, 1 white into each of the next 22 stitches, 2 white into the next stitch, then 1 white into each of the last 8 stitches of this round. 680 total stitches.

**Round 33:** In this round you will begin the motif again, but you will begin it 16 stitches earlier and finish it 16 stitches later, so you will have 18 motifs instead of 16 motifs per side. Crochet 1 white into each of the first 4 stitches, 2 white into the next stitch, 1 white into each of the next 16 stitches, 2 white into the next stitch, then 1 white into each of the next 4 stitches.

Tapestry crochet 8 white and then 8 gray stitches. Repeat this sequence 17 more times.

After the 18th motif has been completed, crochet 1 white into each of the next 4 stitches, 2 white into the next stitch, 1 white into each of the next 16 stitches, 2 white into the next stitch, 1 white into each of the next 8 stitches, 2 white into the next stitch, 1 white into each of the next 16 stitches, 2 white into the next stitch, and then 1 white into each of the next 4 stitches.

Tapestry crochet 8 white and then 8 gray stitches. Repeat this sequence 17 more times.

Crochet 1 white into each of the next 4 stitches, 2 white into the next stitch, 1 white into each of the next 16 stitches, 2 white into the next stitch, then 1 white into each of the last 4 stitches of this round. 688 total stitches.

**Round 34:** Crochet 1 white into each of the first 8 stitches, 2 white into the next stitch, 1 white into each of the next 10 stitches, 2 white into the next stitch, then 1 white into each of the next 8 stitches.

Tapestry crochet 8 white and then 8 gray stitches. Repeat this sequence 17 more times.

After the 18th motif has been completed, crochet 1 white into each of the next 8 stitches, 2 white into the next stitch, 1 white into each of the next 10 stitches, 2 white into the next stitch, 1 white into each of the next 16 stitches, 2 white into the next stitch, 1 white into each of the next 10 stitches, 2 white into the next stitch, and then 1 white into each of the next 8 stitches.

Tapestry crochet 8 white and then 8 gray stitches. Repeat this sequence 17 more times.

Crochet 1 white into each of the next 8 stitches, 2 white into the next stitch, 1 white into each of the next 10 stitches, 2 white into the next stitch, then 1 white into each of the last 8 stitches of this round. 696 total stitches.

**Round 35:** Crochet 1 white into each of the first 5 stitches, 2 white into the next stitch, 1 white into each of the next 18 stitches, 2 white into the next stitch, then 1 white into each of the next 5 stitches.

Tapestry crochet 2 white, 4 gray, 2 white, 2 gray, 4 white, and then 2 gray stitches. Repeat this sequence 17 more times.

After the 18th motif has been completed, crochet 1 white into each of the next 5 stitches, 2 white into the next stitch, 1 white into each of the next 18 stitches, 2 white into the next stitch, 1 white into each of the next 10 stitches, 2 white into the next stitch, 1 white into each of the next 18 stitches, 2 white into the next stitch, and then 1 white into each of the next 5 stitches.

Tapestry crochet 2 white, 4 gray, 2 white, 2 gray, 4 white, and then 2 gray stitches. Repeat this sequence 17 more times.

Crochet 1 white into each of the next 5 stitches, 2 white into the next stitch, 1 white into each of the next 18 stitches, 2 white into the next stitch, then 1 white into each of the last 5 stitches of this round. 704 total stitches.

**Round 36:** Crochet 1 white into each of the first 10 stitches, 2 white into the next stitch, 1 white into each of the next 10 stitches, 2 white into the next stitch, then 1 white into each of the next 10 stitches.

Tapestry crochet 2 white, 4 gray, 2 white, 2 gray, 4 white, and then 2 gray stitches. Repeat this sequence 17 more times.

After the 18th motif has been completed, crochet 1 white into each of the next 10 stitches, 2 white into the next stitch, 1 white into each of the next 10 stitches, 2 white into the next stitch, 1 white into each of the next 20 stitches, 2 white into the next stitch, 1 white into each of the next 10 stitches, 2 white into the next stitch, and then 1 white into each of the next 10 stitches.

Tapestry crochet 2 white, 4 gray, 2 white, 2 gray, 4 white, and then 2 gray stitches. Repeat this sequence 17 more times.

Crochet 1 white into each of the next 10 stitches, 2 white into the next stitch, 1 white into each of the next 10 stitches, 2 white into the next stitch, then 1 white into each of the last 10 stitches of this round. 712 total stitches.

**Round 37:** Crochet 1 white into each of the first 3 stitches, 2 white into the next stitch, 1 white into each of the next 26 stitches, 2 white into the next stitch, then 1 white into each of the next 3 stitches.

Tapestry crochet 2 white, 4 gray, 2 white, 2 gray, 4 white, and then 2 gray stitches. Repeat this sequence 17 more times.

After the 18th motif has been completed, crochet 1 white into each of the next 3 stitches, 2 white into the next stitch, 1 white into each of the next 26 stitches, 2 white into the next stitch, 1 white into each of the next 6 stitches, 2 white into the next stitch, 1 white into each of the next 26 stitches, 2 white into the next stitch, and then 1 white into each of the next 3 stitches.

Tapestry crochet 2 white, 4 gray, 2 white, 2 gray, 4 white, and then 2 gray stitches. Repeat this sequence 17 more times.

Crochet 1 white into each of the next 3 stitches, 2 white into the next stitch, 1 white into each of the next 26 stitches, 2 white into the next stitch, then 1 white into each of the last 3 stitches of this round. 720 total stitches.

**Round 38:** Crochet 1 white into each of the first 9 stitches, 2 white into the next stitch, 1 white into each of the next 16 stitches, 2 white into the next stitch, then 1 white into each of the next 9 stitches.

Tapestry crochet 8 white and then 8 gray stitches. Repeat this sequence 17 more times.

After the 18th motif has been completed, crochet 1 white into each of the next 9 stitches, 2 white into the next stitch, 1 white into each of the next 16 stitches, 2 white into the next stitch, 1 white into each of the next 18 stitches, 2 white into the next stitch, 1 white into each of the next 16 stitches, 2 white into the next stitch, and then 1 white into each of the next 9 stitches.

Tapestry crochet 8 white and then 8 gray stitches. Repeat this sequence 17 more times.

Crochet 1 white into each of the next 9 stitches, 2 white into the next stitch, 1 white into each of the next 16 stitches, 2 white into the next stitch, then 1 white into each of the last 9 stitches of this round. 728 total stitches.

**Round 39:** Crochet 1 white into each of the first 15 stitches, 2 white into the next stitch, 1 white into each of the next 6 stitches, 2 white into the next stitch, then 1 white into each of the next 15 stitches.

Tapestry crochet 8 white and then 8 gray stitches. Repeat this sequence 17 more times.

After the 18th motif has been completed, crochet 1 white into each of the next 15 stitches, 2 white into the next stitch, 1 white into each of the next 6 stitches, 2 white into the next stitch, 1 white into each of the next 30 stitches, 2 white into the next stitch, 1 white into each of the next 6 stitches, 2 white into the next stitch, and then 1 white into each of the next 15 stitches.

Tapestry crochet 8 white and then 8 gray stitches. Repeat this sequence 17 more times.

Crochet 1 white into each of the next 15 stitches, 2 white into the next stitch, 1 white into each of the next 6 stitches, 2 white into the next stitch, then 1 white into each of the last 15 stitches of this round. 736 total stitches.

**Round 40:** Crochet 1 white into each of the first 6 stitches, 2 white into the next stitch, 1 white into each of the next 26 stitches, 2 white into the next stitch, then 1 white into each of the next 6 stitches.

Tapestry crochet 8 gray and then 8 white stitches. Repeat this sequence 17 more times.

After the 18th motif has been completed, crochet 1 white into each of the next 6 stitches, 2 white into the next stitch, 1 white into each of the next 26 stitches, 2 white into the next stitch, 1 white into each of the next 12 stitches, 2 white into the next stitch, 1 white into each of the next 26 stitches, 2 white into the next stitch, and then 1 white into each of the next 6 stitches.

Tapestry crochet 8 gray and then 8 white stitches. Repeat this sequence 17 more times.

Crochet 1 white into each of the next 6 stitches, 2 white into the next stitch, 1 white into each of the next 26 stitches, 2 white into the next stitch, then 1 white into each of the last 6 stitches of this round. 744 total stitches.

**Round 41:** Crochet 1 white into each of the first 13 stitches, 2 white into the next stitch, 1 white into each of the next 14 stitches, 2 white into the next stitch, then 1 white into each of the next 13 stitches.

Tapestry crochet 8 gray and then 8 white stitches. Repeat this sequence 17 more times.

After the 18th motif has been completed, crochet 1 white into each of the next 13 stitches, 2 white into the next stitch, 1 white into each of the next 14 stitches, 2 white into the next stitch, 1 white into each of the next 26 stitches, 2 white into the next stitch, 1 white into each of the next 14 stitches, 2 white into the next stitch, and then 1 white into each of the next 13 stitches.

Tapestry crochet 8 gray and then 8 white stitches. Repeat this sequence 17 more times.

Crochet 1 white into each of the next 13 stitches, 2 white into the next stitch, 1 white into each of the next 14 stitches, 2 white into the next stitch, then 1 white into each of the last 13 stitches of this round. 752 total stitches.

**Round 42:** Crochet 1 white into each of the first 19 stitches, 2 white into the next stitch, 1 white into each of the next 4 stitches, 2 white into the next stitch, then 1 white into each of the next 19 stitches.

Tapestry crochet 2 gray, 4 white, 2 gray, 2 white, 4 gray, and then 2 white stitches. Repeat this sequence 17 more times.

After the 18th motif has been completed, crochet 1 white into each of the next 19 stitches, 2 white into the next stitch, 1 white into each of the next 4 stitches, 2 white into the next stitch, 1 white into each of the next 38 stitches, 2 white into the next stitch, 1 white into each of the next 4 stitches, 2 white into the next stitch, and then 1 white into each of the next 19 stitches.

Tapestry crochet 2 gray, 4 white, 2 gray, 2 white, 4 gray, and then 2 white stitches. Repeat this sequence 17 more times.

Crochet 1 white into each of the next 19 stitches, 2 white into the next stitch, 1 white into each of the next 4 stitches, 2 white into the next stitch, then 1 white into each of the last 19 stitches of this round. 760 total stitches.

**Round 43:** Crochet 1 white into each of the first 4 stitches, 2 white into the next stitch, 1 white into each of the next 36 stitches, 2 white into the next stitch, then 1 white into each of the next 4 stitches.

Tapestry crochet 2 gray, 4 white, 2 gray, 2 white, 4 gray, and then 2 white stitches. Repeat this sequence 17 more times.

After the 18th motif has been completed, crochet 1 white into each of the next 4 stitches, 2 white into the next stitch, 1 white into each of the next 36 stitches, 2 white into the next stitch, 1 white into each of the next 8 stitches, 2 white into the next stitch, 1 white into each of the next 36 stitches, 2 white into the next stitch, and then 1 white into each of the next 4 stitches.

Tapestry crochet 2 gray, 4 white, 2 gray, 2 white, 4 gray, and then 2 white stitches. Repeat this sequence 17 more times.

Crochet 1 white into each of the next 4 stitches, 2 white into the next stitch, 1 white into each of the next 36 stitches, 2 white into the next stitch, then 1 white into each of the last 4 stitches of this round. 768 total stitches.

**Round 44:** Crochet 1 white into each of the first 12 stitches, 2 white into the next stitch, 1 white into each of the next 22 stitches, 2 white into the next stitch, then 1 white into each of the next 12 stitches.

Tapestry crochet 2 gray, 4 white, 2 gray, 2 white, 4 gray, and then 2 white stitches. Repeat this sequence 17 more times.

After the 18th motif has been completed, crochet 1 white into each of the next 12 stitches, 2 white into the next stitch, 1 white into each of the next 22 stitches, 2 white into the next stitch, 1 white into each of the next 24 stitches, 2 white into the next stitch, 1 white into each of the next 22 stitches, 2 white into the next stitch, and then 1 white into each of the next 12 stitches.

Tapestry crochet 2 gray, 4 white, 2 gray, 2 white, 4 gray, and then 2 white stitches. Repeat this sequence 17 more times.

Crochet 1 white into each of the next 12 stitches, 2 white into the next stitch, 1 white into each of the next 22 stitches, 2 white into the next stitch, then 1 white into each of the last 12 stitches of this round. 776 total stitches.

**Round 45:** Crochet 1 white into each of the first 20 stitches, 2 white into the next stitch, 1 white into each of the next 8 stitches, 2 white into the next stitch, then 1 white into each of the next 20 stitches.

Tapestry crochet 8 gray and then 8 white stitches. Repeat this sequence 17 more times.

After the 18th motif has been completed, crochet 1 white into each of the next 20 stitches, 2 white into the next stitch, 1 white into each of the next 8 stitches, 2 white into the next stitch, 1 white into each of the next 40 stitches, 2 white into the next stitch, 1 white into each of the next 8 stitches, 2 white into the next stitch, and then 1 white into each of the next 20 stitches.

Tapestry crochet 8 gray and then 8 white stitches. Repeat this sequence 17 more times.

Crochet 1 white into each of the next 20 stitches, 2 white into the next stitch, 1 white into each of the next 8 stitches, 2 white into the next stitch, then 1 white into each of the last 20 stitches of this round. 784 total stitches.

**Round 46:** Crochet 1 white into each of the first 10 stitches, 2 white into the next stitch, 1 white into each of the next 30 stitches, 2 white into the next stitch, then 1 white into each of the next 10 stitches.

Tapestry crochet 8 gray and then 8 white stitches. Repeat this sequence 17 more times.

After the 18th motif has been completed, crochet 1 white into each of the next 10 stitches, 2 white into the next stitch, 1 white into each of the next 30 stitches, 2 white into the next stitch, 1 white into each of the next 20 stitches, 2 white into the next stitch, 1 white into each of the next 30 stitches, 2 white into the next stitch, and then 1 white into each of the next 10 stitches.

Tapestry crochet 8 gray and then 8 white stitches. Repeat this sequence 17 more times.

Crochet 1 white into each of the next 10 stitches, 2 white into the next stitch, 1 white into each of the next 30 stitches, 2 white into the next stitch, then 1 white into each of the last 10 stitches of this round. 792 total stitches.

**Round 47:** Crochet 1 white into each of the first 5 stitches, 2 white into the next stitch, 1 white into each of the next 42 stitches, 2 white into the next stitch, 1 white into each of the next 298 stitches, 2 white into the next stitch, 1 white into each of the next 42 stitches, 2 white into the next stitch, 1 white into each of the next 10 stitches, 2 white into the next stitch, 1 white into each of the next 42 stitches, 2 white into the next stitch, and then 1 white into each of the next 298 stitches, 2 white into the next stitch, 1 white into each of the next 42 stitches, 2 white into the next stitch, then 1 white into each of the last 5 stitches of this round. 800 total stitches.

**Round 48:** Crochet 1 white into each of the first 20 stitches, 2 white into the next stitch, 1 white into each of the next 14 stitches, 2 white into the next stitch, 1 white into each of the next 328 stitches, 2 white into the next stitch, 1 white into each of the next 14 stitches, 2 white into the next stitch, 1 white into each of the next 40 stitches, 2 white into the next stitch, 1 white into each of the next 14 stitches, 2 white into the next stitch, and then 1 white into each of the next 328 stitches, 2 white into the next stitch, 1 white into each of the next 14 stitches, 2 white into the next stitch, then 1 white into each of the last 20 stitches of this round. 808 total stitches.

**Round 49:** Crochet 1 white into each of the first 8 stitches, 2 white into the next stitch, 1 white into each of the next 40 stitches, 2 white into the next stitch, 1 white into each of the next 304 stitches, 2 white into the next stitch, 1 white into each of the next 40 stitches, 2 white into the next stitch, 1 white into each of the next 16 stitches, 2 white into the next stitch, 1 white into each of the next 40 stitches, 2 white into the next stitch, and then 1 white into each of the next 304 stitches, 2 white into the next stitch, 1 white into each of the next 40 stitches, 2 white into the next stitch, then 1 white into each of the last 8 stitches of this round. 816 total stitches.

**Round 50:** Crochet 1 white into each of the first 15 stitches, 2 white into the next stitch, 1 white into each of the next 28 stitches, 2 white into the next stitch, 1 white into each of the next 318 stitches, 2 white into the next stitch, 1 white into each of the next 28 stitches, 2 white into the next stitch, 1 white into each of the next 30 stitches, 2 white into the next stitch, 1 white into each of the next 28 stitches, 2 white into the next stitch, and then 1 white into each of the next 318 stitches, 2 white into the next stitch, 1 white into each of the next 28 stitches, 2 white into the next stitch, then 1 white into each of the last 15 stitches of this round. 824 total stitches.

**Last Round (Fringe):** In order to make the heavy fringe, put the white and gray yarns together and crochet with them both at the same time (making an eight-ply yarn). Chain 50 (with both white and gray together), then crochet 2 stitches into the next stitch. Repeat this sequence 411 more times around the edge of the shawl.

**To finish:** Cut the white and gray yarns (leaving 6" tails). Yarn over, then pull the yarns all the way through the loop on the hook. Turn the shawl over and with a size one crochet hook, work in the ends by pulling them through the last row of stitches for two inches. Cut the ends flush. Block the body of the shawl (but not the fringe).

# Alpaca

Believe it or not, South American alpacas, llamas, and vicuñas are related to camels. Alpacas and llamas were domesticated in Peru around 3000 years ago, but vicuñas (which produces the finest fiber) have never been successfully domesticated. Alpaca is still an important camelid fiber for textile production and is naturally colored in 22 shades of white, brown, gray, and black. Other colors are obtained by dying the fibers. Llamas have coarse fiber, so it is used for utilitarian textiles. Depending on the individual animal though, or the location of the fiber on the animal, all three can overlap in fiber quality; coarse vicuña can equal fine alpaca or fine llama can equal coarse alpaca. Alpaca produce three grades of fiber; grade one is from the back and sides, grade two is from the neck, and grade three is from the rump and legs.

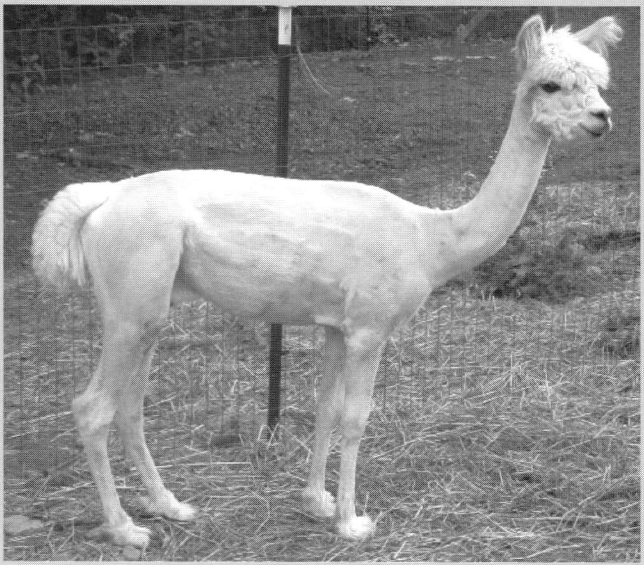

**Before and after shearing.**

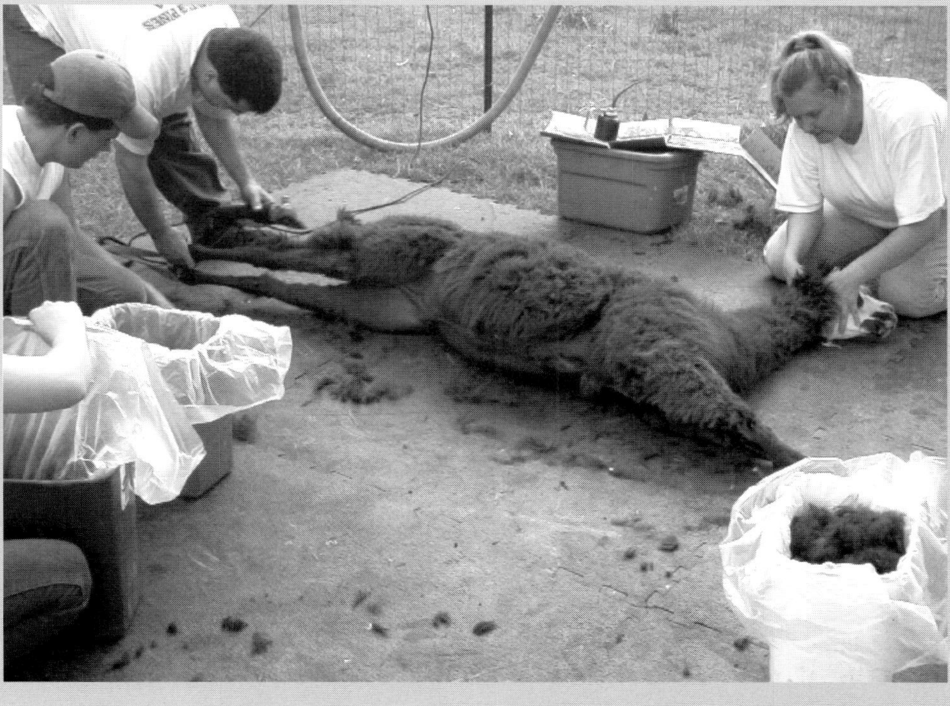

**To secure the alpaca for shearing, the feet are tied and stretched apart and the head is held down. The dust is blown off with an electric blower, then electric shears are used to remove the fiber, beginning with with the legs. Each grade of fiber is placed into a separate bag.**

# An Oval Purse That's "For the Birds!"

The figure/ground reversal motif on this oval purse was inspired by pre-Columbian interlocking designs from Peru and by the graphic designs of the 20th century artist, M. C. Escher. First, the flat oval spiral base is crocheted, then when the diameter of the base is no longer increased, the edges of the spiral move upwards to form the sides. The bird motif is sixteen stitches wide, so the total number of stitches in the base is a multiple of sixteen. It is possible to make a variety of sizes with the same design motif simply by increasing or decreasing the size of the base chain by eight stitches. Feel free to substitute another motif. If you use another motif, be sure that the total number of stitches in the base is a multiple of the number of stitches in your motif.

## Hook
Steel crochet hook size 1 (2.75 mm.) or the size that will give an acceptable gauge

## Gauge
8 stitches equals 1 inch
7 rows equals 1 inch

## Size
9 1/2" wide by 12" high (not including the strap)

## Materials
Four balls (50 grams/1 3/4 oz./114 yards each) of Antique White (color 0020), two balls of Royal Blue (color 5646), and three balls of Red (color 4246) Kolibri mercerized cotton thread (or a similar substitute);
Safety pin or a piece of thread of a contrasting color for counting the rounds.

**Round 1:** Starting with the white thread, make a slip knot (leaving a ten-inch tail), then chain 51 stitches. Increase or decrease in multiples of 8 chain stitches at this point to make a wider or narrower purse. Starting with the second chain, single crochet 49 stitches. Single crochet 4 stitches into the last chain for a total of 53 stitches. Continue to single crochet using the new top of the chain until you come around to the first stitch, carrying the "tail" as you go. Single crochet 3 stitches into the last stitch. This first round should have a total of 104 stitches. This piece is worked as a spiral, not in concentric rings, so it is difficult to tell where each round ends. To keep track of where each round ends, slip a safety pin into the top of the last stitch of the round or lay a two inch piece of thread of a contrasting color across the path of the last stitch. You will remove the safety pin from the last stitch as you come to it again and slip it into the new last stitch or cross the path of the last stitch with the end of the counting thread at the end of each round. Pull a little on the counting thread as it runs out to make it longer.
**Round 2:** Continue to crochet with white. Cut the tail flush and start to carry the red and blue threads. To keep the base flat, you will increase each round by 8 stitches; 4 at each end. So begin this round by crocheting 2 stitches into the first stitch, 2 stitches into the next stitch, 48 stitches (one in each stitch), 2 stitches into each of the

next 4 stitches, 48 stitches (one in each stitch), 2 stitches into the 49th stitch, then crochet 2 stitches into the last stitch. The purse should have 112 stitches when you finish this round.

**Round 3:** Continue to crochet with white while you carry the red and blue threads. Crochet 2 stitches into the first stitch, 1 stitch into the next stitch, 2 stitches into the next stitch, 49 stitches (one in each stitch), 2 stitches into the next stitch, 1 stitch into the next stitch, 2 stitches into the next stitch, 1 stitch into the next stitch, 2 stitches into the next stitch, 1 stitch into the next stitch, 2 stitches into the next stitch, 49 stitches (one in each stitch), 2 stitches into the next stitch, 1 stitch into the next stitch, 2 stitches into the next stitch, then crochet 1 stitch into the last stitch. The purse should have 120 stitches when you finish this round.

**Round 4:** Continue to crochet with white while you carry the red and blue threads. Crochet 1 stitch into the first stitch, 2 stitches into the next stitch, 1 stitch into the next stitch, 2 stitches into the next stitch, 52 stitches (one in each stitch), 2 stitches into the next stitch, 1 stitch into the next stitch, 2 stitches into the next stitch, 2 stitches (one in each stitch), 2 stitches into the next stitch, 1 stitch into the next stitch, 2 stitches into the next stitch, 52 stitches (one in each stitch), 2 stitches into the next stitch, 1 stitch into the next stitch, 2 stitches into the next stitch, then crochet 1 stitch into the last stitch. The purse should have 128 stitches when you finish this round.

**Round 5:** Continue to crochet with white while you carry the red and blue threads. Crochet 2 stitches (one in each stitch), 2 stitches into the next stitch, 1 stitch into the next stitch, 2 stitches into the next stitch, 54 stitches (one in each stitch), 2 stitches into the next stitch, 1 stitch into the next stitch, 2 stitches into the next stitch, 4 stitches (one in each stitch), 2 stitches into the next stitch, 1 stitch into the next stitch, 2 stitches into the next stitch, 54 stitches (one in each stitch), 2 stitches into the next stitch, 1 stitch into the next stitch, 2 stitches into the next stitch, then crochet 2 stitches (one in each stitch). The purse should have 136 stitches when you finish this round.

**Round 6:** Continue to crochet with white while you carry the red and blue threads. Crochet 3 stitches (one in each stitch), 2 stitches into the next stitch, 1 stitch into the next stitch, 2 stitches into the next stitch, 56 stitches (one in each stitch), 2 stitches into the next stitch, 1 stitch into the next stitch, 2 stitches into the next stitch, 6 stitches (one in each stitch), 2 stitches into the next stitch, 1 stitch into the next stitch, 2 stitches into the next stitch, 56 stitches (one in each stitch), 2 stitches into the next stitch, 1 stitch into the next stitch, 2 stitches into the next stitch, then crochet 3 stitches (one in each stitch). The purse should have 144 stitches when you finish this round.

**Round 7:** Continue to crochet with white while you carry the red and blue threads. Crochet 4 stitches (one in each stitch), 2 stitches into the next stitch, 1 stitch into the next stitch, 2 stitches into the next stitch, 58 stitches (one in each stitch), 2 stitches into the next stitch, 1 stitch into the next stitch, 2 stitches into the next stitch, 8 stitches (one in each stitch), 2 stitches into the next stitch, 1 stitch into the next stitch, 2 stitches into the next stitch, 58 stitches (one in each stitch), 2 stitches into the next stitch, 1 stitch into the next stitch, 2 stitches into the next stitch, then crochet 4 stitches (one in each stitch). The purse should have 152 stitches when you finish this round.

**Round 8:** Continue to crochet with white while you carry the red and blue threads. Crochet 5 stitches (one in each stitch), 2 stitches into the next stitch, 1 stitch into the next stitch, 2 stitches into the next stitch, 60 stitches (one in each stitch), 2 stitches into the next stitch, 1 stitch into the next stitch, 2 stitches into the next stitch, 10 stitches (one in each stitch), 2 stitches into the next stitch, 1 stitch into the next stitch, 2 stitches into the next stitch, 60 stitches (one in each stitch), 2 stitches into the next stitch, 1 stitch into the next stitch, 2 stitches into the next stitch, then crochet 5 stitches (one in each stitch). The purse should have 160 stitches when you finish this round.

**Round 9:** Continue to crochet with white while you carry the red and blue threads. Crochet 6 stitches (one in each stitch), 2 stitches into the next stitch, 1 stitch into the next stitch, 2 stitches into the next stitch, 62 stitches (one in each stitch), 2 stitches into the next stitch, 1 stitch into the next stitch, 2 stitches into the next stitch, 12 stitches (one in each stitch), 2 stitches into the next stitch, 1 stitch into the next stitch, 2 stitches into the next stitch, 62 stitches (one in each stitch), 2 stitches into the next stitch, 1 stitch into the next stitch, 2 stitches into the next stitch, then crochet 6 stitches (one in each stitch). The purse should have 168 stitches when you finish this round.

**Round 10:** Continue to crochet with white while you carry the red and blue threads. Crochet 7 stitches (one in each stitch), 2 stitches into the next stitch, 1 stitch into the next stitch, 2 stitches into the next stitch, 64 stitches (one in each stitch), 2 stitches into the next stitch, 1 stitch into the next stitch, 2 stitches into the next stitch, 14 stitches (one in each stitch), 2 stitches into the next stitch, 1 stitch into the next stitch, 2 stitches into the next stitch, 64 stitches (one in each stitch), 2 stitches into the next stitch, 1 stitch into the next stitch, 2 stitches into the next stitch, then crochet 7 stitches (one in each stitch). The purse should have 176 stitches when you finish this round.

**Round 11:** Continue to crochet with white while you carry the red and blue threads. Crochet 8 stitches (one in each stitch), 2 stitches into the next stitch, 1 stitch into the next stitch, 2 stitches into the next stitch, 66 stitches (one in each stitch), 2 stitches into the next stitch, 1 stitch into the next stitch, 2 stitches into the next stitch, 16 stitches (one in each stitch), 2 stitches into the next stitch, 1 stitch into the next stitch, 2 stitches into the next stitch, 66 stitches (one in each stitch), 2 stitches into the next stitch, 1 stitch into the next stitch, 2 stitches into the next stitch, then crochet 8 stitches (one in each stitch). The purse should have 184 stitches when you finish this round.

**Round 12:** Continue to crochet with white while you carry the red and blue threads. Crochet 9 stitches (one in each stitch), 2 stitches into the next stitch, 1 stitch into the next stitch, 2 stitches into the next stitch, 68 stitches (one in each stitch), 2 stitches into the next stitch, 1 stitch into the next stitch, 2 stitches into the next stitch, 18 stitches (one in each stitch), 2 stitches into the next stitch, 1 stitch into the next stitch, 2 stitches into the next stitch, 68 stitches (one in each stitch), 2 stitches into the next stitch, 1 stitch into the next stitch, 2 stitches into the next stitch, then crochet 9 stitches (one in each stitch). The purse should have 192 stitches when you finish this round.

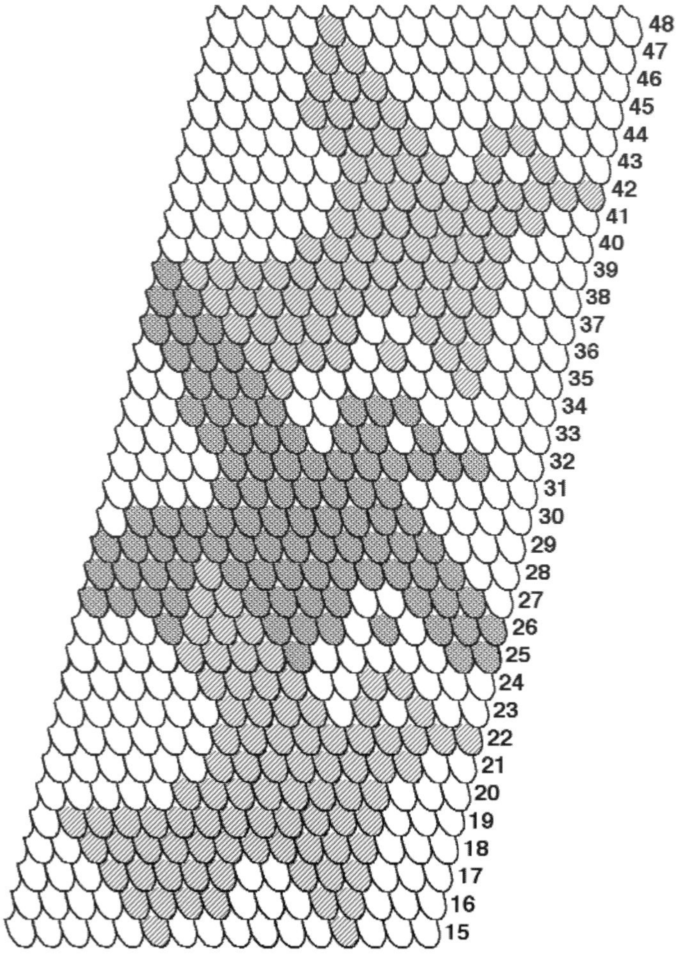


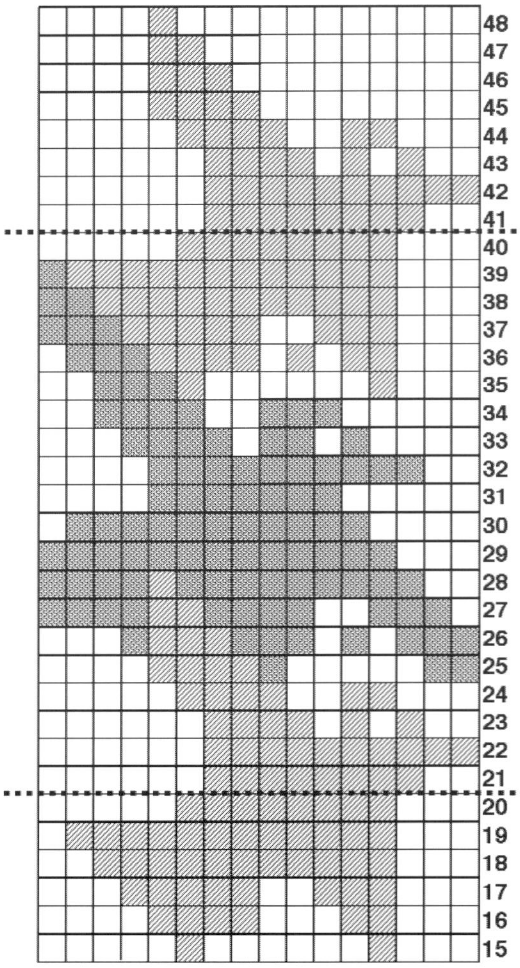


***The above graphs are for right-handed crocheters.***
***Left-handed crocheters should look at the reversed image of the graphs in a mirror.***

***Begin sides:***

**Round 13:** Continue to crochet with white while you carry the red and blue threads. Crochet a round without any increases. The number of stitches will now remain constant from round to round. The purse should still have 192 stitches when you finish this round.
**Round 14:** Continue to crochet with white while you carry the red and blue threads. Crochet another round without any increases. The purse should still have 192 stitches when you finish this round.
**Round 15:** Rounds 15 through 48 correspond to the illustrated birds motif (read from right to left and bottom to top). You will now begin to tapestry crochet the bird motif. Remember, that to do a tapestry crochet stitch, colors are switched while 2 loops are still on the hook; yarn over with the next color and pull it through the loops to prepare for the tapestry crochet stitch. Tapestry crochet 3 white, 1 red, 6 white, 1 red, and 5 white. Repeat around. Every once in a while, untwist the carried threads. You can avoid twisted threads if you separate the three balls. One way to separate them is to place one thread to your right, another in your lap, and the third to your left. As you change colors, you will see a twist in the threads where they cross over one another. The twist will not show in the finished piece.
**Round 16:** Tapestry crochet 3 white, 2 red, 3 white, 4 red, and 4 white stitches. Repeat around.
**Round 17:** Tapestry crochet 3 white, 3 red, 2 white, 5 red, and 3 white stitches. Repeat around. Turn the purse inside out (to make it right side out). As you tapestry crochet each stitch, the hook should point toward the inside of the purse.
**Round 18:** Tapestry crochet 3 white, 11 red, and 2 white stitches. Repeat around.
**Round 19:** Tapestry crochet 3 white, 12 red, and 1 white stitch. Repeat around.
**Round 20:** Tapestry crochet 3 white, 8 red, and 5 white stitches. Repeat around.
**Round 21:** Tapestry crochet 2 white, 8 red, and 6 white stitches. Repeat around.
**Round 22:** Tapestry crochet 10 red and 6 white stitches. Repeat around.
**Round 23:** Tapestry crochet 2 white, 1 red, 1 white, 1 red, 1 white, 4 red, and 6 white stitches. Repeat around.
**Round 24:** Tapestry crochet 3 white, 2 red, 2 white, 4 red, and 5 white stitches. Repeat around.
**Round 25:** Tapestry crochet 2 blue, 5 white, 1 blue, 4 red, and 4 white stitches. Repeat around.
**Round 26:** Tapestry crochet 3 blue, 1 white, 1 blue, 1 white, 3 blue, 3 red, 1 blue, and 3 white stitches. Repeat around.
**Round 27:** Tapestry crochet 1 white, 3 blue, 2 white, 4 blue, 2 red, and 4 blue stitches. Repeat around.
**Round 28:** Tapestry crochet 2 white, 9 blue, 1 red, and 4 blue stitches. Repeat around.
**Round 29:** Tapestry crochet 3 white and 13 blue stitches. Repeat around.
**Round 30:** Tapestry crochet 4 white, 11 blue, and 1 white stitch. Repeat around.
**Round 31:** Tapestry crochet 5 white, 7 blue, and 4 white stitches. Repeat around.
**Round 32:** Tapestry crochet 2 white, 10 blue, and 4 white stitches. Repeat around.
**Round 33:** Tapestry crochet 4 white, 1 blue, 1 white, 2 blue, 1 white, 4 blue, and 3 white stitches. Repeat around.
**Round 34:** Tapestry crochet 5 white, 3 blue, 2 white, 4 blue, and 2 white stitches. Repeat around.
**Round 35:** Tapestry crochet 3 white, 1 red, 6 white, 1 red, 3 blue, and 2 white stitches. Repeat around.
**Round 36:** Tapestry crochet 3 white, 2 red, 1 white, 1 red, 1 white, 4 red, 3 blue, and 1 white stitches. Repeat around.
**Round 37:** Tapestry crochet 3 white, 3 red, 2 white, 5 red, and 3 blue stitches. Repeat around.
**Round 38:** Tapestry crochet 3 white, 11 red, and 2 blue stitches. Repeat around.
**Round 39:** Tapestry crochet 3 white, 12 red, and 1 blue stitch. Repeat around.
**Round 40:** Tapestry crochet 3 white, 8 red, and 5 white stitches. Repeat around.

***Repeat Rounds 21 through 40 as many times as you wish (I repeated it three times for the pictured project).***

**Round 41:** Tapestry crochet 2 white, 8 red, and 6 white stitches. Repeat around.
**Round 42:** Tapestry crochet 10 red and 6 white stitches. Repeat around.
**Round 43:** Tapestry crochet 2 white, 1 red, 1 white, 1 red, 1 white, 4 red, and 6 white stitches. Repeat around.
**Round 44:** Tapestry crochet 3 white, 2 red, 2 white, 4 red, and 5 white stitches. Repeat around.
**Round 45:** Tapestry crochet 8 white, 4 red, and 4 white stitches. Repeat around.
**Round 46:** Tapestry crochet 9 white, 3 red, and 4 white stitches. Repeat around.
**Round 47:** Tapestry crochet 10 white, 2 red, and 4 white stitches. Repeat around.
**Round 48:** Tapestry crochet 11 white, 1 red, and 4 white stitches. Repeat around.

***Strap and Border:***

**Round A:** Tapestry crochet 12 white stitches. Chain 175 stitches with white. If you would like a longer or shorter shoulder strap, increase or decrease at this point. Cut the blue and red threads flush. Insert the hook into the 96th stitch away from the base of the chain, connecting the end of the chain to the other side of the top of the shoulder bag. Make sure that the chain is not twisted.
**Round B:** Start to carry the blue and red threads. Tapestry crochet 96 stitches across the top of the bag with white. Continue to crochet onto the chain. You should have 271 stitches when you finish this round.
**Round C:** Tapestry crochet 271 stitches around with white while carrying the white and red threads.
**Round D:** Tapestry crochet 271 stitches around with the blue thread while carrying the white and red threads.
**Round E:** Tapestry crochet 271 stitches around with the blue thread while carrying the white and red threads.
**Round F:** Tapestry crochet 271 stitches around with the red thread while carrying the white and blue threads.
**Round G:** Tapestry crochet 271 stitches around with the red thread while carrying the white and blue threads. Cut the white and blue threads flush at the end of the round. Do a slip stitch, cut the red thread (leaving a 6 inch tail), then yarn over and pull it all the way through the loop. Work in the end for 2 inches to secure it, then cut it flush.

**Round H:** Turn over the shoulder bag. Have the side facing you that needs a border. Insert the hook into the stitch in the upper right hand corner of the bag next to the shoulder strap. Pull through a loop of white thread, leaving a 2” piece hanging out of the back. Chain 1 with the white, then tapestry crochet 1 stitch into the same stitch. Start to carry the blue and red threads along with the 2” white tail. Tapestry crochet 95 more stitches across the top of the purse. Continue to tapestry crochet onto the shoulder strap, inserting the hook into the bottom loop of the original chain. You should have 271 stitches when you finish this round.
**Round I:** Repeat Round C.
**Round J:** Repeat Round D.
**Round K:** Repeat Round E.
**Round L:** Repeat Round F.
**Round M:** Repeat Round G.
Block the purse.

**Detail of the strap.**

# 8 SQUARE SPIRAL PROJECT

## Square Woolen Hats/Baskets

Depending upon which way they are turned, these pieces may function as hats or baskets. The square hat/baskets begin in the center, and then work outward and upward. A flat square spiral base is crocheted first, then when the diameter of the base is no longer increased, the edges of the spiral move upwards to form the sides. The motif is eight stitches wide, so the total number of stitches in the base is a multiple of eight. It is possible to make a variety of sizes with the same design motif simply by increasing or decreasing the size of the base by eight stitches. Since the number of stitches of every round of the base is a multiple of eight, you can start the sides at any point and the motif will still work out perfectly. Feel free to substitute another motif, just be sure that the total number of stitches in the base is a multiple of the number of stitches in your motif.

### Hook
Steel crochet hook size 1 (2.75 mm.) or the size that will give an acceptable gauge

### Gauge
6 stitches equals 1 inch
5 rows equals 1 inch

## Medium Hat/Basket
### Size
7 3/8" diameter by 4 1/2" high (23" circumference)

### Materials
One skein (100 grams/3.5 ounces/140 yards) of Mattullgarn 509 and 1 skein of Mattullgarn 581 by Blomqvist (or a similar substitute);
Safety pin or a piece of wool of a contrasting color for counting the rounds.

# Large Hat/Basket

## Size

8 1/2" diameter by 4 1/4" high (27" circumference)

## Materials

One skein (100 grams/3.5 ounces/140 yards) of Mattullgarn 770 and 2 skeins of Mattullgarn 577 by Blomqvist (or a similar substitute);
Safety pin or a piece of thread of a contrasting color for counting the rounds.

**Round 1:** Since Mattullgarn is sold in skeins, must wind it into balls before you can crochet. Ask a friend to hold the skein while you wind it. Then, starting with the light color yarn, make a slip knot (leaving a six-inch tail), then chain 5 stitches. Join the ends together to form a ring by working a slip stitch into the first chain stitch. Single crochet 8 stitches loosely into the ring (while carrying the tail of the yarn). The piece should have a total of 8 stitches when you finish this round. This piece is worked as a spiral, not in concentric rings, so it is difficult to tell where each round ends. To keep track of where each round ends, slip a safety pin into the top of the last stitch of the round or lay a two inch piece of yarn of a contrasting color across the path of the last stitch. You will remove the safety pin from the last stitch as you come to it again and slip it into the new last stitch or cross the path of the last stitch with the end of the counting yarn at the end of each round. Pull a little on the counting thread as it runs out to make it longer.
**Round 2:** Continue to carry the tail. Increase by crocheting 2 stitches into each stitch. The spiral should have a total of 16 stitches when you finish this round.
**Round 3:** Cut the tail flush and start to carry the other yarn. Increase by crocheting 2 stitches into the first stitch, then crochet one stitch in each of the next two stitches, then increase again by crocheting 2 stitches into the next stitch. Repeat this sequence (two increases in each corner) three more times. The piece should have 24 stitches when you finish this round
**Round 4:** Increase in the first stitch, crochet 4 stitches, then increase in the next stitch. Repeat this sequence three more times. The piece should have 32 stitches when you finish this round.
**Round 5:** Increase in the first stitch, crochet 6 stitches, then increase in the next stitch. Repeat this sequence three more times. The piece should have 40 stitches when you finish this round.
**Round 6:** Increase in the first stitch, crochet 8 stitches, then increase in the next stitch. Repeat this sequence three more times. The piece should have 48 stitches when you finish this round.
**Round 7:** Increase in the first stitch, crochet 10 stitches, then increase in the next stitch. Repeat this sequence three more times. The piece should have 56 stitches when you finish this round.
**Round 8:** Increase in the first stitch, crochet 12 stitches, then increase in the next stitch. Repeat this sequence three more times. The piece should have 64 stitches when you finish this round.
**Round 9:** Increase in the first stitch, crochet 14 stitches, then increase in the next stitch. Repeat this sequence three more times. The piece should have 72 stitches when you finish this round.
**Round 10:** Increase in the first stitch, crochet 16 stitches, then increase in the next stitch. Repeat this sequence three more times. The piece should have 80 stitches when you finish this round.
**Round 11:** Increase in the first stitch, crochet 18 stitches, then increase in the next stitch. Repeat this sequence three more times. The piece should have 88 stitches when you finish this round.
**Round 12:** Increase in the first stitch, crochet 20 stitches, then increase in the next stitch. Repeat this sequence three more times. The piece should have 96 stitches when you finish this round.
**Round 13:** Increase in the first stitch, crochet 22 stitches, then increase in the next stitch. Repeat this sequence three more times. The piece should have 104 stitches when you finish this round.
**Round 14:** Increase in the first stitch, crochet 24 stitches, then increase in the next stitch. Repeat this sequence three more times. The piece should have 112 stitches when you finish this round.
**Round 15:** Increase in the first stitch, crochet 26 stitches, then increase in the next stitch. Repeat this sequence

three more times. The piece should have 120 stitches when you finish this round.
**Round 16:** Increase in the first stitch, crochet 28 stitches, then increase in the next stitch. Repeat this sequence three more times. The piece should have 128 stitches when you finish this round.
**Round 17:** Increase in the first stitch, crochet 30 stitches, then increase in the next stitch. Repeat this sequence three more times. The piece should have 136 stitches when you finish this round. Don't worry if your piece is not flat, it will become flat after blocking.

***For the medium hat, go to round 21.***
**Round 18:** Increase in the first stitch, crochet 32 stitches, then increase in the next stitch. Repeat this sequence three more times. The piece should have 144 stitches when you finish this round.
**Round 19:** Increase in the first stitch, crochet 34 stitches, then increase in the next stitch. Repeat this sequence three more times. The piece should have 152 stitches when you finish this round.
**Round 20:** Increase in the first stitch, crochet 36 stitches, then increase in the next stitch. Repeat this sequence three more times. The piece should have 160 stitches when you finish this round.

***Begin sides:***
**Round 21:** Rounds 21 through 40 correspond to the illustrated motif (read from right to left and bottom to top). Crochet one round without any increases. The number of stitches will now remain constant from round to round.
**Round 22:** Crochet one more round without any increases.

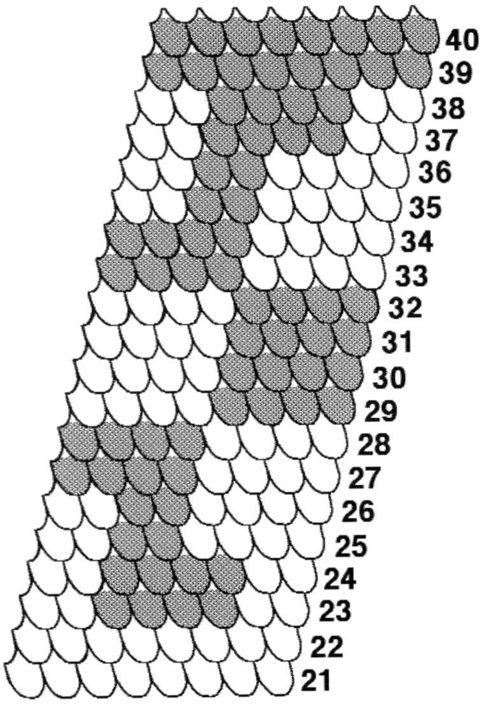


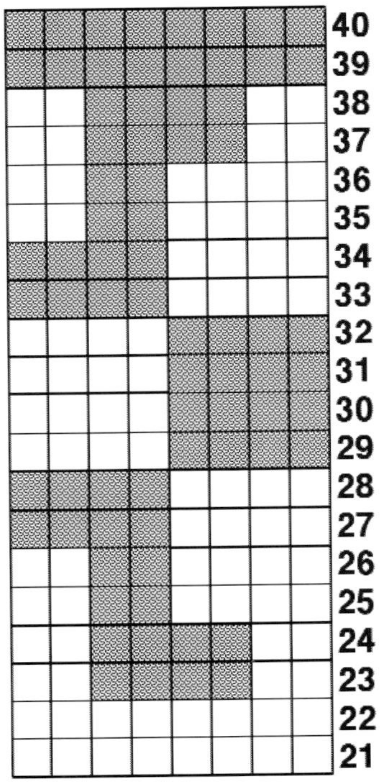


***The graphs on the left are for right-handed crocheters. Left-handed crocheters should look at the reversed image of the graphs in a mirror.***

***Begin motif:***
**Round 23:** You will now begin to do the tapestry crochet stitch. Remember, that to do a tapestry crochet stitch, colors are switched while 2 loops are still on the hook; yarn over with the next color and pull it through the loops to prepare for the tapestry crochet stitch. Tapestry crochet 2 light color, 4 dark color, and 2 light color stitches. Repeat around. Every once in a while, untwist the yarns by holding the hat/basket up in the air with one of the yarns while pulling on the other yarn. Let the piece spin around in the air so that the yarns untangle.
**Round 24:** Tapestry crochet 2 light, 4 dark, and 2 light stitches. Repeat around. Turn the hat/basket inside out (to make it right side out). As you tapestry crochet each stitch, the hook should point toward the inside of the hat/basket.

**Round 25:** Tapestry crochet 4 light, 2 dark, and 2 light stitches. Repeat around.
**Round 26:** Tapestry crochet 4 light, 2 dark, and 2 light stitches. Repeat around.
**Round 27:** Tapestry crochet 4 light and 4 dark stitches. Repeat around.
**Round 28:** Tapestry crochet 4 light and 4 dark stitches. Repeat around.
**Round 29:** Tapestry crochet 4 dark and 4 light stitches. Repeat around.
**Round 30:** Tapestry crochet 4 dark and 4 light stitches. Repeat around.
**Round 31:** Tapestry crochet 4 dark and 4 light stitches. Repeat around.
**Round 32:** Tapestry crochet 4 dark and 4 light stitches. Repeat around.
**Round 33:** Tapestry crochet 4 light and 4 dark stitches. Repeat around.
**Round 34:** Tapestry crochet 4 light and 4 dark stitches. Repeat around.
**Round 35:** Tapestry crochet 4 light, 2 dark, and 2 light stitches. Repeat around.
**Round 36:** Tapestry crochet 4 light, 2 dark, and 2 light stitches. Repeat around.
**Round 37:** Tapestry crochet 2 light, 4 dark, and 2 light stitches. Repeat around.
**Round 38:** Tapestry crochet 2 light, 4 dark, and 2 light stitches. Repeat around.
**Round 39:** Crochet around with dark while you carry the light yarn.
**Round 40:** Crochet around with dark while you carry the light yarn.

**To finish:** Cut the carried yarn flush. Slip stitch with the dark yarn, cut it (leaving a 6 inch tail) then yarn over and pull it all the way through the loop. Work in the end for 2 inches to secure it, then trim it off flush. Block the hat/basket.

# WOOL

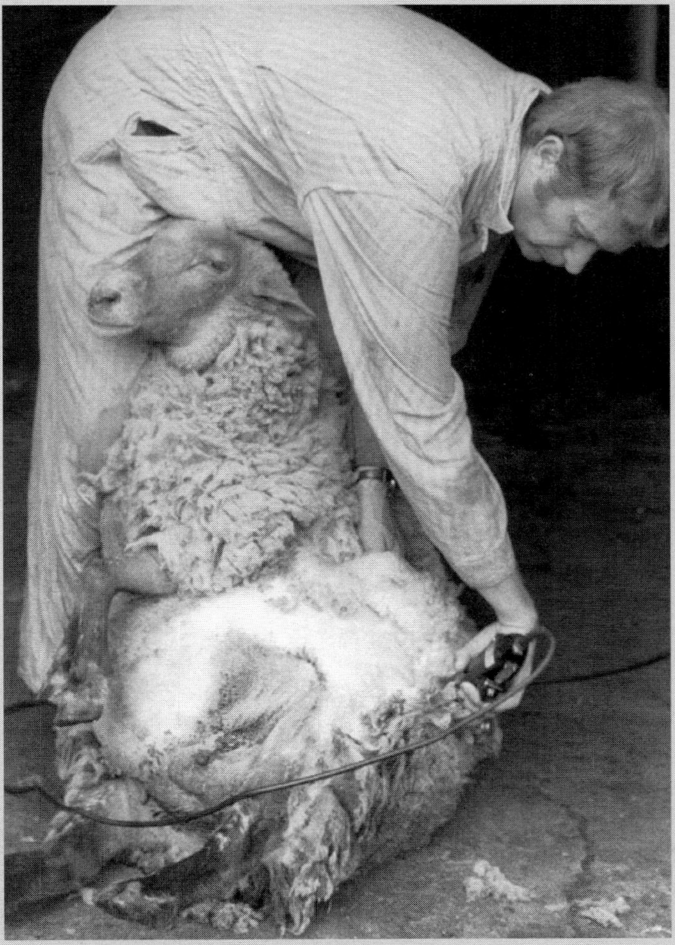

Wool has been spun and woven in the Old World for over 4,000 years. In ancient times it was collected as sheep shed their wool when warm weather began. Today it is removed in the Spring with scissors or electric shears.

Wool grows from a follicle in sheep's skin. These follicles also produce lanolin. Wool fiber is actually keratin, a protein also present in horns and hoofs. Keratin consists of helical chains of amino acids. Because the chains are coiled, they stretch when pulled, and then recoil back into shape, so wool doesn't shrink; it just recoils.

Sheep were first domesticated in ancient Mesopotamia. They were introduced to the Americas by the Spaniards during the Colonial period. The more than 450 breeds of domestic sheep in the world today produce a wide variety of wool, from fine to course, in many shades of white, brown, and black. Since wool can be easily dyed in a rainbow of hues, it continues to warm and color our lives, as it has for countless generations.

**Wool is removed with electric shears.**

# 9 FLAT PROJECTS

## Flat Heart

This small project is a good introduction to flat tapestry crochet. Flat pieces with a distinct front and back can be made by using *Reverse Crochet* or *Alternate-Row Switch-Hands Crochet* on every other row. Whichever method you choose, use it consistently throughout the piece. At first, the unusual working method may feel awkward, however the result is well worth the initial extra effort. This piece begins on the bottom and works it's way up.

### Hook:
Steel crochet hook size 4 (2.00 mm.) or the size that will give an acceptable gauge

### Gauge:
8 stitches equals 1 inch
7 rows equals 1 inch.

### Size:
2 1/8"wide by 2 1/2" high

### Materials:
One partial ball (100 yards) each of White (color 001) and Spanish Red (color 126), size 3 J. & P. Coats Speed-Cro-Sheen 100% mercerized cotton, article C-45 (or a similar substitute);

**Row 1:** Starting with white, make a slip knot, then chain 15 stitches. Starting with the second chain, single crochet 14 stitches.
**Row 2 >:** Chain 1 and work across. You need to choose *Reverse Crochet* (see page 44) or *Alternate-Row Switch-Hands Crochet* (see page 45) to work each even-numbered row.

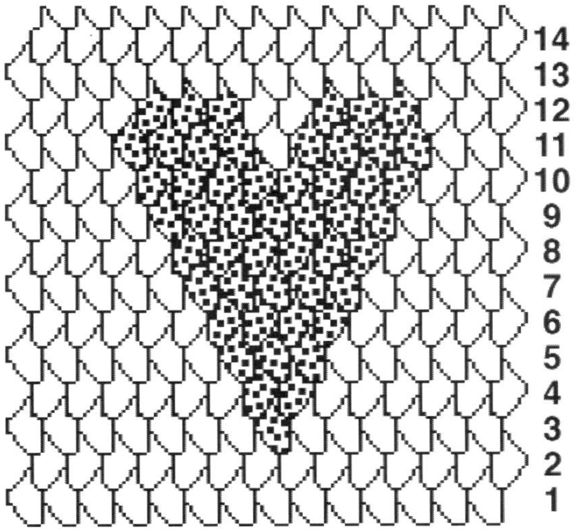


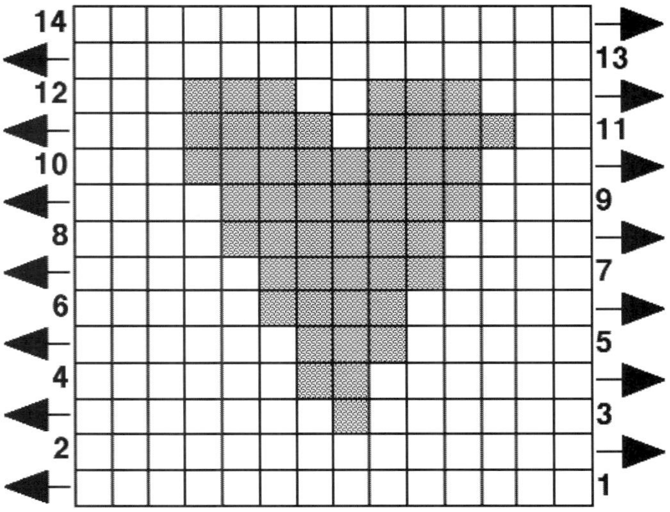


***Arrows indicate the working direction of the stitches for that row.***
***The above graphs are for right-handed crocheters.***
***Left-handed crocheters may follow the graphs, as long as an extra row is crocheted at the beginning of the piece so that the arrows may be followed correctly.***

**Row 3 <:** Start to carry the red thread. You will begin to tapestry crochet the heart motif on this row. Remember, that to do a tapestry crochet stitch, colors are switched while 2 loops are still on the hook; yarn over with the red thread and pull it through the white loops to prepare for the next tapestry crochet stitch. Chain 1, then tapestry crochet 6 white, 1 red, and then 7 white stitches.
**Row 4 >:** Chain 1, then tapestry crochet 6 white, 2 red, and then 6 white stitches.
**Row 5 <:** Chain 1, then tapestry crochet 5 white, 3 red, and then 6 white stitches.
**Row 6 >:** Chain 1, then tapestry crochet 5 white, 4 red, and then 5 white stitches.
**Row 7 <:** Chain 1, then tapestry crochet 4 white, 5 red, and then 5 white stitches.
**Row 8 >:** Chain 1, then tapestry crochet 4 white, 6 red, and then 4 white stitches.
**Row 9 <:** Chain 1, then tapestry crochet 3 white, 7 red, and then 4 white stitches.
**Row 10 >:** Chain 1, then tapestry crochet 3 white, 8 red, and then 3 white stitches.
**Row 11 <:** Chain 1, then tapestry crochet 2 white, 4 red, 1 white, 4 red, and then 3 white stitches.
**Row 12 >:** Chain 1, then tapestry crochet 3 white, 3 red, 2 white, 3 red, and then 3 white stitches.
**Row 13 <:** Chain 1, tapestry crochet across with white.
**Row 14 >:** Chain 1, tapestry crochet across with white

**Border:** Chain 1, tapestry crochet across with red. Crochet 2 more stitches into the last (corner) stitch. Continue to carry the white thread. Crochet 3 stitches into the next corner stitch and continue across the bottom. Crochet 3 stitches into the next corner stitch and continue up the side, carrying the white thread until the end, then cut the white thread flush. Do a slip stitch, cut the red thread (leaving a 6 inch tail), then yarn over and pull it all the way through the loop. Work in the end for one inch to secure it, then cut it flush. Block the piece.

# Flat Tapestry

This is one of the most difficult projects in the book. Only the bravest crocheters should consider it, but you can do it if you are patient! In order to allow for a three color motif, two threads are carried. Actually, this tapestry could be a wonderful collaboration piece. If you are right-handed, find a left-handed crocheter; if you are left-handed, locate a right-handed crocheter. Then, crochet every-other row (all of the "from right to left" or "left to right" rows), and let your partner crochet every other row. I suggested this to a right-handed crocheter who has a daughter that crochets with her left hand. What a wonderful project to do together! In fact, wouldn't it be even better if they traced their own hands for the motif!

This piece features my husband's left hand and my right hand. As I was crocheting it, I realized that the colors and theme are very similar to one of the flat tapestry crochet projects that I did for my first *Tapestry Crochet* book. I even chose the same colors! This piece is crocheted with another fiber, though, and it is mounted differently.

Learn from my mistakes! This is what happens when you do not make a sampler to determine the gauge (which tells you which graph to use). The compressed piece is above, and the stretched piece is below.

Instead of crocheting a two by two inch sample piece to determine the gauge (rows per inch and stitches per inch measurement) for this project, which would have told me which graph paper I should have used, I went ahead and selected the paper that I thought was appropriate. Unfortunately, I crocheted twenty-eight rows before I realized that the motif looked "compressed". So, I measured the gauge on the compressed piece, selected what I thought was the correct graph paper, and redrew the design. This time, I almost finished crocheting the tapestry before I realized that the motif looked "stretched." Since I was so close to finishing the piece, I went ahead and completed it. Then I decided to measure the gauge again (this time I did it correctly) and I also decided that the tapestry needed more contrast, so I selected a darker background color.

To determine the appropriate graph paper, measure ten stitches across the row, then use that measurement to see how many rows it equals. In this case, ten stitches is the same measurement as eight rows. So, the correct graph paper turned out to be the "10 stitches = 8 rows" graph paper.

This flat tapestry was designed with a traced motif. To design your own piece, tapestry crochet a two by two inch sample and measure the gauge. Then, photocopy two pieces of the appropriate graph paper, cut off one of the side edges of one of the graph papers, place the papers side by side, face down on a light table or against a window, line them up (with the cut edge overlapping a half inch on top of the grid pattern of the other paper), then tape them together.

After I taped two graph papers together, I turned them over (face side up), placed my husband's left hand on the paper, matching up the edges of his fingers with the edges of the stitches wherever possible, then I traced his hand onto the paper. Next, I lined up the fingers of my right hand and traced my hand onto the graph paper. Next, I colored in the hands. When the traced line fell in the middle of a stitch, I had to decide whether to fill that particular stitch in or not. I hope that you will design your own piece by tracing your own hand together with the hand of your special loved one.

The acid present in most cardboard and paper will eventually cause art work to yellow, so I prefer acid free framing materials. This tapestry is sewn to a piece of acid free board and protected by Plexiglas in a shadow box frame. Besides needing protection from dust, acid, and UV light, fabric also needs an air space to breathe.

## Hooks
Steel crochet hook size 8 (1.50 mm.) or the size that will give an acceptable gauge, and a steel crochet hook size 10 (1.30 mm.) for pulling the carried threads of the finished tapestry.

## Gauge
13 stitches equals 1 inch
11 rows equals 1 inch

### Tools
Pencil;
Ruler;
Sewing machine;
Hand sewing needle;
Screw driver;
Wire cutters.

## Size (without frame)
8 3/16" wide by 6 3/16" high

## Materials
One partial tube of Beige (color 470), one partial tube of Light Blue (color 515), and one partial tube of Red (color 517) of Bockens Lingarn (16/2 linen/120 grams);
9" x 11" (or the size that will frame your piece) Shadowbox sectionals, acid-free framing kit with foam core, acrylic sheet, and uncut mat board.

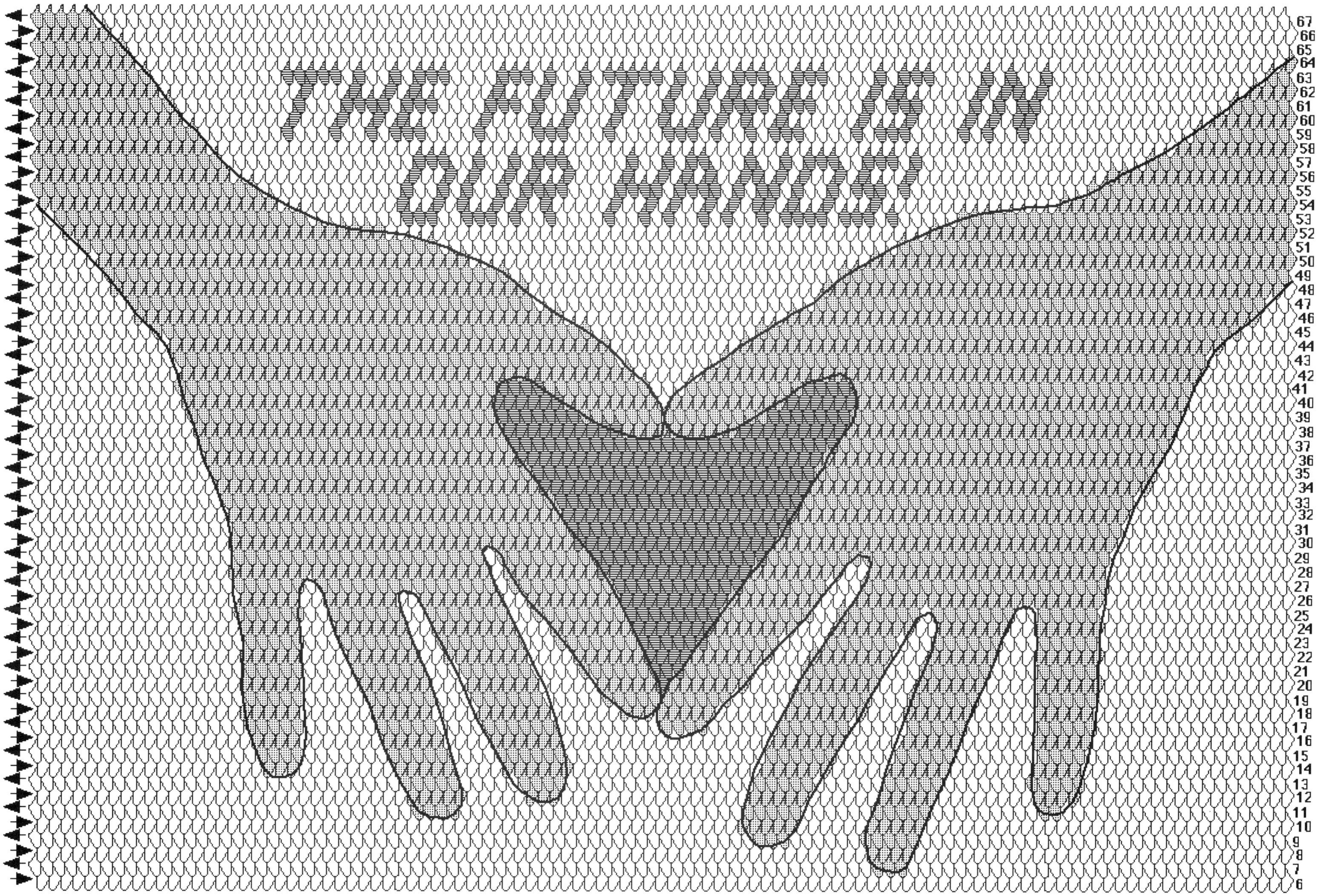


**When the traced line falls in the middle of a stitch, a decision must be made about whether or not to to fill in that particular stitch.**

67 66 65 64 63 62 61 60 59 58 57 56 55 54 53 52 51 50 49 48 47 46 45 44 43 42 41 40 39 38 37 36 35 34 33 32 31 30 29 28 27 26 25 24 23 22 21 20 19 18 17 16 15 14 13 12 11 10 9 8 7 6

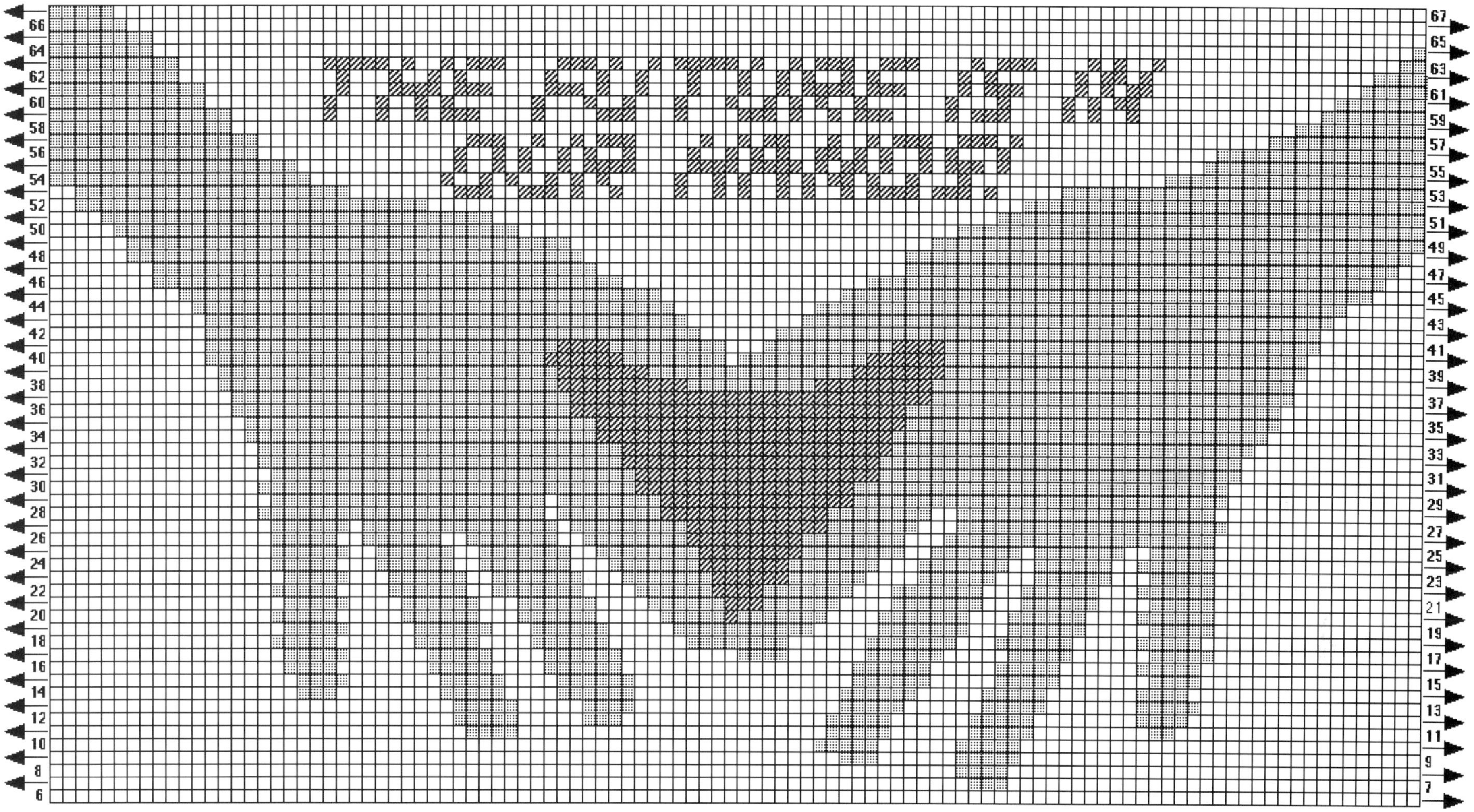

*This graph is for right-handed crocheters. Arrows indicate the working direction of the stitches for that row. Left-handed crocheters may follow this graph, as long as an extra row is crocheted at the beginning of the piece so that the arrows may be followed correctly.*

**Row 1:** Starting with the blue linen, make a slip knot (leaving a twelve-inch tail), then chain 107 stitches. Starting with the second chain, single crochet 106 stitches.
**Row 2 >:** Chain 1 with blue. In this row you need to choose *Reverse Crochet* (see page 44) or the *Alternate-Row Switch-Hands Crochet* (see page 45) to work each odd-numbered row. Carry the blue tail as you crochet across this row. Do not cut the tail off at the end of the row.
**Row 3 <:** Start to carry the red and beige linen (leave a 2" tail hanging out where you start to carry them, at the edge of the row). Chain 1 with blue, then single crochet across with blue.
**Row 4 >:** Chain 1 with blue, then crochet across with blue with the *Reverse Crochet* or the *Alternate-Row Switch-Hands Crochet* while you carry the beige and red linen.
**Row 5 <:** Chain 1 with blue, then crochet across with blue while you carry the beige and red linen.
**Row 6 >:** Chain 1 with blue, then crochet across with blue with *Reverse Crochet* or *Alternate-Row Switch-Hands Crochet* while you carry the beige and red linen.
**Row 7 <:** On this row you will begin tapestry crocheting the motif. Chain 1 with blue, then crochet 32 stitches. To prepare for the tapestry crochet stitch, partially crochet another blue stitch, then switch to the beige linen while two blue loops are still on the hook. The final yarn over and loop are made with the beige linen. Tapestry crochet 3 stitches with beige, then crochet 71 blue stitches, while you carry the beige and red linen. You can follow the graph (made up of squares) or these written instructions for color changes. The graphs are read from the bottom up. The arrows at the left edge of the graphs indicate the working direction of the stitches for that row.

It is very easy to lose your place when you are crocheting a complicated tapestry like this one, so I suggest that you either mark through each row of the instructions or graph with a highlighter-marker as you complete it or use a metal board with a magnetic ruler to keep your place.
**Row 8 >:** Chain 1 with blue, crochet 70 blue, 4 beige, and then 32 blue stitches.
**Row 9 <:** Chain 1 with blue, crochet 31 blue, 5 beige, 6 blue, 3 beige, and then 61 blue stitches. Do not worry if the piece curls. When it is finished and blocked it will be flat.
**Row 10 >:** Chain 1 with blue, crochet 60 blue, 5 beige, 6 blue, 5 beige, and 31 blue stitches.
**Row 11 <:** Chain 1 with blue, crochet 19 blue, 2 beige, 9 blue, 5 beige, 6 blue, 5 beige, 24 blue, 4 beige, and then 32 blue stitches.
**Row 12 >:** Chain 1 with blue, then crochet 31 blue, 5 beige, 5 blue, 3 beige, 16 blue, 5 beige, 6 blue, 5 beige, 8 blue, 4 beige, and then 18 blue stitches.
**Row 13 <:** Chain 1 with blue, crochet 17 blue, 5 beige, 7 blue, 5 beige, 6 blue, 5 beige, 16 blue, 4 beige, 5 blue, 5 beige, and then 31 blue stitches.
**Row 14 >:** Chain 1 with blue, then crochet 19 blue, 3 beige, 8 blue, 5 beige, 4 blue, 6 beige, 16 blue, 6 beige, 5 blue, 5 beige, 7 blue, 4 beige, and then 18 blue stitches.
**Row 15 <:** Chain 1 with blue, crochet 17 blue, 4 beige, 7 blue, 5 beige, 5 blue, 6 beige, 17 blue, 6 beige, 4 blue, 5 beige, 7 blue, 4 beige, and then 19 blue stitches.
**Row 16 >:** Chain 1 with blue, then crochet 18 blue, 4 beige, 7 blue, 5 beige, 4 blue, 6 beige, 18 blue, 6 beige, 5 blue, 5 beige, 6 blue, 5 beige, and then 17 blue stitches.
**Row 17 <:** Chain 1 with blue, crochet 16 blue, 5 beige, 6 blue, 5 beige, 5 blue, 6 beige, 6 blue, 4 beige, 9 blue, 6 beige, 4 blue, 5 beige, 6 blue, 5 beige, and then 18 blue stitches.
**Row 18 >:** Chain 1 with blue, then crochet 17 blue, 5 beige, 6 blue, 5 beige, 4 blue, 6 beige, 6 blue, 8 beige, 6 blue, 7 beige, 3 blue, 6 beige, 5 blue, 5 beige, and then 17 blue stitches.
**Row 19 <:** Chain 1 with blue, crochet 16 blue, 5 beige, 5 blue, 6 beige, 3 blue, 7 beige, 5 blue, 11 beige, 5 blue, 6 beige, 3 blue, 6 beige, 5 blue, 5 beige, and then 18 blue stitches.
**Row 20 >:** Chain 1 with blue, then crochet 17 blue, 5 beige, 5 blue, 6 beige, 3 blue, 6 beige, 5 blue, 5 beige, 1 red, 7 beige, 4 blue, 7 beige, 3 blue, 6 beige, 4 blue, 6 beige, and then 16 blue stitches.
**Row 21 <:** Chain 1 with blue, crochet 16 blue, 5 beige, 4 blue, 6 beige, 3 blue, 7 beige, 4 blue, 6 beige, 3 red, 6 beige, 4 blue, 6 beige, 3 blue, 6 beige, 4 blue, 5 beige, and then 18 blue stitches.
**Row 22 >:** Chain 1 with blue, then crochet 17 blue, 5 beige, 4 blue, 6 beige, 2 blue, 7 beige, 4 blue, 6 beige, 4 red, 7 beige, 3 blue, 7 beige, 3 blue, 6 beige, 3 blue, 6 beige, and then 16 blue stitches.

**Row 23 <:** Chain 1 with blue, crochet 16 blue, 5 beige, 3 blue, 6 beige, 3 blue, 6 beige, 4 blue, 6 beige, 6 red, 7 beige, 3 blue, 7 beige, 2 blue, 6 beige, 3 blue, 5 beige, and then 18 blue stitches.
**Row 24 >:** Chain 1 with blue, then crochet 17 blue, 5 beige, 3 blue, 6 beige, 2 blue, 7 beige, 3 blue, 7 beige, 7 red, 7 beige, 3 blue, 7 beige, 2 blue, 6 beige, 2 blue, 6 beige, and then 16 blue stitches.
**Row 25 <:** Chain 1 with blue, crochet 16 blue, 5 beige, 2 blue, 7 beige, 1 blue, 7 beige, 2 blue, 8 beige, 8 red, 8 beige, 2 blue, 7 beige, 2 blue, 6 beige, 2 blue, 6 beige, and then 17 blue stitches.
**Row 26 >:** Chain 1 with blue, then crochet 17 blue, 5 beige, 2 blue, 6 beige, 2 blue, 7 beige, 2 blue, 8 beige, 9 red, 8 beige, 3 blue, 21 beige, and then 16 blue stitches.
**Row 27 <:** Chain 1 with blue, crochet 15 blue, 21 beige, 3 blue, 7 beige, 11 red, 9 beige, 1 blue, 15 beige, 1 blue, 6 beige, and then 17 blue stitches.
**Row 28 >:** Chain 1 with blue, then crochet 16 blue, 22 beige, 1 blue, 8 beige, 13 red, 8 beige, 2 blue, 20 beige, and then 16 blue stitches.
**Row 29 <:** Chain 1 with blue, crochet 15 blue, 29 beige, 15 red, 8 beige, 1 blue, 21 beige, and then 17 blue stitches.
**Row 30 >:** Chain 1 with blue, then crochet 16 blue, 29 beige, 17 red, 29 beige, and then 15 blue stitches.
**Row 31 <:** Chain 1 with blue, crochet 14 blue, 28 beige, 19 red, 28 beige, and then 17 blue stitches.
**Row 32 >:** Chain 1 with blue, then crochet 16 blue, 28 beige, 20 red, 28 beige, and then 14 blue stitches.
**Row 33 <:** Chain 1 with blue, crochet 13 blue, 28 beige, 21 red, 28 beige, and then 16 blue stitches.
**Row 34 >:** Chain 1 with blue, then crochet 15 blue, 27 beige, 23 red, 29 beige, and then 12 blue stitches.
**Row 35 <:** Chain 1 with blue, crochet 11 blue, 29 beige, 24 red, 27 beige, and then 15 blue stitches.
**Row 36 >:** Chain 1 with blue, then crochet 14 blue, 26 beige, 26 red, 29 beige, and then 11 blue stitches.
**Row 37 <:** Chain 1 with blue, crochet 10 blue, 28 beige, 28 red, 26 beige, and then 14 blue stitches.
**Row 38 >:** Chain 1 with blue, then crochet 13 blue, 26 beige, 10 red, 10 beige, 9 red, 28 beige, and then 10 blue stitches.
**Row 39 <:** Chain 1 with blue, crochet 9 blue, 28 beige, 7 red, 16 beige, 7 red, 26 beige, and then 13 blue stitches.
**Row 40 >:** Chain 1 with blue, then crochet 12 blue, 26 beige, 6 red, 8 beige, 1 blue, 10 beige, 6 red, 28 beige, and then 9 blue stitches.
**Row 41 <:** Chain 1 with blue, crochet 8 blue, 29 beige, 4 red, 10 beige, 3 blue, 9 beige, 4 red, 27 beige, and then 12 blue stitches.
**Row 42 >:** Chain 1 with blue, then crochet 12 blue, 38 beige, 6 blue, 42 beige, and then 8 blue stitches.
**Row 43 <:** Chain 1 with blue, crochet 7 blue, 41 beige, 9 blue, 37 beige, and then 12 blue stitches.
**Row 44 >:** Chain 1 with blue, then crochet 11 blue, 37 beige, 11 blue, 41 beige, and then 6 blue stitches.
**Row 45 <:** Chain 1 with blue, crochet 4 blue, 41 beige, 14 blue, 37 beige, and then 10 blue stitches.
**Row 46 >:** Chain 1 with blue, then crochet 8 blue, 36 beige, 19 blue, 40 beige, and then 3 blue stitches.
**Row 47 <:** Chain 1 with blue, crochet 2 blue, 38 beige, 24 blue, 34 beige, and then 8 blue stitches.
**Row 48 >:** Chain 1 with blue, then crochet 6 blue, 35 beige, 25 blue, 39 beige, and then 1 blue stitch.
**Row 49 <:** Chain 1 with beige, crochet 38 beige, 28 blue, 34 beige, and then 6 blue stitches.
**Row 50 >:** Chain 1 with blue, then crochet 5 blue, 31 beige, 34 blue, and then 36 beige stitches.
**Row 51 <:** Chain 1 with beige, crochet 33 beige, 39 blue, 30 beige, and then 4 blue stitches.
**Row 52 >:** Chain 1 with blue, then crochet 2 blue, 27 beige, 46 blue, and then 31 beige stitches.
***Begin the letters:***
**Row 53 <:** Chain 1 with beige, crochet 28 beige, 5 blue, 1 red, 1 blue, 3 red, 1 blue, 4 red, 1 blue, 1 red, 2 blue, 1 red, 1 blue, 1 red, 2 blue, 1 red, 1 blue, 1 red, 2 blue, 1 red, 4 blue, 1 red, 2 blue, 1 red, 1 blue, 3 red, 2 blue, 3 red, 8 blue, 21 beige, and then 2 blue stitches.
**Row 54 >:** Chain 1 with beige, crochet 20 beige, 10 blue, 1 red, 2 blue, 1 red, 1 blue, 1 red, 2 blue, 1 red, 1 blue, 1 red, 1 blue, 1 red, 5 blue, 1 red, 2 blue, 1 red, 1 blue, 1 red, 2 blue, 1 red, 1 blue, 1 red, 1 blue, 2 red, 1 blue, 1 red, 2 blue, 1 red, 3 blue, 1 red, 15 blue, and then 20 beige stitches.
**Row 55 <:** Chain 1 with beige, crochet 17 beige, 15 blue, 1 red, 1 blue, 3 red, 1 blue, 1 red, 2 blue, 1 red, 1 blue,

2 red, 1 blue, 1 red, 1 blue, 4 red, 1 blue, 4 red, 4 blue, 4 red, 1 blue, 1 red, 2 blue, 1 red, 1 blue, 1 red, 2 blue, 1 red, 12 blue, and then 19 beige stitches.
**Row 56 >:** Chain 1 with beige, crochet 16 beige, 15 blue, 1 red, 2 blue, 1 red, 1 blue, 1 red, 2 blue, 1 red, 1 blue, 1 red, 2 blue, 1 red, 4 blue, 1 red, 2 blue, 1 red, 1 blue, 1 red, 1 blue, 1 red, 2 blue, 2 red, 1 blue, 1 red, 1 blue, 1 red, 2 blue, 1 red, 1 blue, 1 red, 3 blue, 1 red, 16 blue, and then 16 beige stitches.
**Row 57 <:** Chain 1 with beige, crochet 12 beige, 19 blue, 1 red, 1 blue, 3 red, 2 blue, 3 red, 1 blue, 1 red, 2 blue, 1 red, 3 blue, 2 red, 1 blue, 1 red, 2 blue, 1 red, 5 blue, 3 red, 1 blue, 1 red, 2 blue, 1 red, 2 blue, 3 red, 16 blue, and then 16 beige stitches.
**Row 58 >:** Chain 1 with beige, crochet 14 beige, 82 blue, and then 10 beige stitches.
**Row 59 <:** Chain 1 with beige, crochet 8 beige, 14 blue, 1 red, 2 blue, 1 red, 1 blue, 1 red, 4 blue, 3 red, 1 blue, 1 red, 4 blue, 3 red, 1 blue, 1 red, 2 blue, 1 red, 1 blue, 3 red, 4 blue, 1 red, 3 blue, 3 red, 4 blue, 1 red, 4 blue, 3 red, 1 blue, 1 red, 2 blue, 1 red, 3 blue, 1 red, 7 blue, and then 14 beige stitches.
**Row 60 >:** Chain 1 with beige, crochet 12 beige, 9 blue, 1 red, 3 blue, 1 red, 2 blue, 1 red, 1 blue, 1 red, 6 blue, 1 red, 3 blue, 1 red, 2 blue, 1 red, 3 blue, 1 red, 3 blue, 1 red, 2 blue, 1 red, 1 blue, 1 red, 1 blue, 1 red, 2 blue, 1 red, 6 blue, 1 red, 3 blue, 1 red, 4 blue, 1 red, 1 blue, 1 red, 1 blue, 2 red, 15 blue, and then 7 beige stitches.
**Row 61 <:** Chain 1 with beige, crochet 5 beige, 16 blue, 2 red, 1 blue, 1 red, 1 blue, 1 red, 4 blue, 3 red, 1 blue, 1 red, 4 blue, 3 red, 1 blue, 4 red, 1 blue, 1 red, 2 blue, 1 red, 3 blue, 1 red, 3 blue, 1 red, 2 blue, 1 red, 1 blue, 3 red, 4 blue, 3 red, 1 blue, 4 red, 3 blue, 1 red, 10 blue, and then 12 beige stitches.
**Row 62 >:** Chain 1 with beige, crochet 10 beige, 12 blue, 1 red, 3 blue, 1 red, 2 blue, 1 red, 1 blue, 1 red, 6 blue, 1 red, 3 blue, 1 red, 2 blue, 1 red, 3 blue, 1 red, 3 blue, 1 red, 2 blue, 1 red, 1 blue, 1 red, 2 blue, 1 red, 1 blue, 1 red, 6 blue, 1 red, 1 blue, 1 red, 6 blue, 1 red, 1 blue, 2 red, 1 blue, 1 red, 17 blue, and then 4 beige stitches.
**Row 63 <:** Chain 1 with beige, crochet 2 beige, 18 blue, 1 red, 2 blue, 1 red, 1 blue, 1 red, 4 blue, 3 red, 1 blue, 1 red, 4 blue, 3 red, 2 blue, 3 red, 1 blue, 1 red, 2 blue, 1 red, 1 blue, 5 red, 1 blue, 1 red, 2 blue, 1 red, 1 blue, 3 red, 4 blue, 3 red, 1 blue, 1 red, 2 blue, 1 red, 1 blue, 5 red, 11 blue, and then 10 beige stitches.
**Row 64 >:** Chain 1 with beige, crochet 8 beige, 97 blue, and then 1 beige stitch.
**Row 65 <:** Chain 1 with blue, crochet 98 blue, and then 8 beige stitches.
**Row 66 >:** Chain 1 with beige, crochet 6 beige, and then 100 blue stitches.
**Row 67 <:** Chain 1 with blue, crochet 101 blue, and then 5 beige stitches.

***Border:***

Crochet two more stitches into the last stitch of Row 67. Turn the piece around a quarter of the way ($90^{o}$) until the left side is on the top. Continue to crochet across the side of the piece, inserting the hook into the spaces at the end of each row, carrying the beige and red threads, changing the color where necessary. Depending upon the tension you use, usually one crochet stitch per row is about right. If the piece starts to pucker, increase a stitch or two along the border. If the piece starts to look wavy, decrease a stitch or two along the side border.

Crochet three stitches into the next corner stitch. Turn the piece $90^{o}$ again so that the bottom of the piece is now on the top. Continue to crochet across, inserting the hook into the bottom loop of the original foundation chain. Again, crochet three stitches into the corner stitch. Turn the piece $90^{o}$, then continue to crochet across the side of the piece as you did for the previous side. Crochet three stitches into the corner stitch. Cut the beige and red threads flush. Finish the border with a slip stitch. Work in the end.

Is your finished piece lumpy, or is the bottom wider than the top? Don't worry - this is normal. Lumps or uneven edges can be fixed during mounting and blocking. Major problems can be fixed in several ways. To make the piece flat and rectangular, begin by pulling the blue tail and the tails of the carried linen on the bottom of the piece. Then turn the tapestry over. Using a small crochet hook, pull some of the carried threads from the back until the hanging flattens out or gets narrower. The loops formed from pulling the carried threads can be cut flush as long as they are secured with several crochet stitches on each side.

*Mounting and Framing:*

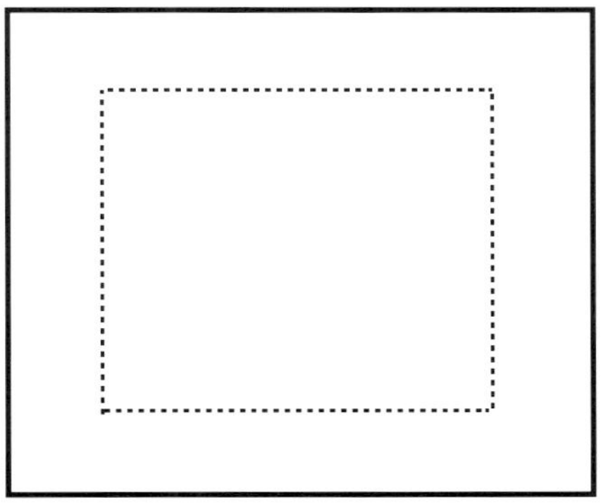

To mount the tapestry in the center of the mat board you must determine the size of the border. First, measure the width of the tapestry. Subtract 3/16" from the width measurement (to allow for the stitches), then subtract the width measurement of the tapestry from the width of the mat board and divide by two. This will be the size of the right and left side border. The pictured tapestry is 8 3/16" wide and the board is 10 7/8" wide. My calculations were: 8 3/16" - 3/16" = 8"; (10 7/8" - 8" = 2 7/8") / 2 = 1 7/16". Mark the back side of the mat board in several places (1 7/16" for the pictured tapestry) so that you can place a ruler parallel to the edge of the mat board. Lightly draw a line with a pencil along the ruler to create the side border line.

Do the same thing to determine the upper and lower border. Measure the height of the tapestry. Subtract 3/16" from the height measurement (to allow for the stitches), then subtract the height measurement of the tapestry from the height of the mat board and divide by two. This will be the size of the top and bottom border. The pictured tapestry is 6 3/16" high and the board is 9" high. My calculations were: 6 3/16" - 3/16" = 6"; (9" - 6" = 3") / 2 = 1 1/2". Mark the back side of the mat board in several places (1 1/2" for the pictured tapestry) so that you can place a ruler parallel to the edge of the mat board. Lightly draw a line with a pencil along the ruler to create the top and bottom border.

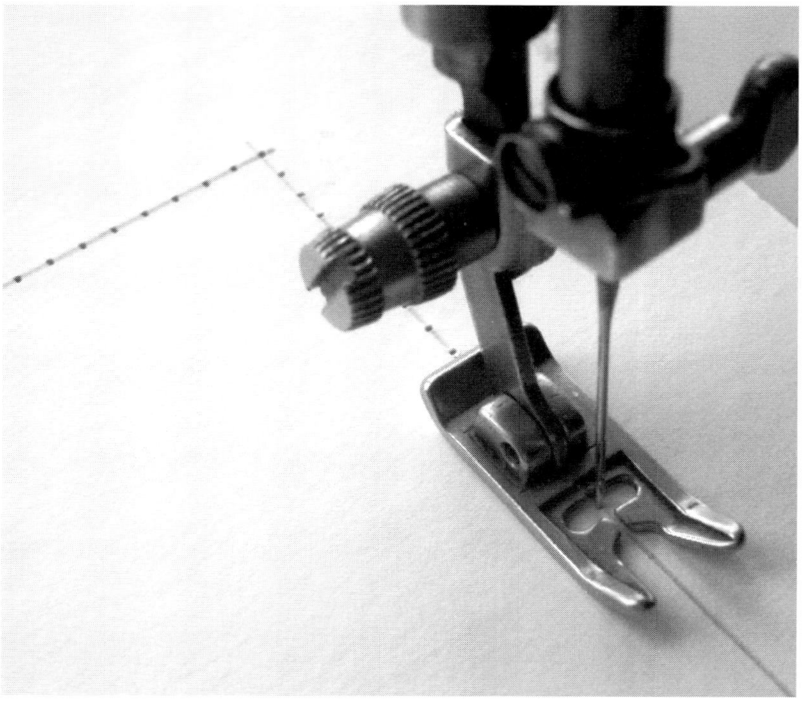

**An unthreaded sewing machine is used to punch holes in the mat board over the pencil lines.**

Use an unthreaded sewing machine (set to 8 stitches per inch) to punch holes all around the border, stitching on top of the pencil lines.

Thread a hand-sewing needle with the background color linen and put a knot in one end. Push the threaded needle through the lower left corner hole of the mat board, from the back to the front, then through the lower left hand corner of the tapestry from the back to the front. Pull the thread tight, then continue stitching the tapestry to the mat board. Once the bottom has been attached, make a knot on the back of the mat board, then cut off the thread.

Rethread the needle, then attach the top of the tapestry to the mat board with appropriate thread colors (I used beige and then blue). Once the top has been attached, sew the sides of the tapestry to the mat board. Once the tapestry has been sewn to the mat board, it can be blocked with a steam iron.

Don't worry if the piece is lumpy at this point, because blocking will shrink and flatten the tapestry. Use a steam iron to make the tapestry flat. Repeated blocking might be necessary if the tapestry is distorted. I blocked the pictured tapestry four times, waiting until it cooled between each blocking because it had several large bulges after I sewed it to the mat board. The tapestry still had a large bulge in it, so I pulled some of the carried threads (from the front this time), cut the loops that I had pulled out, then blocked the piece a few more times. The tapestry did eventually flatten out after the last blocking.

Assemble three sides of the sectional frame (following the manufacturer's instructions), then insert the foam core, matted tapestry, and acrylic sheet before screwing the last part of the frame together. Attach the hanging wire to the loops in the back of the frame. Ammonia will damage the acrylic sheet, so use a window cleaner that is specially formulated for Plexiglas and plastics when you clean the acrylic sheet.

# SUPPLIERS

Blomqvist/Nordiska Textil-Garner AB
Box 4039
S-512 84 Överlida
Sweden
Phone: +46 325 32290
Fax: +46 325 32500
e-mail: blomqvist@swipnet.se
web site: http://www.clb.se
***Square Hats/Baskets Project***
*Mattullgarn available in around a hundred colors. This firm yarn was one of the easiest wools to work with because it's twisted tighter than most other wool, so it doesn't split as often while being crocheted.*
***Flat Tapestry Project***
*Bockens Lingarn is available in around fifty colors.*

The Daisy Chain
Phone: 1-800-311-8061
Kreinik Threads

Dale
N16 W23390 Stoneridge Drive
Suite A
Waukesha, WI 53188
Phone: 1-800-441-3253
***Pillow and Oval Purse Projects***
*Kolibri mercerized cotton thread is available in around twenty seven beautiful colors.*

The DMC Corporation
10 Port Kearny
South Kearny, NJ 07032-4688
web site: http://www.dmc-usa.com
***Yarmulke/Kippa/Skullcap Project***
*DMC Size 8 Pearl Cotton thread is available in around two hundred beautiful colors.*

Fire Mountain Gems
28195 Redwood Highway
Cave Junction, OR 97523-9304
Phone: 1-800-423-2319
***Beaded Bracelet/Necklace Project***
*Beading needles, silk thread in over twenty five colors, and over hundreds of colors, shapes, and sizes of beads are available.*

Graphik Dimensions, Ltd.
2103 Brentwood Street
High Point, NC 27263
Phone: 1-800-221-0262
web site: http://www.pictureframes.com
***Flat Tapestry Project***
*UV-blocking acrylic, acid-free Foamcore backing board, metal shadowbox frames in six colors and acid-free mat board in forty four colors.*

Halcyon Yarn
12 School Street
Bath, ME 04530
Phone: 1-800-341-0282
web site: http://www.halcyonyarn.com
***Shawl Project***
*Four-Ply Knitting Worsted Indiecita Peruvian Alpaca is available in black, two grays, three browns, beige, and white.*

J. & P. Coats
Greenville, SC 29615
***Change Purse, Hats/Baskets, Beaded Basket, Hacky-Sack/Ball, and Flat Heart Projects***
*J. & P. Coats Speed-Cro-Sheen is available in a large variety of colors. This thread was one of the easiest to work with because it's twisted tighter than most other cotton threads, so it doesn't split as often while crocheting.*

Kreinik Consumer Info Line
Phone: 1-800-537-2166
e-mail: kreinik@kreinik.com
web site: http://www.kreinik.com
***Amulet Pouches Project***
*Kreinik silk and metallic threads are available in many thicknesses and over one hundred colors.*

Lion Brand Yarns
34 West 15th Street
New York, NY 10011
Phone: 1-800-258-YARN (9276)
web site: http://www.lionbrand.com
***Blanket/Throw Project***
*Lion Brand Art. No. 760 four ply worsted weight Kitchen Cotton is available in over twenty colors that are sold in four and five ounce balls and one pound cones.*

Nordic Needle
Phone: 1-800-433-4321
Kreinik Threads

Patons Yarns
P.O. Box 40
Listowel, Ontario
Canada N4W 3H3
Phone: 1-416-782-2969
***Jewelry Basket Project***
*Patons four ply 100% Mercerized Cotton is available in 33 colors and is sold in one and three quarter ounce balls.*

Reynolds Yarns
JCA, Inc.
35 Scales Lane
Townsend, MA 01469-1094
***Eyeglass Case, Cat's Meow Purses, and Scrunchies Projects***
*Sedona mercerized Egyptian cotton thread is available in a variety of colors - including several variegated combinations.*

Unicorn Books and Crafts
1338 Ross Street
Petaluma, CA 94954-6502
Phone: 1-800-289-9276
***Scarf Project***
*Klippan Berga 16/2 linen is available in around one hundred colors and is sold in 100 gram cones.*

# BIBLIOGRAPHY


Altman, Patricia B., and Caroline D. West, *Threads of Identity: Maya Costume of the 1960s in Highland Guatemala,* Los Angeles, CA: Fowler Museum of Cultural History, 1992.

Anderson, Marilyn, *Guatemalan Textiles Today,* NY: Watson Guptill Publications, 1978.

Baizerman, Suzanne, "The Kippa and the Social Construction of Gender," pages 92-105, in *The Anthropology of Dress and Gender,* edited by Ruth Barnes and Joanne B. Eicher, NY:Berg Publishers, 1992.

Coburn, Kate, *Crocheting With Beads,* Gilbert, AS, KTB Publishers, 1996.
This book, the first of several by Kate about crocheting with beads, covers the basics and includes instructions for six different projects.

Davis, Eli and Elise, *Hats and Caps of the Jews,* Israel: Massada Ltd. Publishers, 1983.
This book covers the history of the various Jewish hats and caps and features several tapestry crocheted caps. The word "knit" is used to describe both knit and tapestry crocheted caps in this book; most of the "knit" caps are actually crocheted.

Dittrick, Mark, *Hard Crochet,* NY: Hawthorn Books, Inc., 1978.
This book features a number of interesting hard (tapestry) crochet projects, including baskets and men's hats, belts, and a briefcase.

Harter, Legs Pierre, *Les Rois Sculpteurs,* Paris: Musée national des Artes d'Afrique et d'Océanie, 1993.
Although the focus of this book is the sculpture of Western Cameroon, some of the men pictured in the historical photographs are wearing tapestry crocheted hats.

Koch, Elly, *Schweizer Kreuzstichmuster, aus dem Bergell, Engadin, Safiental und anderen Graubünder Tälern,* Rosenheimer Verlag, Book 1: 1982; Book 2: 1984.
This book has Swiss cross stitch patterns. A note on the title page of this book says that these patterns were the basis for Mosaic (Tapestry) Crochet, Filet Crochet, and Cross Stitch.

Norton, Carol, *Tapestry Crochet Video,* Colfax, CA: Victorian Video Productions, 1992.
This video was produced when my name was Carol Norton. It is available through Yarn Barn, 930 Massachusetts, Lawrence, KS 66044, 1-800-848-0284.

Norton, Carol, *Tapestry Crochet,* Saint Paul, MN: Dos Tejedoras, 1991.
This book was published when my name was Carol Norton. It is available through Interweave Press, 201 East Fourth Street, Loveland, CO 80537-5644, 1-800-272-2193.

Osborne, Lilly de Jongh, *Indian Crafts of Guatemala and El Salvador.* Norman, OK: University of Oklahoma Press, 1975.

Schevill, Margot Blum, editor, *The Maya Textile Tradition,* NY: Harry N. Abrams, Inc., Publishers, 1997.

Schevill, Margot Blum, *Costume as Communication: Ethnographic Costumes and Textiles from Middle America and the Central Andes of South America,* Bristol, RI: Brown University, 1986.

Taylor, Colin F., editor, *The Native Americans,* NY: Smithmark Publishers, 1991.
Woolen Navajo sock/leggings and a cap that date to 1874 are illustrated on Page 60 and 61. The cap is said to be knit, but I believe that it was tapestry crocheted. These items are owned by the Smithsonian.

Ventura, Carol, "Duck Motif Tote," QUICK & EASY CROCHET, March/April, 1996:3, 10-11.

Ventura, Carol, "The Striking Tapestry Crochet of Guatemala," PIECEWORK, September/October, 1995:38-45.

Ventura, Carol, "A Tapestry Technique in Crochet," SHUTTLE, SPINDLE & DYEPOT, Fall 1993:28-29.

Ventura, Carol, "Tapestry Crochet Shoulderbag," CRAFTS, January 1985:32-33.

Wolbrom, Ricky, and Mati Jacobovits, *The Complete Guide to Yarmulka Design,* Brooklyn, NY: Judaica Press, Inc., third edition, 1995.
This book is available from the press at 1-800-972-6201. It does not have exact how-to instructions, but it does include lots of charted designs.

Wolf-Bearth, Maria, project leader, *Kreuz und Quer, durch die textile Volkskunst in Graubünden (Over and Across: through the textile Folk Art in Graubünden, Grisons, Switzerland),* Lehrmittelverlag des Kantous Graubünden, Chur, November 1996.
This Swiss schoolbook (commissioned by the government of Graubünden) is written in German. Pages 8 and 55 through 58 feature Swiss Mosaic (Tapestry) Crochet.

Yarhi, Leah Marmorstein, *Book of Samples,* Jerusalem, Israel: S. Zack & Co., 1994.
Even though this wonderful book is written in Hebrew, it has over 300 illustrations of skullcap designs for adults, children, and soldiers that can be understood by non-Hebrew speaking people.

I hope that you have enjoyed this book! It was truly a labor of love.
Please send your comments, suggestions, or corrections to me at

**cventura@tntech.edu**

or

**163 Big Spring Circle**
**Cookeville, TN 38501**

Thank you!

**Other books by Carol Ventura:**

*Tapestry Crochet,* 1991.

*Mayan Hair Sashes Backstrap Woven in Jacaltenango,* Guatemala, 1996.

*Cintas Mayas Tejidas con el Telar de Palitos en Jacaltenango,* Guatemala, 1996.

For more information about these books, please go to:

**http://www.tapestrycrochet.com**